MAKING
MARRIAGE
WORK

MAKING MARRIAGE WORK

THE ADVICE YOU NEED FOR A LIFETIME OF HAPPINESS

by

Joyce Meyer

New York   Boston   Nashville

Warner Books Edition
Copyright © 2000 by Joyce Meyer
Life In The Word, Inc.
P.O. Box 655
Fenton, Missouri 63026
All rights reserved.

Previously published as *Help Me—I'm Married!*

Warner Faith

Hachette Book Group USA
1271 Avenue of the Americas, New York, NY 10020
Visit our Web site at www.warnerfaith.com.

Warner Faith and the "W" logo are trademarks of Time Warner Inc. or an affiliated company. Used under license by Hachette Book Group USA, which is not affiliated with Time Warner Inc.

Printed in the United States of America

First Warner Faith Edition: October 2002
Reissued: June 2005
10 9 8 7 6 5 4 3 2

ISBN: 0-446-57726-X
LCCN: 2004105621

CONTENTS

INTRODUCTION

The blending of two individuals into one harmonious marriage is a process that takes time. God said that marriage will bring two people together and cause them to become as one flesh. I will be the first to admit that making a relationship work is hard and sometimes even painful. Doing what God says to do is not always easy, but my life is a living testimony that obeying God has greater rewards than I could have ever expected. If you had told me twenty-five years ago that one day I would be in such agreement with my husband that we would be as one heart focused on common goals, I would have laughed and asked you what science fiction movie you had been watching. Yet, we are living proof that two opposites can attract and become a strong force together in achieving God's plan for both our own pleasure and our impact in the world.

A popular morning news show in America recently reported an upward trend in the nation of more couples living together who aren't married. The research also showed that these same couples are less likely to be together for life than those who commit to each other through marriage. What's the difference? Both groups claim to love each other, but only the married couples made a promise to keep working at that love for each other.

Only time and trials can prove whether their promise to each other will be kept and thus magnify the presence of their love. To enjoy triumph instead of tragedy in a marriage, couples today need to learn how to keep the promise they made to each other on their wedding day. In keeping the promise of marriage, the mystery of how two people become one flesh will unfold and God's plan for our own relationship with Him will be revealed.

To enjoy triumph instead of tragedy in a marriage, couples today need to learn how to keep the promise they made to each other on their wedding day.

In this book we will examine what God meant when He said that a husband and wife would **become** one flesh. The *King James Version* of the Bible states in Ephesians 5:31 that a man and his wife *shall be one flesh,* but many versions of the Bible use the word *become* rather than *be* (AMP, NKJV, NIV, NASB). Thank goodness we get a chance to *become* or most of us would disqualify ourselves by the end of the honeymoon.

BECOMING ONE TAKES TIME

Becoming one takes time and too many couples are giving up on God's plan before the benefit of His design is manifested in their lives. The marriage vows do not supernaturally bring two individuals into perfect harmony. On the contrary, the wedding vows are a promise that they will not give up on each other, in spite of their differences, sickness, and successes, but will commit to waiting on God's plan to work in their lives. The Bible says that the process of a man becoming one with his wife is a profound mystery, but in it the heart of Christ to His church will be revealed.

As you read the unlikely love story that developed between Dave and me, you will see that God most certainly can work miracles. Dave asked God to lead him to a woman who needed help and when he saw me, he claims it was a "love-at-first-sight story." I wasn't looking for anyone but was determined to face life my own way. Dave met with conflict the first day he said "hello" to me, but God smiled on that day and was faithful to complete the good work He had started in us.

We will look at God's heart and purpose for marriage and see that He is trustworthy and His plans are for us and not against us. Then as we consider His goals for our marriage we will be able to embrace the reasons God wanted a man and woman to become a family. God gives clear direction on how to achieve the goals He sets before us. His ways are not our ways, but He gives us the power and the grace we need to act right so that we can see His face and reflect His goodness through our lives.

We will examine the differences between men and women and how those differences can either build up or tear down the other. The choice of whether we will help or hinder our spouse is our own. If we choose to help, we must draw from God's source of supernatural love that is available to us on a daily basis.

I will give you examples of my own mistakes and shortcomings. If you have listened to me teach or have read my previous books, you know that I am full of illustrations on "what not to do." But I can also prove that God is faithful to bless those who repent of their stubbornness and follow His leading.

I'll show you that happiness is not about finding a spouse who acts right all the time. Dave knows I think he sometimes watches too many sports on TV and plays too much golf, but we'll see the surprise twist of what God says to do with a mate who "doesn't believe" they are in the wrong.

I will not end this discussion without showing you godly principles on how to "fight fair" and confront the threats that come against your relationship with your mate. This is an important book, and I believe that God will reveal to you spiritual truths and powerful applications that will heal, restore, and renew your relationship with your spouse no matter where you are in your relationship with each other.

My goal for this book is to encourage people with bad marriages to believe that they can be healed. People with good marriages need to continue to do what they have to do to keep their relationship thriving. A majority of people don't know how to maintain what they have. Galatians 5:1 says, *In [this] freedom Christ has made us free [and completely liberated us]; stand fast then,* and do not be hampered and held ensnared and submit again to a yoke of slavery [which you have once put off]. So, once couples get this freedom, that doesn't mean they're going to keep it without a healthy focus on their relationship.

In fact, if people have a real weakness in an area, Satan will come back around and try them in that area the first time he thinks they're asleep and not paying any attention. But God will help us through the power of His Holy Spirit. We can anticipate and wait for the blessing and good, which come to those who conform to His will in purpose, thought, and actions.

> *Love sees the best in the other person when they can't see it themselves.*

Love between two people creates a safe place for them to come when they are weary and not on their best behavior. Love sees the best in the other person when they can't see it themselves. God is not mocked; we will reap what we sow. If we love our spouse, we will in turn be loved when we need grace in our lives. Someone needs to be first to sow the right seeds. Read on to refresh yourself with biblical principles on how to plant love into your relationship that will bring you a harvest of happiness from God's abundant supply.

PART 1

TRIUMPH OR TRAGEDY?

1

ONE FLESH?
ARE YOU SURE?

*Therefore a man shall leave his father
and his mother and shall become united and
cleave to his wife, and they shall become one flesh.*
Genesis 2:24

Marriage begins with a promise between a man and a woman to honor and cleave to each other for life. Too many couples depend on love to keep their marriage together, but commitment is the adhesive of marriage, and love is the reward of keeping the promise to stand beside each other through both good and bad times, in both sickness and in health, in both poverty and wealth. The process of keeping that promise is what makes love grow between the two of them.

The story of how Dave and I met is probably much like many other people's first encounter. However, not every couple started out with as many problems as I had, nor has every couple enjoyed the victory and triumphs we have celebrated through our marriage. Our relationship didn't always bear the good fruit that is now overflowing into the lives of others. Without God, we were headed for tragedy, but God showed us life principles that helped us through the struggles and difficulties that most all couples face.

Our story proves that with God, all things are possible, and that commitment to a promise bears the fruit of love.

By the time I was twenty-three years old, I was filled with great disappointment. Injury upon injury had been inflicted upon my heart, and I had never known what it meant to be happy or at peace with life. When I met Dave, I had already suffered an abusive relationship from my father and from a five-year marriage to a young man who had as many problems as I did.

I was born during the Second World War, right in the heat of it, in 1943. My father was inducted into the service the day after I was born, and I only saw him one time during the first three years of my life. When he came home from the war, he was bitter, angry, and addicted to alcohol, which left our family with painful memories. I endured nearly fifteen years of sexual abuse from him, which obviously had a devastating effect on my personality.

I didn't understand how to loose myself from the evil root of rejection that developed in my soul, and after being abused sexually I thought nobody would ever want me. So I married the first young man who came along in my life even though he had as many problems as I had. He had been raised improperly, too, and was allowed to quit school at a very young age. We had a five-year relationship that was riddled with pain and more rejection. We were separated maybe twenty times during those five years. My brief marriage ended in divorce, and my first husband, who was living with other women, ended up going to prison for writing bad checks.

Although we divorced, I had one child from that relationship, whom I named David after my brother, and when my son was about nine months old, I met Dave Meyer. Dave worked with a young man who lived in the upstairs apartment over my mom and dad's two-family flat.

One night I was washing my mother's car when Dave pulled up in front of my house with the young man who lived upstairs. Trying to flirt with me, Dave said, "When you are finished with that car, would you like to wash mine?" I was really sarcastic and snapped back, "If you want your car washed, wash it yourself."

Dave was twenty-six years old and was going with three girls at the time, ardently looking for a wife. He says he knew none of them were right for him. He was praying for somebody "who needed help." When he gave our tenant, with whom he had worked for years, a ride home, he says I caught his attention. He recently told the following story in his own words to a friend of ours.

"She was in short shorts and I thought she was pretty nice looking, so I said to myself, **Well, I'm going to try this.** Leaning out of my car window, I said, 'Hey, after you're done with that car, how about washing my car?'

"She snarled back at me and said, 'If you want your car washed, buddy, you wash it yourself.' Immediately, the thought hit me, **That's the girl for me.** That voice inside me just blurted out, 'That's the one, the one you've been looking for."

Dave says he has always enjoyed that original "fire" in my personality. There have been many times that fire has caused arguments, but over the years God has changed both of us. I used to think Dave was actually entertained by my temper tantrums. I can remember times when we would be in a heated spat and Dave would change my direction by saying with a smile, "Hey, there's that old fire that I like so much — keep that fire lit!"

Dave obviously likes a challenge. He reminds me of Caleb, from the Old Testament book of Joshua, who said, "Give me a mountain," when he and Joshua were dividing up the property in the promised land. Why would someone want to take on a mountain? But Dave likes a challenge and I am convinced that his wanting me had to be a supernatural act in his heart from God. There was nothing inviting in my personality that would have made somebody want me that much.

I am thankful that Dave continued to pursue his "mountain." On our first date we went to the bowling alley and I almost beat him. Then we went to a basketball game together, played poker one night with his brother, went to see a movie, and then went for a drive on a Sunday. We basically had five dates and he asked me to marry him. It was really a whirlwind courtship.

When Dave asked me to marry him, I was all messed up emotionally. I was living at home and dealing with the challenges of my dad again. I desperately wanted out of that situation, and I was farther away from knowing what love was than ever before. Dave said he loved me so when he asked me to marry him, I basically thought, **Well, why not? He is good looking!** I couldn't know whether or not I loved him because I didn't know what love was after the way I had been treated before I met Dave.

Anyone who had ever said they loved me, hurt me, and so I didn't trust anyone. My walls were carefully positioned to protect my heart. I was afraid of being hurt again so I kept a certain distance, but Dave seemed to understand the reason for my fears and chose to love me anyway.

From the time Dave asked me to marry him, I thought he was going to jilt me. The night that he proposed, he kept saying, "I need to talk to you about something."

I felt hurried because my dad was away from home on a drinking spree and I wanted to get home before he did. Dad became violent sometimes so I kept saying, "I have to get home."

But he insisted, "I have something important I want to talk to you about." I thought he was going to break up with me. Finally, I conceded to let him say it so the bad news would be over. When he asked me to marry him, I was shocked. I had a negative outlook about everything. It was difficult for me to believe that anything good would happen to me.

My answer to Dave when he said he wanted to marry me was, "Well, you know, I have a son." And he said, "If I love you, then I love anything that's part of you." So we decided to get married in six months. We ended up getting married about three months after meeting each other. I divorced my first husband in September, met Dave in October, and we were married by January 7 of the next year.

Dave says he could have asked me to marry him the first night we went out, but he knew it would just freak me out. He said he **knew** that I was the girl that he was supposed to marry. But, too many disappointments preceded his offer of love, and I doubted his commitment right up to the moment that I walked into the church and saw him at the altar. During all our preparations for the wedding, I kept thinking we probably wouldn't go through with the ceremony.

In fact, I was late for the service. My mother was literally on the verge of having a nervous breakdown at that time. She was upset because I wouldn't let her take more pictures at the house, and she had me all upset. By the time I reached the church, everyone wondered where in the world I had been.

We both agree that our marriage was a supernatural event. Dave was a Spirit-filled Christian and was obviously hearing from God. God could see the end result, beyond the person that I was the day Dave pulled up in my driveway. We married, and then the fun began.

YOUR FLESH OR MINE?

If two people are to become one flesh, as God frequently repeats in His Word, it was obvious that one of us was going to have to make some changes. It seemed right to me at the time that Dave was the one who needed amendments.

When Dave and I were first married, we already had David, then I became pregnant with Laura a few months later. She was born in April 1968, and we were married in January of 1967. Then eighteen months later, we had Sandy. With three kids, we lived in a three-room apartment. There was just a living room, one bedroom, and the kitchen. The apartment was part of a four-family flat. Everyone else who lived there was quite a bit older than us.

We had one car and hardly any money. Dave went to work every day, and I stayed home with the kids. The first place we lived had mice. I was seven months pregnant with Laura, and mice were all over the house. I think that in one day we caught seventeen mice.

One time I called Dave to tell him that I had a mouse tied up in the bathroom. I had thrown a plunger over the mouse, tied a rope around the bathroom doorknob, strung the rope across the hall to a closet, and from there tied it around the bedpost. It took Dave half an hour to get my barricade unraveled. By the time he reached the plunger, that baby mouse had died and was on its back with all four feet stuck up in the air.

When I was in the hospital with Laura, Dave decided we should move out of our five-room apartment into the three-room flat to save money. The rent for the apartment where we had been living was ninety-five dollars a month, and the rent at the three-room flat, about sixty-five dollars a month. Without telling me anything about it, Dave moved all our things to the three-room apartment. Can you imagine how furious I was when Dave took me home from the hospital to a different, and smaller, apartment? After all, we had finally caught all the mice, or had become used to the ones that remained! He says now that he knew I would be mad, but since I was mad all the time anyway, he didn't think this would make any difference!

The new apartment had roaches. There was one that was so big we decided to name him Harvey. When I sat up in the middle of the bed at night to feed Laura, Harvey would come flying around the corner. I was petrified of him, and at the sight of him I would go into a screaming fit! Then after screaming from seeing Harvey, I'd start yelling at Dave for moving us to that stupid place. Dave finally caught Harvey, and after failing to successfully set him on fire with lighter fluid, he delivered the lively pest to his sister, who had lived there previously and talked him into moving there in the first place.

The neighborhood where we lived was small. There was a dime store on the corner, a bakery, a grocery store, a little confectionery, and a beauty shop across the street. I never went anywhere beyond that neighborhood. Every Friday I'd walk across the street and get my hair done, and the rest of the time I stayed locked up with the kids. I was trying to baby-sit to make extra money, but I was the last person in the world who needed to baby-sit — I was on the edge myself!

But even in the midst of all that, we had a certain amount of fun. It wasn't all a nightmare and crazy, but it was the right setting for chaos and trials. Dave was always good to me and he tried to make me lighten up. He'd go to the grocery store with me, walk over into the next aisle and throw things over the top of the shelves at me! Then he would chase me around with the grocery cart until I became upset with him. Whatever he did, Dave was determined to have fun.

I had never been allowed to have fun when I was growing up. I was very insecure and felt as though everyone was inspecting me. Because I thought nobody really liked me, I acted as though I didn't need anybody — like I didn't care. Yet down deep inside, I really did care and tried to be what I thought others expected of me. But because I wasn't at peace with myself, the process of becoming one with Dave had a rough start.

I entered our marriage feeling as though each of us was out for ourself. Dave would do what was best for him, and I would do what was best for me. If Dave watched football on Sunday when I wanted to do something else, I felt that he wasn't interested in me. My thoughts nagged me with repeated agonies, **You don't care about me; you are not taking care of me.**

And I regularly had temper tantrums. When Dave watched football on Sundays, I cleaned the house, slamming and banging things around to make noise so that he could tell I was angry. I dragged the vacuum sweeper around while having a pity party, then went into the back bathroom to cry. With all my carrying on, I was trying to get him to do what I wanted. That kind of behavior is what I now call "emotional manipulation."

I did this so many times that Dave became immune to my noise. He watched the ball game because he knew I was going to throw a fit anyway. Sometimes he played with the kids when he knew I was mad at him. They would be on the floor with the kids putting rollers in Dave's hair, all oblivious to my demand for attention. When you are hopping mad and obviously are not affecting anybody, it just drives you crazy.

I was always looking for worth in what I did. Even where I worked, I tried to climb the corporate ladder. And in church I tried to be in with the right groups and the head of this and the head of that. Of course, I did have a natural leadership personality, but my personality was so messed up that I wanted all this stuff for the wrong reasons. I wasn't trying to serve God; I was searching for ways to look important. My struggles to do good things were just for "appearances" from a works mentality, and my sarcastic mouth was not working to help me get what I really wanted.

About six years into our marriage, I nearly exhausted Dave's patience. He was always the optimist, always trying to help me look beyond my situation. But I couldn't understand why my efforts to manipulate him weren't working, and, of course, our sex life was messed up from all my anger. Finally one day Dave said, "You know, Joyce, you just about have me to the point where I can hardly stand you." And he added, "The only thing I can tell you is if you continue the way you are, I cannot guarantee you a hundred percent what I'll end up doing." His comments put the fear of God in me to seriously look at the value I placed on Dave and our marriage.

All during this time, we were going to church. I really loved God. I was born again and knew that I would go to heaven when I died. But I wasn't Spirit-filled. Dave was an elder in the church, and I was on the church board. We went out every week, knocked on doors for the evangelism program and told people about Jesus. We were seen as leaders in the church. We were living the pretend life, but behind closed doors, it was another whole world and existence.

Happiness doesn't come from doing the right thing for the wrong reason.

I needed real answers from a real God. Of course I wanted the answers real fast, too. But one of the first things I learned was that happiness doesn't come from doing the right thing for the wrong reason. You can't do what's right to get something right to happen to you. You have to do what's right just because it's right. Then God will reward you. If your motive is, "OK, I'm going to do this to get you to change, but if you don't change, then eventually I'll quit doing it," we will never enjoy the reward that comes from God. He sees our heart and knows whether we are trying to manipulate others or obey Him purely out of love for Him alone.

Dave wanted me to change, and I wanted him to change. But I had to reach the point of knowing that I had to do what was right whether or not Dave ever changed. Even if he played golf every Saturday and watched football every Sunday for the rest of his life, I had to reach the point of acting right no matter what Dave did.

It's amazing how God changes things. Dave wanted to play golf recently when I had some other things I wanted him to do with me. He countered me with, "Well, you can do those things by yourself."

I said, "I'd really rather that you go with me. "

He said, "OK."

Fifteen years ago, he wouldn't have done that. I nagged him and was mad all the time, and he had learned to ignore me. But now, most of the time he can go do what he wants, and it's not a problem. But if once in a while I want him to do something different with me, he has the freedom to choose to be with me. He knew I wouldn't be mad at him if he really wanted to play golf, but he also knew that it must be important to me to want him with me this time or I wouldn't have asked him.

Bottom line, if he would have said, "No, I really want to play golf on Friday," then I would have said, "OK, then I'm going to go pick out the things we need for the house, and you will need to trust my decisions." And he would have agreed.

The same conditions still exist that used to bring separation and strife between us, but they no longer have the divisive effect on us. We've learned to be honest with our feelings without threatening each other's security. We've learned to find the right time to confront each other with the issues that used to throw us into opposite corners of the ring.

Dave and I learned to love each other, and out of our love a worldwide ministry was birthed. It was never my goal to start a huge ministry; I was just loving God and trying to learn to love Dave because that was what God was asking me to do. God has made big changes in our lives.

Dave and I learned to love each other, and out of our love a worldwide ministry was birthed.

We learned to be good stewards when we were paying the sixty-five dollars a month rent we needed for our apartment. Today God provides all the funds needed each month for a world outreach. I share this with you only to show you the vast expanse of God's ability to take plain, common, and ordinary people like Dave and me through gigantic steps of faith.

I was a housewife with a twelfth grade education, making my bed in a town nobody ever heard of, Fenton, Missouri, when God called me to do this. I was not looking for some big ministry; I was trying to survive sexual abuse, failed relationships, a messed up mind, and messed up emotions. But I loved God.

It's amazing what God will do for you if you just love Him. We complicate Christianity to the point of losing the joy of our salvation. The primary thing we need to do is receive the love of God, learn how to love ourselves in a balanced way, love God back, and then let that love flow through us to the world full of hurting, dying people.

God will give back to us not only what we give away but will also give us a great deal of joy with it. The world is full of rich people who have "things" but are miserable. It's good to be materially prosperous, but it's even better to be happy and biblically blessed along with prosperity.

The doors that God has opened for us amaze us. I can't figure it out, but I am determined that as long as I can breathe, I will keep walking through them in trying to help as many people receive God's joy in their lives as I can. Our society today is in a major, major, major mess, and people don't realize that they need God!

So many people have an impression of God that is just not true, and they don't know to turn to Him to solve their problems. God called Dave and me to a ministry in which we can show the world an exciting God Who is fun, generous, wonderful, and Who can solve their problems. We receive thousands of letters confirming that our simple message of trusting God by doing what He says to do is getting through to people.

One woman who wrote me said that she'd been living with a man for fifteen years. They weren't married; they had an eight-year-old son; they were drug addicts and they both had been abused in their childhood. She ran away from home when she was fifteen. She wrote:

> *God called Dave and me to a ministry in which we can show the world an exciting God Who is fun, generous, wonderful and Who can solve their problems.*

> *We believed in God, but we lived in sin. One morning, I came across [your television program] Life In The Word. I don't even know why I stopped to watch you. But I began to watch you every morning as I cleaned my house, and I felt like you were talking directly to me.*

> *Now I get up every day looking forward to watching Life In The Word. I watch you first, then I read my Bible, then I pray. Me and my boyfriend and our son started attending the same church that I went to when I was young. We both got saved two weeks ago. Joyce, we gave up drugs and we are getting married next month.*

> *I wanted to let you know that you reached me and helped me and my family turn our lives around. Please continue doing what you are doing.*

When Dave and I read the next sentence, we both stood in our bedroom and cried. She said,

> *Now our son will be raised in church by Christians and not by drug addicts.*

There are many people like her who believe in God, but live in sin. Christianity is not just a trip to the altar to say the sinner's prayer. It is not just marching off to church on Sunday morning or having a bumper sticker, a tape recorder, and a Jesus pin. Christianity has to be walked out in a lifestyle that solves problems. We must learn to die to self and live like Christ.

Another woman wrote to us saying:

My husband had a gambling addiction. One night we had an argument because he was going to go out and gamble more of our money away. We were already in such a deep financial hole it was unbelievable.

We were arguing, and he was going to leave. He came into the bedroom to grab the keys off the dresser. I reached out and turned on the television. There you were and said, "You with the gambling addiction . . ." He stopped dead in his tracks.

We film these shows to be aired months later, so only God could orchestrate something like that. Isn't God powerful? The woman said her husband it still working through some things, but he's been attending Gambler's Anonymous and has made a real commitment to conquer his addiction.

One woman who started watching me said she didn't even believe in women preachers because she had been taught that it was wrong for women to teach or preach. The only reason she started watching was because she liked my clothes. (I told Dave, "You see Dave, my clothes are helping the cause of Christ. I have no choice but to shop!")

The woman who liked my clothes was a seamstress and went out and bought a sketchpad. Every night at 11 o'clock, she sat and drew the outfit I had on. She said:

I added all the sparkles, and I'd look at the backs of your sleeves and draw them all out so I could make them. I have no idea when I started listening to you, but somewhere in the process of all that, God deeply touched my heart. I'm closer to God now than I've ever been in my whole life.

I've been a Christian thirty years, but I never had a really close relationship with God. [Your messages] drew me so close to God. My husband did not believe in women preachers, but he saw such a change in me that now if I get in a little bit of a bad mood, he says, "You'd better be sure to watch Joyce Meyer tonight."

My favorite letter came from Rick Renner who has a ministry in Latvia. I have the privilege of being on television there, all over the former Soviet Union. The letter told how God was moving in a woman's life in a powerful way through the ministers she saw on TV. In many small Russian villages where it looks as though people don't have much of anything, most families still manage to have a television.

Rick wrote: "I think this story will bless you, Joyce." He said a Ukrainian pastor took an evangelistic team into a little Russian village where they knew for certain there had never been a church or a gospel outreach. They believed it was brand new territory and anticipated awesome opportunities.

They knocked on the door of the first little house in the village and a little woman opened the door. When they began to share the Gospel with her, she said, "Oh, wait, wait, wait; come in. Let me tell you what's happened to me."

When they went in, she shared that she had been watching "Good News with Rick Renner" and was saved while watching television. She said that on the lower part of her back, she had, had a cantaloupe-sized tumor that could not be removed because it was too dangerous. The tumor, which she had, had most of her life, caused her to slump over when she walked. She wore loose fitting clothes to keep people from seeing it. The tumor was very uncomfortable and had affected her whole life.

A month after being saved, she watched a minister on TV who pointed at the screen and said, "Healing belongs to you." In an instant she believed. She heard a loud pop on her back, ran to the bathroom and saw that all the stuff that had been in the tumor was running down her back and the back of her legs. By the end of the day, the thing was completely gone — not one trace of it remained.

Another month passed. She was watching a different minister who began to share about the baptism in the Holy Spirit. The Russian woman said she received the baptism of the Holy Spirit and began to pray in the Spirit right there in her little home, in that Russian village. She was born again, healed, and baptized in the Holy Ghost, but felt there was something still missing. Then she told them, "Now I've found 'Life In The Word with Joyce Meyer.' I am getting my soul healed and am maturing as a Christian." .

In 1999, we had a rare opportunity to go on a popular network in Asia called "Starworld." It is a secular network, but it's an English-speaking channel that reaches up to one-half billion homes of people who want to practice their English. They've never had any kind of religious broadcasting on that channel. This letter came from Asia where we are sharing the Good News of the Gospel every morning:

> *One day, at 6 A.M., I happened to get up early and turn on the television. I saw you for the first time. I've been watching Starworld for ten years, and I've never felt any program as inspiring as the lecture you gave. I was totally amused.*
>
> *I've been feeling depressed for many years; sometimes I even felt like I was going to explode, although my students would never feel it. I never showed it outwardly.*

Do you have any idea how many people are unhappy, but they never show it outwardly? They live phony lives, putting a plastic smile on their face every day and just trying to hide their misery from everybody. Jesus died for us to have more than a phony life.

> *At my work post, I think I can say I'm a qualified professor, but as a person, I always felt that I was unhappy inside. I tried to analyze myself — tried to find out what psychological problems I had — but I always failed. Really I was just very miserable.*
>
> *But when I saw you, you said, "I want to share something with you that can help you come into a place of rest." You said, "Frustration comes from works of the flesh," and I'll never forget your description about the seeds in your hands, which was so impressive.*
>
> *Your paraphrases are so amazing I can't even tear myself away from it. So from the first time I saw you, I've never missed the chance to meet you at 6 A.M. every day for nearly two weeks now. I'm totally obsessed with your lectures. I'm sure I'll follow your course.*
>
> *I managed to borrow a Bible in English in order to follow your reading. I found no bookshops within my reach that sells the Book. When you asked us to open the Book and turn to*

1 Peter chapter 5, I opened up the Book I borrowed. It was not the Word you were reading. (The reason is that I read from The Amplified Bible.) She continued:

To tell you the truth, before listening to your lectures, I never thought that I would be interested in any religious beliefs because I knew too little about them. I think maybe the one I borrowed is not the same edition as the one you have. Mine is like this: 'Holy Bible placed by the Gideons.'

Could you please tell me where and in which way I can get the Book that you use. Thank you very much.

Sincerely,

Your listener . . .

Of course, we sent her "The Book" right away, and we are believing for her salvation. It is amazing how many people have never heard godly principles to apply to their lives.

Christianity has so much to offer people. It is a lifestyle. Christianity has to be walked out in our everyday lives if we are going to affect anybody else's life.

After I made a decision to become a Christian, I had to learn how to live like a Christian. I learned that God's blessings cannot be enjoyed with one worldly foot stuck in stubbornness, fear, and rebellion and the other foot trying to touch the kingdom. I also learned that God's blessings are not just for ourselves. When we do what is right, it affects the lives of others.

That is part of the miracle that God works between two people. His plan is to restore our relationship with Him, then our relationships with each other. He didn't change our individual style or approach to life; He simply changed our hearts to be more accepting toward each other. He taught us to adapt to each other and attend to each other's needs when at all possible. He taught us to take care of each other as well as we would take care of ourselves.

God simply changed our hearts to be more accepting toward each other. He taught us to adapt to each other and attend to each other's needs when at all possible.

If husbands and wives could practice this ability to accept and attend to each other at home, these relational standards could spread to how we treat people at work, in our neighborhoods, and in our world. Then the *mystery* of relationships that God spoke of in Ephesians 5:32 would begin to unfold its secret.

2

BUT WON'T
THAT HURT?

For no man ever hated his own flesh, but nourishes and
carefully protects and cherishes it, as Christ does the church,
Because we are members (parts) of His body. For this reason
a man shall leave his father and his mother and shall be
joined to his wife, and the two shall become one flesh.
Ephesians 5:29-31

What was God thinking when He designed two unique, never to be copied again, strangely wonderful individuals with their own visions, dreams, and goals, and then told them, "Now you will become one flesh"? And which one of us are we to become? Is he to become like me, or am I to become like him? What is God really asking us to do and what is His purpose in all of this?

First, we must understand that the instruction that husbands and wives would become one was given to those who fellowship with God. "Becoming one" was not something we were told to **do**, but was something that He said would **happen** to us through the process of His plan.

God wants Christian couples to be subject to one another out of a reverence for Christ. His purpose lies in the fact that we are members (parts) of His Own body. Christian couples are to become as one flesh in their goals and decisions in order to demonstrate to

*"Becoming one" was not something we were told to **do**, but was something that God said would **happen** to us through the process of His plan.*

the world on a small scale the power that takes place from the oneness that a personal relationship with Him should reflect. Look at the verse that follows the comment that couples would become one flesh.

This mystery is very great, but I speak concerning [the relation of] Christ and the church.

Ephesians 5:32

Married couples, who submit themselves to God's leading, are examples of the love relationship that is available between a believer and Jesus. In other words, unbelievers who can't see Christ should be able to see His love when they observe the relationship between Christian couples. As believers, we are to put our attention on the Lord. But when we focus on Christ, He always empowers us to achieve or receive our heart's desire.

Delight yourself also in the Lord, and He will give you the desires and secret petitions of your heart.

Commit your way to the Lord [roll and repose each care of your load on Him]; trust (lean on, rely on, and be confident) also in Him and He will bring it to pass.

Psalm 37:4,5

Likewise, when a wife delights in her husband as unto the Lord, the Lord will in turn attend to the desires and secret petitions of her heart. God has also instructed the husband to nourish and carefully protect his wife as he would his own flesh. God has not called us into bondage but into the mystery of His way that leads to freedom. God's best will be returned to us if we trust in Him and do His Word.

God said, *the two **shall** become* as one. There is finality to God's Word that points to the end rather than to the process. He promises that the husband and wife **will** become one just as Christ is one with the church. God is doing this work in us. It is not something that we **make** happen; it is something that we **let** happen as we trust God to do what He promised to do in us.

SOMEONE HAS TO BE FIRST

To let God's plan work, at least one of the two people involved must start trusting the plan. Either the wife must trust God enough to turn her attention on her husband, or the husband must love his wife and care for her needs as Christ cares for us. What a profound mystery that Christ came as a servant to us, yet we find it hard to serve others. The more we adapt ourselves to His ways, the more His blessings will fill our lives.

God loved us first, and we loved Him back. He reaffirms us concerning His love and we start loving others and eventually, the love becomes so intertwined in us that it no longer matters who was first to love the other. Ephesians 5:1 continues:

Therefore be imitators of God [copy Him and follow His example], as well-beloved children [imitate their father].

The book of Ephesians explains this lesson of love by saying that we are to be useful and helpful and kind to one another, tenderhearted, compassionate, and understanding with the other. In becoming like Christ, we will naturally turn our attention on the needs of others.

Neither the husband nor the wife sets the standard of what the other one should become. Only Christ is the role model to Whom we must adapt. Reaching the goal of becoming one with each other is a daily process just as becoming like Christ is a lifetime study course. It is painful to work at a relationship, but it is more painful to reap failure, dissension, and separation from those we love because we have simply neglected them and sown bad seed.

So, to become "one" with each other, we must first come into agreement with God by drawing near to Christ and becoming like Him. Once we invite Jesus into our relationships, and do what He says to do, we become like Him in our thoughts and deeds, and consequently, we become loving like He is and we develop and maintain good relationships.

> There is [now no distinction] neither Jew nor Greek, there is neither slave nor free, there is not male and female; for you are all one in Christ Jesus.
>
> Galatians 3:28

LOVE GROWS WHERE IT IS SOWN

When I met Dave, he was well on his way to adapting to the mind of Christ. He was willing to take me as I was, just as God is willing to accept all of us the way we were when we found Him. God loves us, "flaws and all," and I guess you could say that Dave was overlooking mine. But just as God's love changes us to be more like Him, His love between two people can cause them to adapt and be at peace with each other as they become more like Christ in each other's presence.

God's love between two people can cause them to adapt and be at peace with each other.

If Dave had not been walking with God, our marriage would have suffered longer than it did, or perhaps not survived at all. He was very patient with me during the years when I was struggling so much. The fact that I was born again did help — at least I made some tiny effort to be pleasing to God. I wanted to do what was right, but I either did not know what that was due to a lack of strong biblical teaching, or I was unwilling and often unable to choose the right actions due to all the bondage and strongholds in my personality.

I was born again when I was nine years old. The night I was saved, I had to sneak out of the house to go to church with some relatives that were visiting us because my dad wouldn't have permitted us to go if we had asked. I knew that I went to be saved that night, and I don't even know how I knew that I needed salvation.

The pastor did not have an altar call that evening. I was really scared, but at the end of service I walked to the front of the church, taking two of my cousins with me. I looked at the pastor and said, "Can you save me?"

He was sorry that he hadn't offered an altar call, but I had a glorious cleansing of my soul that night. I knew I was born again, but the next day I cheated in a game of hide-and-go-seek with my cousins by peeking to see where they were going, and I thought I lost my salvation! I was in my twenties before I realized that Jesus had promised not to abandon me. Hebrews 13:5 confirms this promise, . . . *For He [God] Himself has said, I will not in any way fail you nor give you up nor leave you without support. [I will] not, [I will] not, [I will] not in any degree leave you helpless nor forsake nor let [you] down (relax My hold on you)! [Assuredly not!]*

Looking back I can see that since my conversion experience I was determined to break loose from the situation that I was in and become something more than my father thought of me. I realize now that when I received the Lord, His strength came into me to overcome that situation. Throughout my teenage life, I still prayed and talked to God when I needed help to get out of various situations.

God was with me all those years, and He helped me to endure and to come out of the circumstances that had held me captive. I always hoped that my mother would leave my dad, but she never did and I couldn't understand why she stayed with him. Once, when seeking for answers, God showed me that parents have an awesome authority over children's lives and that my father made a lot of bad choices — I was in the bull's eye of his aim.

When God gives a child to someone, He gives parents the authority to make decisions for them, good or bad. Yet the amazing thing is that God can take a child who was raised by parents who made bad decisions and transform the child's heart to be as pure as though nothing had happened to him or her. There isn't anything that God cannot turn around for the good if we love and obey Him. God has taken all the bad in my life and used it to reach many lives with His love and transforming power. I encourage you not to spend your life trying to understand why things happen the way they do, just close the door on the past and let God lead you into a wonderful future.

Hurting people hurt other people. Satan wants the one who was hurt to spend the remainder of his life hating the one who hurt him, but God's plan is just the opposite. God teaches us to forgive by faith, trust Him to heal our emotions, then get on with life. Life is not always fair, but God is. He is the God of justice and He will bring compensation to those who have been hurt if they place their trust in Him instead of taking matters into their own hands.

LOVE TURNS THINGS AROUND FOR THE GOOD

God promises that if we love Him, **He** will turn all things for our good. What a wonderful promise! Look at God's promise to fulfill our hopes in Romans 8:24-28.

For in [this] hope we were saved. But hope [the object of] which is seen is not hope. For how can one hope for what he already sees?

But if we hope for what is still unseen by us, we wait for it with patience and composure.

So too the [Holy] Spirit comes to our aid and bears us up in our weakness; for we do not know what prayer to offer nor how to offer it worthily as we ought, but the Spirit Himself goes to meet our supplication and pleads in our behalf with unspeakable yearnings and groanings too deep for utterance.

And He Who searches the hearts of men knows what is in the mind of the [Holy] Spirit [what His intent is], because the Spirit intercedes and pleads [before God] in behalf of the saints according to and in harmony with God's will.

We are assured and know that [God being a partner in their labor] all things work together and are [fitting into a plan] for good to and for those who love God and are called according to [His] design and purpose.

Does it help you to realize that the Holy Spirit is praying for you, even when you don't know what to pray for? (See Romans 8:27.) He is praying that God's design and plan will bring us into God's will. This means that our marriage partner can also come into God's perfect design and purpose as we continue to love God and put our hope in His promises.

When Dave and I were first married, I had many problems, but I didn't even know I was headed for deep trouble. Dave, on the other hand, was Spirit-filled, which was unheard of in the Protestant church he attended at that time. He was in the fourth grade when he was born again and only eighteen when he received the baptism of the Holy Spirit which I will explain more about in a later chapter. He testifies of a tremendous experience with the Lord when he was a young boy. Then as a teenager he felt as though there was a wall he had to climb in order to know more of God. He wanted more out of life than he was getting, and he sought it for the longest time.

One day, while on break at an engineering company, he went in the bathroom and said to God, "I'm not coming out of here until You give me what I am looking for." I think it is pretty funny that he was sitting in the stall in the men's room when God answered Him. This proves that God is willing to meet us where we are.

Dave was very serious about it. He was **not** leaving until God gave him what he was seeking after, and that's when it happened. His face shines when he retells the story of how God just filled him up, right there. Prior to this infiltration of God's Spirit, his eyesight was pretty bad, and God healed his eyes! God began to reveal Himself to Dave and teach him about grace. Instruction from God continued for days on the subject of grace. Then God taught Dave about love, and over the next few years Dave grew into a very strong, mature believer in Jesus Christ.

GOD'S LOVE IS THE BEGINNING OF ROMANCE

I want to tell you more about Dave's story because I am convinced that marriages work if at least one of two people is

> *Be willing to make the changes that God directs so that love begins to grow in the relationship.*

seeking God for direction. Someone has to be first — it doesn't matter if it is the wife or the husband. But one of them needs to know how to hear from God concerning the conflicts and challenges they face and be willing to make the changes that God directs so that love begins to grow in the relationship. In our case, Dave knew how to hear from God.

Through supernatural events and strange coincidences, God showed Dave how to slow down his life to almost a slow motion pace where it would be synchronized with Him. As Dave understood the process, he intentionally slowed down so he could be in step with God, focusing on listening to God for days and days. Dave said that he functioned almost in a slow-motion pace during that time of renewal, then God speeded up his life up to the normal pace again. But when He did, Dave felt synchronized with God.

Isaiah spoke of a similar experience with God in chapter 50, verse 4:

[The Servant of God says] The Lord God has given Me the tongue of a disciple and of one who is taught, that I should know how to speak a word in season to him who is weary. He wakens Me morning by morning, He wakens My ear to hear as a disciple [as one who is taught].

After that experience, Dave found that in everything he did, he seemed to know what God wanted him to say. It no longer satisfied Dave to have just a **good** answer; he was now aware that God had a **perfect** answer for every situation. It was a supernatural revelation that, at the time, Dave didn't realize how miraculous it was.

By the time he went into the army, Dave had spent years walking intimately with God, but he was already taking God's supernatural voice for granted because it had been such a natural part of his life. His understanding of God's will had come to him from close communion with God, rather than through study of the Word. Then when Dave was in the service, he experienced a time that felt as though God's presence had left him.

GOD'S WORD ESTABLISHES HIS LOVE IN OUR HEARTS

Dave didn't understand why God didn't speak to him as He did before. But since we have been married and are both in full-time ministry, Dave can see God's purpose in letting him experience that time of silence. When he felt all alone, he had to learn how to live all over again because he had depended on God's voice for every-thing. When his feelings changed he had to seek security that transcended "feelings." He had to learn that God's promises are true regardless of what our five senses experience.

God wanted Dave to establish their relationship on the Word that had been given to him. Dave needed to discover the promises that had been made to him in God's Word and learn that God is faithful to keep His promises no matter how Dave felt. This time, he had to learn how to come back to the intimate position with God through the Word and faith alone.

As he began to study God's promises, he saw that God was still as close to him as the days he first began to love God. While feelings waver, God's Word stands firm as Isaiah also expressed in chapter 40, verse 8:

The grass withers, the flower fades, but the word of our God will stand forever.

God wanted Dave to depend on His Word — His promises. During that time, Dave became familiar with the Scriptures that confirmed what God had taught him about grace and love. Three years after he left the service he met and married me. God had well prepared him for all of my problems. He had firmly learned **not** to operate by his feelings. He explains that God's grace made him able to be patient with me and love me in the midst of my upsets.

When I was angry, Dave didn't let it steal his joy. He knew that God was working in us, and he didn't let our arguments tear him down. By God's grace during those early years of our marriage and then by faith in His Word, Dave continued to enjoy life even when I was mad. His happiness during my trials made me angry and upset, but at the same time, drew me to him. I wanted what he had.

I saw stability in Dave that I had never seen in anybody in my whole life. No matter what I did, he remained the same. As the years went by, Dave could look back and see that God was preparing him the whole time for our marriage. When God was revealing Himself to me in those early years, I didn't realize that He was making me think more like He thinks. And when it seemed that God had left me, He was actually wooing me or drawing me after Him so that I would get into the Word, then depend on His Word.

DON'T LET ANYONE STEAL YOUR JOY

Many disagreements could be avoided if we didn't depend upon our spouse to make us happy.

It was a key factor to our success that Dave didn't let me make him unhappy. Many disagreements could be avoided if we didn't depend upon our spouse to make us happy. Dave's contentment was in God's promise not in my compliance.

When I have shared that in meetings, it really ministers to people. People feel that if they have a problem, they are almost obligated to be unhappy. I was a dependent person with irrational behavior, and I wanted to make Dave codependent on me so I could control him. It seemed fair to me that if I wasn't happy, he shouldn't be either!

Dave was a role model to me, who showed me new ways to handle disappointment and disagreement. I challenged Dave's stability to the extremes. Sometimes for two and three weeks I wouldn't say one word to him. Not one word. I would just shut up and not say a word. But Dave loved me and showed me the agape love of God. I saw God's unconditional love in him and if I wanted to receive it, I could benefit from it, but if I didn't, it didn't stop him from loving me. His stability amazed me. He did get angry with me sometimes, but somehow he was always able to demonstrate his love while disapproving of my actions. He was the closest thing I had ever seen to what I might have conjectured peace or love to be like.

It is important for people who are married to a troubled person, or married to somebody who is having problems, or who isn't saved, or whatever the case might be, to strive for stability in God. This can be a painful process but it is the direct path to eventual peace and joy. People must not let a troubled spouse's behavior dictate their joy. They should strive to be stable and solid, so their behavior can witness to the other person.

The only way I had ever seen anything handled as I was growing up was with anger, force, and manipulation. Disagreements were handled by controlling people with temper tantrums. In other words, "I'm mad at you and I'm going to stay mad at you until you do what I want you to." And that was the way I fought for what I wanted. I grew up in a negative atmosphere where I was taught, "You cannot trust anybody. Anybody who even wants to do anything or even says they want to do something nice for you has some ulterior motive."

I'm using the example of the people who influenced my childhood, not to disrespect them, but to demonstrate that I believe people repeat what they were taught as children unless God does a work in them. Later, I will discuss how we learned to have healthy confrontations. But I was taught in the earlier years of my life to be negative.

HAPPINESS IS YOUR OWN RESPONSIBILITY

Six years into our marriage, Dave was beginning to tire of the fight. When I saw that Dave was no longer trying to give me "pep talks," I realized it was my turn to do something about my unhappiness. If a spouse can make everything all right for someone, then Dave had been doing all the right things for our marital bliss. But I couldn't be in harmony with him until I was in harmony with God.

I wasn't aware at the time how painful my unhappiness was for Dave. He reflects on that time of challenge with both fond and fretful memories. When I pushed him to the edge, he would go out alone and pray and cry. In the beginning he would try to share with me about things, saying, "You have to change or this has to change." And nothing ever happened. It made me worse. So Dave realized that I couldn't change from the outside in. It had to be from the inside out. From that time on, he realized that all he could do was pray when I was being sarcastic or belligerent. He would cry, "God, I can't change this! Only You can get on the inside of her and change this."

It was at this time in our marriage that I began to read the Word of God with new interest and enthusiasm. The Word was beginning to make sense to me and draw me to desire more of God in my life. I know that people don't like "pat answers" for life, but the Good News of the Gospel is very simple. I think that every person has to pick up the Bible and be willing to do what it says no matter what any other person does. And they have to do it as unto the Lord. Only then does an individual find the true path to happiness and wholeness.

3

BEFORE STARTING OVER,
TRY THIS . . .

Do not fret or have any anxiety about anything,
but in every circumstance and in everything, by prayer
and petition (definite requests), with thanksgiving,
continue to make your wants known to God.
And God's peace [shall be yours, that tranquil state of a
soul assured of its salvation through Christ, and so fearing
nothing from God and being content with its earthly lot
of whatever sort that is, that peace] which transcends
all understanding shall garrison and mount guard over
your hearts and minds in Christ Jesus.
Philippians 4:6,7

If more people would actually pray for their struggling relationships, I believe they would see peaceful changes in their marriages. Too often, people spend all their waking thoughts on their problems instead of on their relationship with God. Consequently, they miss out on the peace that God wants to bring them.

Peace was not even a concept in the early days of our marriage. Six years into our marriage, Dave was possibly at a point that if he could have asked for a second chance, he would have offered God another rib and said, "Lord, how 'bout a new model; this one isn't working!" Fortunately, Dave didn't trade me in on a new wife. He did ask God to change me in the areas that were causing us so much pain, and after a period of time, I did begin to change in those areas. It was during his time of intercession that I began reading and studying the Word.

I began to study the Word, but typical to when a person is changing, I appeared to get worse before I got better. The Word was convicting me and fortunately, Dave didn't stop praying for me. When we share about this time in our lives, I have heard Dave say, "When you are praying for somebody in an area and they get worse, that's not the time to stop praying. That's the time to get encouraged. Most people give up when they pray for somebody and a person gets worse because they think their prayers are not working. But in reality God is beginning to deal with them, and their flesh is getting all upset."

There will be a transition period so if you keep praying during that period of time, they'll get through it and will be changed in that area. Too often Christians give up praying because they want instantaneous success and immediate answers.

Jesus told us to ask and keep asking, to seek and keep seeking, and to knock and keep knocking until the door opens that we want to enter. Matthew 7:8 promises a response:

For everyone who keeps on asking receives; and he who keeps on seeking finds; and to him who keeps on knocking, [the door] will be opened.

When God was dealing with me, I felt more stubborn than ever before I started to improve. It can make you mad to find out that you are the one who needs to make changes instead of the one who you think is irritating your life. When Dave saw how irritable I was becoming, he became encouraged instead of discouraged.

It is so important to understand that a process takes time, and time is something of which God has plenty. He is not in a hurry when it comes to working things out. He knows that eternity outweighs the longevity of today. He will work with us until the work is complete, no matter how long it takes. When you see that

God is dealing with your loved one, don't give up but rejoice and keep praying.

It takes time to receive the blessing. So many people want everything to be big **now**. It's not going to be big now. You are going to have to go through a learning process or a transition of metamorphosis like the caterpillar turning into a butterfly. There are many things that must happen in that process. When God completes the work in your marriage, you won't regret any of the process that it took to get where He wants you. The happiness will be so complete that the process will no longer matter. But don't give up in the middle of the process. God had something great in store for both partners of a marriage when He promised that they would become one. If you are having problems in your marriage: **Don't give up!**

> *God had something great in store for both partners of a marriage when He promised that they would become one.*

STAND FIRM

I believe many couples are divorcing after years of marriage because they are not given proper direction on how to stand against the enemies of marriage, of which pride and selfish self-centeredness are two of the worst. There are some good role models, but we have to search for them: people with loving, stable relationships, who have been willing to be patient and work through their difficulties, who realize the grass is not always greener on the other side as we are often tempted to believe it is. The church should demonstrate to the world what a godly marriage is suppose to be like, but instead we now have percentages of divorce among Christians so high that they barely differ from the world.

Because we live in a society that expects things instantaneously, most people want everything to be good immediately. But there's a process that must take place for anything to become solid. That's why I like our motto for the ministry which is **slow and solid; fast**

and fragile. If it's fast, it's not going to last very long, and it's not going to be very effective. But if it's slow, there's going to be a lot of solidity to it.

The letter to the Ephesians has much to say about the process of establishing both the family and the church. Paul clearly teaches that spirit forces of wickedness will come against us as we strengthen ourselves in the Lord (Ephesians 6:10-12) and when they do, we are to put on the full armor of God.

> *Therefore put on God's complete armor, that you may be able to resist and stand your ground on the evil day [of danger], and, having done all [the crisis demands], to stand [firmly in your place].*
>
> *Stand therefore [hold your ground], having tightened the belt of truth around your loins and having put on the breastplate of integrity and of moral rectitude and right standing with God.*
>
> Ephesians 6:13,14

God answers through a process of events, and we must not abandon our hope before we get His answer.

If you study the times when it appeared that God brought instant answers, you will find that someone had been praying and standing on their petitions for that miracle for a long time. God answers through a process of events, and we must not abandon our hope before we get His answer. We may see God's answer manifest suddenly, but work had been going on behind the scenes for probably a long time. It may encourage you to realize that if you are trusting God and praying, He is working on your situation even though you have not seen the evidence yet. This is what faith is: It is the assurance of things unseen.

When I started getting in the Word, God did me a great favor in calling me to preach because I'm a committed, responsible person. And if I was going to do it, I was going to do it right, which meant I had to study a lot. I studied for the home Bible studies that I taught for six, seven, eight hours a day in order to teach for one hour.

Gradually, I started changing and conforming to the Word. One of the first things I had to learn was to respect people. Learning to respect and submit to authority was another major event in my life. It was very hard for me to do because I didn't trust anyone. I could not believe that Dave would make a decision with my best interests at heart. No one had before I met Dave, so I had no positive experience on which to base trust. I had to learn to trust.

As I read the Word, I saw that God had a plan to bless me and not hurt me. Marriage was His idea and He established it for a purpose that was greater than I could understand. He said that He came to bring us peace.

> I have told you these things, so that in Me you may have [perfect] peace and confidence. In the world you have tribulation and trials and distress and frustration; but be of good cheer [take courage; be confident, certain, undaunted]! For I have overcome the world. [I have deprived it of power to harm you and have conquered it for you.]
>
> John 16:33

But I lacked peace and Scriptures pointed to the fact that peace is the goal God had in mind when He established authority and relationships. I was so hungry for stability and peace. And I just made my mind up that I was going to have peace regardless of what changes would be required of me. I understood that to have peace, I must be in Christ and let Christ live in me. At that point, I stopped arguing with Dave so much. I had finally come to the point where arguing just wasn't worth it to me anymore.

Peace is the goal God had in mind when He established authority and relationships.

STAY FOCUSED ON THE PROMISE

As I studied the Word, I could see that God focuses on the end result, not the process that we go through. Our hope is in His answer not in our trials or waiting period. As time went by, God began to change areas in me, and Dave said it was as though I was a whole new person.

The more I fell in love with Jesus, the more I wanted to obey Him. The more I obeyed the Lord, the more I wanted to be involved with Him. The more involved I was, I loved Him even more and soon became eager for opportunities to obey Him. That's why Jesus said, "If you love Me, you will obey Me." And so really, to whatever degree we are obeying Him, it's to that degree that we love him.

I started wanting to have peace, realizing that not having peace was affecting my anointing to minister. It was then that I received a revelation on strife and how to keep strife out of our marriage and our lives.

SEPARATE YOUR WHO FROM YOUR DO

Besides this deep desire for peace, another major breakthrough for me was learning that I had a root of rejection which I share of in my book, *The Root of Rejection*. That problem kept me from communicating with Dave. I didn't know what in the world was wrong with me. We were okay as long as we both thought the same way about something, but if Dave had his own opinion on how something should be that was conflicting with my idea, I felt like he was putting me down.

He would try to tell me, "I'm not trying to put you down. I have an opinion and you have an opinion. We have the right to have separate opinions." But I couldn't understand that because of the way I had been treated. If he rejected my opinion, I **felt** that he was rejecting me.

Although I couldn't work all that out in my head, I honestly did not know why we couldn't talk. We would try to talk about something, and I would get confused. I would get **so** confused that I didn't even know what we were doing anymore, and it was horrible. We went through this time, after time, after time.

During this same time I was actually teaching our home Bible study group on rejection! A couple of other things happened in our relationship during that time. God said to me, "You are reacting to him this way because he doesn't agree with you and you feel he's rejecting you. You are not separating your **who** from your **do**. Dave loves you, but he doesn't agree with you on this one point. And you have to let him have his opinion." It was a major turning point for me.

God wants spouses to work through the obstacles that separate them from each other. Unfortunately, there are few role models in our lives to demonstrate what He had intended for the union of a husband and wife to be. Rebellion, fear, insecurity, and impatience keep us from the blessing God intended for a man and woman to enjoy together.

I had to learn to submit to the authority of God trusting that He has my good in mind. I had to learn that God loves me enough to direct me to actions that will bring blessing not bondage. He told me in His Word to love my husband — "love Dave." I could only prove that God was trustworthy by doing what He said to do.

> *I had to learn that God loves us enough to direct us to actions that will bring blessing not bondage.*

Healing began as I was obedient to what God said to do.

God was asking me to let Dave have a separate opinion without it being a threat to my self-esteem. I had to learn to let God work out the differences between us while learning to respect Dave's differences and personality, which I will discuss more in a later chapter.

Peace comes from trusting God first. I had to learn to trust God when Dave and I differed in our opinions. By letting God into the midst of my concerns, I began to have a new respect for Dave's point of view. Once the threat of rejection was removed from our debate, my heart began to change. The reward of my obedience was a growing sense of admiration for my husband.

GOD CAN MAKE ALL THINGS NEW

God does not have to have good material to build with; He is willing to take all the messes we offer Him and turn them into miracles. He has the ability to make all things new.

> *God does not have to have good material to build with; He is willing to take all the messes we offer Him and turn them into miracles.*

In Ezekiel 36:26 God makes a promise to those who will come to Him, *A new heart will I give you and a new spirit will I put within you, and I will take away the stony heart out of your flesh and give you a heart of flesh.* God can give a tender heart to someone whose old heart was bruised and beaten with the hardness of life.

This promise is made again in 2 Corinthians 5:17: *Therefore if any person is [ingrafted] in Christ (the Messiah) he is a new creation (a new creature altogether); the old [previous moral and spiritual condition] has passed away. Behold, the fresh and new has come!* God makes the past nonexistent as if it never happened so that we can face tomorrow without nagging memories from the past. He has bright and wonderful promises for our marriages if we will trust Him and do what He tells us to do.

4

A MAN SHOULDN'T
BE ALONE

---

*Let marriage be held in honor (esteemed worthy, precious,
of great price, and especially dear) in all things. And thus
let the marriage bed be undefiled (kept undishonored);
for God will judge and punish the unchaste
[all guilty of sexual vice] and adulterous.*
Hebrews 13:4

God has a purpose for marriage. And what God intended marriage to be and what most of us believe it to be are two entirely different things. All that God created was good, but when He looked at man, He said it wasn't good for him to be alone, so He created woman and told them to become one. He blessed them and told them to be fruitful, multiply, and subdue the earth.

To trust God's plan it helps to understand what His purpose is. God always starts out with something good and powerful, but it doesn't take the enemy very long to come in and pervert it in an effort to steal and destroy what God wanted to give to us.

Merriam-Webster's Collegiate® Dictionary defines "marriage" as "**1 a**: the state of being married **b**: the mutual relation of husband and wife . . . **c**: the institution whereby men and women are joined in a special kind of social and legal dependence for the purpose of founding and maintaining a family **2**: an act of marrying or the rite

To trust God's plan, it helps to understand His purpose.

by which the married status is effected; *especially:* the wedding ceremony and attendant festivities or formalities 3: an intimate or close union <the *marriage* of painting and poetry — J. T. Shawcross>."[1]

Marriage is certainly more than the ceremony, but to many people today it has been reduced to merely a day of flowers and festivities. Our divorce rate is extremely high.

Divorce used to just affect non-Christians, and believers were very serious about making their marriages work. Divorce was not an option for the Christian because the Word of God gave only certain conditions under which somebody should just give up on their marriage. People used to be more serious about making their marriages work, but more and more believers, Christian people who love God and know the Word, are giving up on their marriages today. They're throwing in the towel and saying, "Well, forget it. We just can't get along."

I know a woman who loves the Lord, and yet after twenty-three years of marriage her husband left her. There are a lot of different circumstances involved in divorce, and she knows a lot of their problems were her fault. He was willing to try to make it work. She knew if she called him and said, "OK, I'm sorry, let's try and get this thing to work," there was a good chance that he would come back. But she said, "I don't even know if I want to bother. I just don't know if I really love him or if I ever really loved him."

No one really loves anyone unless God puts that love in their heart for them. First John 4:8 says, *He who does not love has not become acquainted with God [does not and never did know Him], for God is love.* That tells me that if God is love, then we must allow God to instruct us in how to treat people. I'm not so sure how many of us loved each other when we got married to start with. Most of the time young couples marry because of a physical attraction. Sometimes, people just get married because they're lonely. There are all kinds of different reasons.

I can tell you right now that when I married Dave, I didn't have the slightest idea what love was. I didn't know how to give love; I didn't know how to receive love. I had never seen real love coming toward me. I didn't know what it was. When Dave started telling me that he loved me, I just couldn't seem to release the words out of my mouth to tell him I loved him, too.

I have grown to love Dave over the years that I have lived with him. Through watching him, hurting with him, laughing with him, crying with him, raising children with him, fighting with him, making up with him, working together and playing golf together, now I can say that I know that I love him very deeply.

Maybe your marriage is not presently in serious trouble, but that doesn't mean that five years from now the devil couldn't launch an attack against your marriage, and you would need to remember something from what I share with you in this book. Believe me, the devil attacks the family unit and the home.

When those doubts begin you think, **I don't know if I ever loved you to start with. This is never going to work. All we ever do is fight.** And then you start to get your eye on somebody else. You need to realize that they probably have more problems than the one you have. As I already said, the grass is never greener on the other side of the fence.

The Bible says that marriage is a union. Now **union** is an interesting word. It means such a joining together of two that they are one. We throw that term around a little bit loosely. We know we are supposed to be one with the Godhead, the body of Christ is supposed to be one, and two people who get married are supposed to be one. But we don't seem to comprehend totally what that means.

Picture that I am holding an empty glass. Beside me are a cup of coffee and a glass of water, the coffee of course is really dark and black, and the water is clear. A lot of times when people get married they are as different as coffee and water. Once in a great while, two people will get married and they're a lot alike, but most of the time people are very different from each other when they first come together.

After having poured that cup of coffee and that glass of water together in this glass, is there any way that I could ever separate them again? Dave and I were so different when we started out, you would think, **How in the world have you guys ever made it more than thirty years?** We were almost like a cup of coffee trying to marry a glass of water. But when God pours the two together you can watch and see what happens.

> *God wants to join us together in such a way when we marry that there is no question about being torn apart. We are one.*

God intended for you and your spouse to become a blend when He joined you together. Just as the coffee and water, you really can't even tell if it's coffee or water now. It looks like a new substance. And we wouldn't have any idea how to ever get it apart again. We become one new person joined together in Christ Jesus. And that's what God wants to do in our marriages. He wants to join us together in such a way that there's no question about being torn apart. We are one.

HOW PRECIOUS IS LOVE?

Look again at Hebrews 13, verse 4, because this is a very powerful Scripture that is going to come up in this discussion several different times. *Let marriage be held in honor, (esteemed worthy, precious. . .).* The marriage relationship should be honored in the home. Marriage should be held in honor. This is something that God created. Marriage is not man's idea. God was the One Who told Adam that he needed a helpmate. God was the One Who brought a woman for him, and He joined the two together and said that the two shall become one flesh.

The minute you were married, you were legally one, but experientially you were not yet one. We make a mistake when we don't realize the difference between legality and experience. Legally, the minute that I was born again and I accepted Jesus

Christ as my Lord and Savior, I legally became a new creature. But I didn't act like a new creature the minute that I was born again.

So legally, when we are married we are bound together as one. But the Bible does say that the two will *become* one flesh. You are in the process of "becoming." While the process is working itself out, marriage should be held in honor and your relationship with each other should be esteemed as worthy and precious. You should treat each other like a piece of fine china.

It's amazing how people treat each other when they're going together compared to the way they treat each other after they get married. When Dave and I were courting, I never even knew the man played golf. I never saw his golf clubs one time. He had eyes only for me. Dave has lifted weights basically all of his life, and he still does every other day or so. He was twenty-six years old when we met, and he had never taken a girl home with him to meet his mother. He told his mother, "When I bring a woman home with me, that will be the woman that I'm going to marry."

But Dave said that the first night he didn't come home to lift weights, his mother knew our relationship was serious. He even laid aside weight lifting some nights for me. I didn't even know he played golf, and all of a sudden, after about five days of marriage, I guess he grew tired of putting up curtain rods for me and decided to drag his golf clubs out of the closet. He said, "I'm going out to the park to hit shag balls."

I said, "What are those and what's a shag ball?"

And from then on, for the first three years of our marriage, we fought over golf. It is amazing how differently we act when we are trying to get **something** from how we treat that **something** we were trying to get when we finally possess it. We are careful about our manners and how we behave and how we act when we are "in pursuit."

Once that thing or "someone" belongs to us we act a different way than the way we acted before it belonged to us. It's sad, isn't it? I exhort you to treat your spouse as if you were still courting because, in effect, you are. If you don't work at your marriage, you are not going to have a good one.

We are to hold marriage in honor, esteem it as worthy and precious. Think about that for a minute. Marriage is precious. It's honorable in the eyes of God, and it is to be esteemed worthy. Keep that fact in your mind's eye.

According to God's Word, we need to esteem marriage as worthy, precious, of a great price, and especially dear.

Avoid getting a loose attitude toward marriage. We begin to treat each other like some old throw pillow tossed in the corner somewhere. We get it when we want to be comfortable, but otherwise ignore it. According to God's Word, we need to esteem marriage as worthy, precious, of a great price, and especially dear.

One morning I was praying because I didn't know what God wanted me to teach at an upcoming couple's advance. I asked the Lord for guidance and found Malachi, chapter 2, confirming that God cares how husbands and wives treat each other. If we would stop treating each other the way we feel like treating each other, and start preferring one another the way God tells us to, we would see God's blessing come into our lives.

We need to understand that if we are not going to follow God's way, then we are opening up doors for the devil to come in to kill, steal, and destroy. But if we'll do it God's way, then we are going to have God's blessing. A good marriage is a tremendous blessing, but a bad one is a curse. There is nothing worse than living in a house with somebody whom you hate and despise and resent. If you are always nit-picking, fighting, and arguing with each other, you will wear each other out. Even when you are not outwardly arguing, you let thoughts constantly run through your head about all these things they do to you that you wish they wouldn't do. I know because I have lived like that, and my marriage was sick. But God can do a tremendously beautiful work in our relationships if we will let Him. But we have to live out our marriage God's way.

It is amazing to me how many Christians think that their home and their lives are going to be blessed while they continue to live in strife. It won't work that way.

The only thing that stands between us and our ability to do what God tells us to do is our flesh. Our hearts are right, or we wouldn't be seeking God for answers or reading books on marriage. We obviously want something to be better than it is now, but our flesh stands between us and doing the perfect will of God. Pride rises up and keeps us from making the first move. That soulish realm blocks us from the perfect will of God. What we **want**, what we **think**, or what we **feel** is not the issue.

The issue is the Word of God. What does the Word of God say about our marriages? The Bible has a lot to say about how men should treat their wives. It also speaks of how wives should treat their husbands. This Scripture in Malachi 2:10-14 addresses the husbands first:

> Have we not all one Father? Has not one God created us? Why then do we deal faithlessly and treacherously each against his brother, profaning the covenant of [God with] our fathers?

> Judah has been faithless and dealt treacherously, and an abomination has been committed in Israel and in Jerusalem; for Judah [that is, Jewish men] has profaned the holy sanctuary of the Lord which He loves, and has married the daughter of a foreign god [having divorced his Jewish wife].

> The Lord will cast out of the tents of Jacob to the last man those who do this [evil thing], the master and the servant [or the pupil] alike, even him who brings an offering to the Lord of hosts.

> And this you do with double guilt; you cover the altar of the Lord with tears [shed by your unoffending wives, divorced by you that you might take heathen wives], and with [your own] weeping and crying out because the Lord does not regard your offering any more or accept it with favor at your hand.

> Yet you ask, Why does He reject it? Because the Lord was witness [to the covenant made at your marriage] between you and the wife of your youth, against whom you have dealt treacherously and to whom you were faithless. Yet she is your

companion and the wife of your covenant [made by your marriage vows.

Now, the issue here is not whether you are Jewish or not. The point God is saying is, "Listen, you have divorced the wife of your youth, and you have married somebody else, and I am not pleased with it." It's pretty simple.

Yet they asked, "Why does He reject our offerings?" It's amazing sometimes how foolish we can be in our thinking. The men of Judah had blatantly disobeyed God, and now God was rejecting their offerings, and yet they come back to the altar saying, "Well, God, why are You mad at us? Why are You rejecting our offerings?" And God just simply says, "Because you didn't do what I told you to do." It's pretty simple.

I am not saying here that there is never a reason to get a divorce. Of course there are cases where divorce is the only option, but certainly not in as many cases as we see and deal with today in our society. Many marriages end in divorce today simply because people are not willing to go through what it takes to make a marriage good. God hates divorce. He does not hate the divorcee, but we should under no circumstances have a loose view of divorce.

As I already mentioned, I was divorced when I was twenty-three years old, after a five-year relationship with a man who was unfaithful and broke the law. He also regularly deserted me for long periods of time. He simply disappeared with no word at all concerning where he was. Then, after several months, he would reappear, begging for another chance, telling me how much he loved me. My hunger to be loved caused me to be deceived by him for a long time, but after giving birth to my first son, I knew my life and his could no longer be subjected to that kind of unstable behavior. My life proves there is "life after divorce," but once again let me stress that marriage is to be held in honor and highly esteemed. We should never pursue divorce without biblical grounds and without having done all we possibly can to make the marriage work.

If you are already divorced, or perhaps even divorced several times, there is no point in spending the rest of your life feeling guilty. Make up your mind from this point on that marriage is intended for a lifetime. If you are married again now, make the marriage work; if you are not, don't get married until you know for sure that you are ready to make a lifetime commitment.

Having a happy life and being blessed is not nearly as complicated as we make it. All we have to do is do what God says to do. It's not really that hard. We get our thinking all fouled up. We are self-centered and self-willed, but there is not a better way than God's way. We don't have a better idea than God has, and we can't come up with a better plan than His. For years, I thought I knew better than God when it came to my own happiness. It took God the better part of twelve years to convince me that my idea was not better than His.

> *Having a happy life and being blessed is not nearly as complicated as we make it.*

Notice why the Lord rejected their offerings. In verse 14 of Malachi 2 it says, . . . *Because the Lord was witness [to the covenant made at your marriage]. . . .* When you got married, were you aware that God was there? He saw it, He watched it, and He calls your union a covenant. It was not just some ceremony you went through with a couple of witnesses. God participated in your marriage.

. . . *Because the Lord was witness [to the covenant made at your marriage] between you and the wife of your youth, against whom you have dealt treacherously. . . .* Now, we are going to get into some pretty serious language here in a minute. The Bible says if a man deals treacherously and faithlessly with his wife, God does not take it kindly. . . . *And to whom you were faithless. Yet she is your companion and the wife of your covenant [made by your marriage vows].*

And now, watch carefully as verse 15 points to God's purpose for marriage.

> *And did not God make [you and your wife] one [flesh]? Did not One (being God) make you and preserve your spirit alive? And why [did God make you two] one? Because He sought a godly offspring [from your union]. . . .*

God makes two people, one, in marriage because He seeks a godly offspring from the union — children and godly fruit.

Now, I think this is interesting. Why did God make the two of you one? Because He sought a godly offspring from your union. Now, I believe that's talking about children, but I believe it's talking about a lot more than that. I think it's talking about godly fruit.

WHAT KIND OF FRUIT ARE YOU BEARING?

I believe that it glorifies God when Dave and I do nice things for each other. We have a little routine in the morning. The first thing we do is I hug up to his back for five minutes, and then I turn over and he hugs up to my back for five minutes. And we set our clock fifteen minutes early because we enjoy that time so much.

That's a personal thing, but married couples need to love each other. We can't just come to each other when we want something. We need to be in the habit of loving each other and being sweet to our spouse. We once had a waterbed, and it was hard to get out of it. So Dave usually got up before I did, then came to help pull me out of the waterbed. Sounds comical, doesn't it? I just kind of fell into his arms and hung there for another few minutes. We've had a housekeeper in recent years, but at one time, Dave used to go off and make the coffee, and I took a shower.

Yes, my husband made the coffee! I needed to wash my hair and allow it time to dry, so he wasn't ashamed to go do that for me. That was a blessing for me, and he did it happily. I believe that is all part of the godly offspring from our union.

God is looking for things in the earth that are going to glorify Him. He's looking for things that are going to give Him praise. And I believe it gives God praise when we love each other. That's why the Bible says that we in the body of Christ should become one. That's why God wants us to love, exhort, and edify each other and not be jealous or envious of each other. That unity and oneness is the presence of His power that gives God glory.

Why did the Lord make you two one? Because He wants a godly offspring from your union. . . . *Therefore take heed to yourselves. . .* (v. 15). God is saying, "You have to watch yourself. Let's be serious about this thing. It's not just going to automatically happen." *. . . And let no one deal treacherously and be faithless to the wife of his youth.* I looked up that word "treacherous," and it means to pillage, to deal deceitfully. There is so much deceit in marriages today because there is a lack of straightforward truthfulness and honesty.

Women buy things and hide them from their husbands. Husbands go out and do things and don't tell their wives. The Bible says we are not to deal deceitfully, unfaithfully. We are not to offend or to depart from each other. Verse 16 says, *For the Lord, the God of Israel, says: I hate divorce and marital separation. . . .* You see, God hates it.

As I have already said, I realize that there are people who are in situations where they feel as though God has told them to get a divorce. My main purpose is not to deal with the issue of divorce. I do believe there are times when that is the only answer. As a matter of fact, I think there are times when people do stay with a mate and it ends up ruining their life and the lives of their children. I believe there are proper grounds, even though God hates divorce.

No one should have a loose attitude toward divorce, but we should do everything we can to avoid it. If you have had a loose attitude toward marriage and divorce in the past, I strongly suggest a time of serious repentance of asking God to forgive you. The attitude may have been the result of a lack of knowledge, but starting from now with a clean conscience and a fresh attitude is very important.

Marriage does require that both partners yield to God, but one may have to put forth more effort in the beginning. Eventually, there will have to be sacrifices from both people. There will have to be giving in and change of heart from both people if their marriage is going to work.

For the Lord, the God of Israel, says: I hate divorce and marital separation and him who covers his garment [his wife] with violence. . . (v. 16). Now, that's an interesting thing to me that the Bible says

> *When the husband is good to his wife, it shows and makes him look good to his community. He is bearing good fruit.*

that a man's garment is his wife. The Bible teaches in both Ephesians and 1 Peter that the wife is the man's glory. How the wife appears to other people reflects on the husband and his headship of the household. When the husband is good to his wife, it shows and makes him look good to his community. He is bearing good fruit.

Dave and I have to eat out a lot because of the nature of our work, and we get tired of eating in the same places. I saw an advertisement for a restaurant while flipping through a magazine and I said, "Oh, why don't you take me to this restaurant sometime?"

And all of a sudden, he whipped a piece of paper out of his wallet and said, "Give me the phone number; let me write it down." I thought, **My goodness, he's going to do it!**

How many times do you tell your marriage mate what you need? How often does your spouse tell you what he needs? Is it possible that you just aren't hearing it? Are you truly paying attention? You must learn to listen to each other. Do you have any idea how happy you'll be if you'll set yourself to meet that other person's needs and quit worrying about getting your own needs met?

The name of the game throughout the Bible is give, give, give. The very principle of love is to forget about yourself, ignore yourself and all your own interests, and get into the relationship to make the other person happy. Your primary goal when you enter marriage should be to make that other person as happy as you can make them. My goal in life is to make Dave happy, and Dave's goal ought to be to make me happy. I'm talking about other than my relationship goals with God.

The next focus after our attention to God ought to be the goal to make each other happy. But most of the time we are trying to get them to make us happy. The Bible says if you give, you will receive.

Jesus came as a servant to those He loved. It's a new twist to think, **Oh, I'm supposed to make you happy? I thought you were supposed to make me happy.** We have to change our thinking.

For the Lord, the God of Israel, says: I hate divorce **and** *marital separation and him who covers his garment [his wife] with violence. Therefore keep a watch upon your spirit [that it may be controlled by My Spirit], that you deal not treacherously and faithlessly [with your marriage mate]* (v. 16). That's pretty interesting, isn't it? He said to, . . . *Keep a watch upon your spirit [that it may be controlled by My Spirit]*. . . . In other words, if we are controlled by the Spirit of God, we are going to always do what love would do, right?

So we are to keep a watch upon our spirit that it may be controlled by the Holy Spirit. If we let our flesh control us, we will deal faithlessly and treacherously with our mate. But if we will let the Holy Spirit control us, we will be surprised how many times we set out to do a certain thing then are quickened by the Holy Spirit to go another way. We must not shut off our ears to the way of God or we will take a selfish route that will lead to loneliness instead of union.

It is virtually impossible to have a good marriage and always get your own way. Realizing that has helped me a lot. Learning to be adaptable, choosing not to make a big deal out of petty things, and being on my guard against selfish behavior on my part have all played a big part in bringing me to the point where I can truly say today: **I have a great marriage!**

5
COUNT TO TEN
BEFORE YOU SPEAK

And be constantly renewed in the spirit of your mind
[having a fresh mental and spiritual attitude].
And put on the new nature (the regenerate self) created in
God's image, [Godlike] in true righteousness and holiness.
Ephesians 4:23,24

Children are sometimes taught to count to ten before they speak if they can't think of something nice to say. That's good advice, but it won't help if the old resentment is still inside after reaching the number ten. As believers, we are to speak life into situations just as the Lord did, but the old, defensive nature too often blurts out its selfish viewpoint. Without help from the Holy Spirit it is difficult to control our tongue. Ephesians 5:18 tells us to be filled and stimulated with the Holy Spirit. To do this we are to ask the Holy Spirit to give us the power that we need to build godly marriages and relationships.

In earlier chapters, I pointed out that marriage is more than a legal institution that binds the property accumulated by two people to an equal right of ownership. Marriage is a promise of companionship and provision for the needs between two people. Marriage is symbolic of God's promise and provision to us. Therefore, to keep the promise of marriage, we need to be full of God's Spirit. We need to let God empower us with His faithfulness and selflessness so that we can attend to the needs of our spouses.

God will fill us with His Own nature. John the Baptist taught that after we are baptized with water, Jesus would come and baptize us with the Holy Ghost and with fire. (Matthew 3:6,11.) As I began studying the Word, I read about this baptism of the Holy Ghost, and because of my ever-increasing desire to have more of God in my life, I asked God for this experience.

Jesus said in Acts 1:5-8 that we would receive power, ability, efficiency, and might when the Holy Spirit comes upon us. This power would cause us to be a witness to Jesus. The book of Acts shows several occasions when the disciples had the power to do what seemed impossible when the Holy Spirit came upon them. When we believe in Christ, His Spirit comes to live **in** us, but the baptism of the Spirit comes **upon** us to empower us with the ability to live the Christian life and serve God according to His will.

When we are filled with God's Spirit, we have the power and strength to love the way He does.

Many couples try to have a Christian marriage by following the laws of God's Word to generate love, but they need a "Spirit-filled" marriage where love generates the laws that operate between them. When we are filled with God's Spirit, we have the power and strength to love the way He does.

As I share in my book entitled *The Most Important Decision You'll Ever Make,* I received the baptism of the Holy Spirit in my car in February 1976, as a sovereign move of the Lord in my life. I had cried out to God asking for more of Him. I said, "God, there has to be more to Christianity than I am experiencing." I wanted victory over my problems, and I did not have it. I had been a Christian for many years prior to this time, but my life was still full of frustration and unhappiness.

That same evening, Jesus baptized me in the Holy Spirit. I did not speak in tongues right away as the accounts in the book of Acts mention, primarily because I knew nothing about such things at that time. It probably would have frightened me since I had never had teaching on it, but I did receive much power, ability, determination, and understanding from that point on. During the next several weeks, God led me to radio programs and books where I learned more about the baptism in the Spirit.

Later, I learned that the gift of tongues is given to believers as a prayer language to communicate with God and to edify and improve oneself. If teaching about the baptism of the Holy Spirit is new to you, I encourage you to read the Scripture references that I added at the end of the book. You can read about the purpose of tongues in 1 Corinthians 14:1-4. If you are struggling with your life, your marriage, and you need power, ability, strength, and miracles in your life and have never asked God to baptize you with His Spirit, I encourage you to stop and pray now. I include information on how to do this in the appendix of this book.

If you have received your prayer language, then praying in the Spirit is much more effective than counting to ten before you speak. But if you will at least ask the Holy Spirit to give you the right words when expressing your heart to your spouse, you will see His power begin to make positive changes in your marriage. He will give you wisdom on how to deal with the conflicts that threaten your unity, and show you ways to build up your love for each other.

If any of you is deficient in wisdom, let him ask of the giving God [Who gives] to everyone liberally and ungrudgingly, without reproaching or faultfinding, and it will be given to him.

James 1:5

We don't have to try to make our marriages successful on our own. God promises to help us, and we should go to Him on a daily, even moment-by-moment, basis and ask for help. I did not know to go to God and I was caught in my old nasty habit of selfish gratification, even though it wasn't gratifying. Dave, who was Spirit-filled, did know to take our struggles to the Lord, and when I finally received the baptism of the Holy Spirit, our relationship took a turn toward God's better plan for us.

> *As I spent time with God, praying in the Holy Spirit, I could hear God speak wisdom to me concerning my marriage.*

Prayer changes us from the inside out. As I spent time with God, praying in the Holy Spirit, I could hear God speak wisdom to me concerning our marriage. I learned that a house divided against itself cannot stand. I had to learn to walk **with** Dave and not **against** him all the time.

When I became Spirit-filled, I was more vocal about it than Dave had been, and we were put out of the Protestant church we attended. We lost almost all our friends who attended there. When we started listening to charismatic faith teachers, our previous friends thought we were crazy. God led me to have a Bible study in my home. That was when I started spending so many hours a day reading God's Word.

I had so many personality problems, and after receiving the baptism in the Holy Spirit, God started confronting me with truth. Truth always brings freedom from bondage and despair, but it was a long, hard battle because I was rebellious, full of fear, and terribly insecure. I acted as if I didn't need anybody, but I knew I did. I acted tough, but I really wasn't. I had rough and grumpy mannerisms, and there was a lot to overcome. But from the minute I started studying, I had a teaching gift. God just put in me the desire and ability to make His Word clear to others.

I have always had a strong gift of communication in both written and oral expressions. Once I was Spirit-filled, I was able to stop communicating rebellion, fear, and insecurity and express agreement, love, and confidence. My gift wasn't worth much until God changed my nature.

WHO CONTROLS YOUR SPIRIT?

Malachi 2:16 tells us to keep a watch on our spirit and be controlled by God's Spirit. We cannot expect a thing to work right if we are not going to listen to God. If we do not listen to God, we are not going to have a good marriage. It's pretty straightforward and simple, isn't it? But, if we will listen to God, we will have a great marriage. Therefore be controlled by God's Spirit. Now, let's read verse 17 of Malachi 2:

You have wearied the Lord with your words. Yet you say, In what way have we wearied Him? . . .

God will tell us, and tell us, and tell us, and tell us what we are doing wrong, then we'll go back to Him and ask, "Well, what am I doing wrong?" In answer to our question of how we have wearied Him, God says, . . . *[You do it when by your actions] you say, Everyone who does evil is good in the sight of the Lord and he delights in them. Or [by asking], Where is the God of justice?* (v. 17). We weary the Lord with our words and the way we act.

In other words, He's saying, "It wearies Me when by your actions you act as if what you are doing is all right when My Word has already told you that it's not all right." That wearies the Lord and He gets tired of it.

When we tell our children what to do, it really makes us happy if they just go do it. If they happily obey, we want to bless them. But if they are rebellious and continue on their own way acting as though everything is OK even though we told them not to do what they are doing, we get tired of that, too.

Some people's perception of God is that He is perfect; therefore, He can't be tired. Yet He says that we have wearied Him with our words. Imagine that if we weary our patient and loving God with the things we say, how much more are we wearing out each other? God wants spouses to serve each other, to be a light in a dark world where the divorce rate is incredibly high, to be a light set on a hill and to nurture a marriage that can literally be an example to other people of God's love.

I believe that Dave and I have a marriage that is an example of God's love between two people without us ever even standing up and telling others that we have a good relationship. People who watch us can tell that we love each other. When couples get involved in our ministry, it doesn't take long to tell if they're putting it on or if they really love each other. You can't hide true love. It doesn't take long to see if somebody's selfish and self-centered, or if they're really pouring out love.

If we love people, it will show as an expressive outpouring of who we are. When we are "in Christ," our actions will demonstrate love. When we are "in ourselves," our actions will demonstrate greed and self-preservation. The words, "I love you," can be expressed to someone whether you are in Christ or outside of Him, but there will be a vast difference in the impact and power of those words if you are not in Christ. True love cannot be felt or expressed without Christ present in the heart that both gives and receives affection.

The words, "I love you," can be expressed whether you are in Christ or outside of Him, but there will be a vast difference in the impact and power.

Yes, it is in giving that we receive, and Christ even gives us the love that we need to give to others. If we want love to fully bloom and bring its manifold blessings to our homes, we must submit ourselves to the work of the Holy Spirit on a daily basis.

Ephesians, chapter 5, supports that women are to be equally good to their husbands, as husbands are taught in Malachi to be faithful to their wives. Verse 21 begins, *Be subject to one another out of reverence for Christ (the Messiah, the Anointed One).* We are to subject ourselves to each other out of respect for Christ. Verse 22 says, *Wives, be subject (be submissive and adapt yourselves) to your own husbands as [a service] to the Lord.* All the men in the room say "amen" when I teach this to couples at weekend advances. They hear what they have been trying to get us to hear from the beginning. Adapt! Submit!

But, you see, this "submitting and adapting thing" is two-sided. It is so clear to me. It's been several years since Dave asked me to sit down and listen to the revelation he had received out of Ephesians. Sometimes when one person gets understanding on a particular subject, no matter how much they tell it to somebody else, the next person doesn't get it. And, when Dave first told me what I am about to share with you, he was all excited about what God had shown him, but I didn't quite get what he was seeing. I just nodded my head and looked at him with a blank expression on my face.

But now I understand what he was so excited about. Dave said, "This is it! The perfect union in marriage is for a man to love his wife as Christ loved the church." We are not talking about a man loving his wife like the guy next door loves his wife. We are talking about a man loving his wife as Christ loved the church. Obviously it will take some time to expound on that fully, but one thing I have learned is that a man loving his wife as Christ loved the church does not mean that she gets her way about everything. I believe Dave's revelation was hard for me to grasp the day he shared it because I was still stubbornly wanting my way all the time. I thought if Dave really loved me, he would want to make me happy. Obviously, I was so caught up in thinking about myself that it never occurred to me to make him happy by letting him have his way. I don't know who I thought was supposed to make him happy, but I certainly wasn't considering that it should have been me.

A woman's response to proper loving care and nurturing should be, then, to submit and adapt to her husband as the church would to the Lord. This is the other major point of Ephesians — a woman is to respect and reverence her husband. This does not mean that she behaves as a vegetable never having an opinion, or being afraid to voice it if she does. Marriage is a partnership, but ultimately someone has to make a final decision when two people don't agree. On relatively unimportant things Dave and I sort of take turns. On major ones the final call is his.

> *When a man loves his wife as Christ loved the church, and the wife submits to her husband and respects him, both doing their part, a glorious relationship will result.*

The man is to love his wife as Christ loved the church, and the woman is to submit to her husband and respect him. If both parties will do their part, a glorious relationship will result. Sometimes one of the spouses is not willing to do their part. Then a standoff begins. The argument begins, "Well, I won't if you don't," and, "I'm not going to if you don't," so we have a big mess.

Somebody needs to start somewhere, and though I hope that both partners are going to be willing to start and do exactly what God says, I want to encourage you to go ahead and be first. But even if it seems that one of you is more willing than the other one, continue doing what is right as a service to the Lord. Love has to start somewhere. If what you are doing now is not working, then you have nothing to lose. Everything will stay the same until someone makes a change. If you want to see what God can do then, wives, be submissive and adapt yourselves to your own husbands as a service to the Lord.

There is probably no one better qualified than I am to try to teach women how to submit and adapt because I was the least likely person to ever want to adapt to anything or anyone. I wanted everything and everybody to adapt to me. And when I first began to read in the Bible that a wife was to adapt to her own husband, it gave me the creeps! Just the thought of adapting made me uncomfortable.

It is amazing how miserable we can make ourselves because we will not adapt to some simple little thing that somebody's asking us to do. But because of pride and rebellion, we are determined to stand our ground and have life our way. Before long we are miserable and so is everyone who knows us. I mentioned that for three years I fought with Dave over his golf. We fought, and fought, and fought, and fought. I was determined that he was not going to play. And he was determined that he was. But as I began to let the Lord work with me, Dave and I reached the place of peace and agreement, which release joy.

You have made known to me the ways of life; You will enrapture Me [diffusing my soul with joy] with and in Your presence.
Acts 2:28

The great standoff between two people is inevitable unless the Lord intervenes and fills their hearts with love. Dave and I fought and fought, but we also prayed and prayed. Keep reading to see who won this battle.

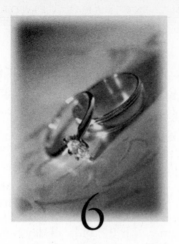

6

MAYBE *SOME* OF IT WAS MY FAULT

Now to Him Who is able to keep you without stumbling or slipping or falling, and to present [you] unblemished (blameless and faultless) before the presence of His glory in triumphant joy and exultation [with unspeakable, ecstatic delight].
Jude 24

When two people spend quality time together, they begin to see life the same way. But when two people stand back to back, facing opposite directions, they have little chance of sharing a common viewpoint. When those same two people are determined, but she is determined that he's **not** going somewhere, and he is determined that he **is,** they have a problem. I will share more about healthy confrontations later in this book, but first I want to point out the difference that spending time with each other can make in a relationship.

I made myself miserable for those three years that I stayed mad at Dave for playing golf. I made him miserable because I refused to adapt to his love for the game. Of course, I made our children miserable, too, because they saw me argue with their dad over it. It unsettles a child when they see their parents fight because many times, they think it's their fault. It produces all kinds of insecurity and fear in children when their parents fight all the time and of course it didn't build a healthy relationship between Dave and me.

With three little kids running around at our feet, Dave and I continued to fight over golf. I was frequently mad and pouted all the time. Dave was not going to quit, and I was determined that he was. The more I nagged, the more he played.

Dave said if you want to be a good golfer, then you have to practice all the time. So he played golf, and he practiced during the week, too. I was home with the kids all day by myself, while several times a week Dave would come home, have dinner, then get out the golf clubs and go to the driving range to hit golf balls. I couldn't understand why he insisted on doing this, nor was I willing to believe there was a valid explanation for such desire. None of it made any sense to me.

The Lord is able to keep us from stumbling, slipping, or falling even though we are sometimes determined to race towards a head-on collision with our blemished plan for life. I believe that prayers intervened and spared us from the tragedies that would have resulted if I had continued down my destructive path of anger and resentment.

When I began to see the Scriptures in the Bible that a woman should adapt to her husband, I thought, **I'd die first. I just can't do it.** Have you ever had such rebellion in your flesh that you honestly thought if you had to give in, you would shrivel and die? I felt that it would kill me if I had to humble myself and do what Dave wanted me to do.

I liked finding Scriptures in the Bible that Dave was supposed to listen to. The Word says in 1 Peter 3:7 (NASB), *You husbands likewise, live with your wives in an understanding way, as with a weaker vessel, since she is a woman; and grant her honor as a fellow heir of the grace of life, so that your prayers may not be hindered.* I was convinced that Dave needed to understand how difficult it was for me to be home with the kids all day long, day in and day out. After all, he was out with adults, normal people, who don't slobber and make strange faces at you. Like other women at home with their young children, I longed to get out and talk to "grown-ups."

JUST ME AND YOU, TOGETHER

It is important for couples to do things together. Spending time with each other increases understanding of each other's viewpoint and needs. At this time in our marriage, I was so hard to get along with that Dave probably went to play golf a lot more than he would have, just to get

It is important for couples to do things together.

away from me. The Bible says that a quarrelsome, nagging wife annoys like constant dripping on a rainy day. (Proverbs 19:13 NIV, TLB; Proverbs 27:15 NIV.) Poor Dave!

Because I really didn't believe that anybody could love me, I wanted Dave to dote on me all the time to make me feel secure. I wanted him to want to be with me rather than want to be on the golf course. I wanted him to fuss over me all the time. Everything was about me and my desperate plight to nurture that root of rejection in my life. I needed constant "fixing." I didn't want to lose control of what made me feel secure, so I tried throwing fits to get him to stay home.

Dave always invited me to go with him. The issue wasn't that he was taking off without me. He would invite me to go, but I was too bullheaded to do it. I didn't want to play golf; and I didn't think that he ought to either, so I was not giving in. At least two or three times a week I was mad over golf to the point that I hated it.

Finally, one afternoon I went to the driving range to find him. I don't even remember how I got there now, maybe we had two cars by then, or maybe he went out with somebody else. I was pouting in my dark little corner of the apartment, crying and unhappy with our three kids, and he was at the driving range having a good time in the sunshine. Somehow, by the mercy of God, I was given the grace to swallow my pride. I put those three kids in the car and drove out to that driving range. I took them out of the car, walked up to Dave, and lined up the kids behind his tee box. He was leaning over, placing his golf ball on the tee when he looked up at me and said, "What happened? Did the house burn down?"

Looking at his surprised face I said, "No, I just give up. Here I am. Teach me to play golf."

SURRENDER MEANS TO "GIVE UP"

I just gave up. God's grace brought me to a place where I realized that I wasn't going to change Dave. We were having such trouble over this golf that it had to have been an act of grace for God to give me a desire to play golf with Dave. The whole issue could have easily caused us some serious, serious problems.

Dave taught me the fundamentals for three months before I ever went out to play a game of golf. I eventually learned to play well. But the first time we went out to play on a nine-hole golf course, I was on the first tee box, and there were a **lot** of men standing around waiting for their turn to tee off.

I swung and missed the ball thirteen times in a row on that first tee because I was nervous. Seeing that I was embarrassed, Dave came up to me and gently said, "Take your time, take your time." Under my breath I threatened, "If I miss this ball again, I'm picking it up and throwing it down!" then I dribbled it off the tee, and thus began my golf career.

> *If I hadn't been willing to do what God said to do, I would have missed out on the fun that God and Dave had planned for me.*

We've enjoyed many years of golf together. If I hadn't been willing to do what God said to do and go play golf with Dave, I would have missed out on the fun that they both had planned for me. When you play golf, you can't think about anything else but your stance, grip, and focus. The clearer your head, the better your swing. It is a nice break from the busyness of our daily life.

I had to surrender my old thinking to try out Dave's way of relaxation. I had to surrender my fears of being unloved, to join the love of my life in a game that we could both enjoy. I had to lay aside my stubbornness and rebellion against God's Word in order to receive the joy of His presence. But with God it is possible to break loose from our old nature and become a new creation.

Having great relationships and a terrific marriage is possible. It is simply a matter of surrender and letting God lead us to the pleasant plan He has in mind for us. I couldn't have my own way and God's way, too.

When I studied the Word, after I was Spirit-filled, I well remember the first confrontation I had with the Holy Ghost. I was praying one day for Dave to change, and God actually spoke to me saying, "Dave is not the problem."

I couldn't believe it! I had a list of things that would be better if Dave would do "this" and our kids would do "that." I was unhappy and hard to get along with because they weren't treating me right. Isn't that the way most people think? Almost everyone blames their bad behavior, their past, and their lack of money on someone else.

When God said, "Dave is not the problem," it was as if my eyes were opened and I could finally see what it was like to live with me. I saw that I was a nag, critical, and hard to get along with. I cried for three days.

DYING TO SELF

I felt as though nobody loved me and couldn't understand why. After all, hadn't I done all the things a good Christian was supposed to do? Didn't I study the Word and teach others God's way? Now even God seemed to be on Dave's side instead of mine.

James 1:26 and 27 are two foundational Scriptures for anyone who feels their life and ministry are worthless, futile, and barren. There might be a valid reason for those feelings and these Scriptures give us a hint of what might be wrong in our lives. Read the verses carefully:

If anyone thinks himself to be religious (piously observant of the external duties of his faith) and does not bridle his tongue but deludes his own heart, this person's religious service is worthless (futile, barren).

External religious worship [religion as it is expressed in outward acts] that is pure and unblemished in the sight of God the Father is this: to visit and help and care for the orphans and widows in their affliction and need, and to keep oneself unspotted and uncontaminated from the world.

Now that's a pretty strong statement. It's saying, if we think we are religious and are attending to all these outward duties of our faith, but we are not bridling our tongue, then all of our efforts are useless and worthless. First Corinthians 13 says that if we don't have a strong love walk, we can speak in tongues all day long and all we are doing is making noise! We can have so much faith that we can move mountains, but we are nothing if we don't really love people.

We are nothing if we don't really love people.

God said another thing that makes our religious service worthless is if we don't bridle our tongue. He didn't say He would do it all for us. We have to use self-control concerning the things we say.

I remember how God taught me the lesson that I do have control over my words. I used to have "fits," just all-out temper tantrums, and unleash my unhappiness on my kids. I'd get mad at Dave, then I'd rant and rave at my kids all day. I didn't like the mess their toys made, so I would yell at them to go clean up. I'd clean the house; they'd make another mess, and I'd go into another fit.

One day I was performing one of my expected fits, yelling, "Pick this stuff up! All I ever do is clean this place and you guys mess it up all the time! You act like I'm your slave around here."

Of course, after the kids were crying and everybody had a fit of their own, I felt guilty for the atmosphere I had inspired. Don't be fooled, the same devil who leads you into temptation is the same one who'll come around and condemn you for the temptation he led you into. So then I would confess, "Oh, God, I'm so sorry, but I just can't help it! I don't want to act like that, but I just lose my temper. I just can't help it, God!"

I had a vision of something God showed me. He said, "Joyce, if your pastor pulled up while you were in the middle of one of those fits, by the time he rang the doorbell you'd get over it." He said, "You would exercise perfect self-control in his presence." You would open the door and you would say, "Well, Pastor, praise the Lord! It's so good to see you. Oh, the children. Oh, well, the little darlings, they're playing in their room, the little dears. Yes, come in, praise the Lord." That truth taught me a major lesson.

When we are around people that we want to impress, or that we don't want to think badly of us, it is amazing how well we can behave. When we want people to "love us" we demonstrate plenty of "self-control" so that they see the lovable side of us. If our focus were to love others, we would also demonstrate self-control over what we do and say so that we wouldn't hurt the people we love.

Verse 27 of James 1 is saying that our worship and faith in Christ are to have some outward expression that others can see. It's called good works, but these good works must be done with a right motive. If good things are done with a wrong motive, then God doesn't call them good works. He calls them "works of the flesh," which stink in His nostrils. James explains that worship that is expressed in outward acts should be pure and unblemished in the sight of God the Father. Examples are to visit, help, and care for the orphans and the widows in their affliction and to keep oneself unspotted and uncontaminated from the world. This is acceptable worship in the eyes of God.

So, if you want your religion to be real, you must have three outward expressions of your faith:
- you must bridle your mouth
- you must help hurting people
- you must live a holy life

If you focus on these three things, you will bless yourself, your spouse, your family, and your friends. You will see the blessing of God poured out into your relationships. Happiness will abound, and success will follow all that you do. God's ways are simple and true. Obedience to His instruction leads to what I call radical and outrageous blessings. **Don't spin your wheels trying to bless yourself. Simply obey God's principles, and God will bless you.**

HOW TO LIVE A HOLY LIFE

Obedience to God's instruction leads to radical and outrageous blessings.

Holy living begins with getting rid of selfishness in your life. The paradox of happiness is that it comes when you forget about yourself and live to help somebody else. I found out that you can't be happy if you have yourself on your mind all the time. I spent so many years as an unhappy Christian. If we don't have righteousness, peace, and joy, then we have missed the kingdom.

Prosperity, healing, success, and promotions on our jobs are all kingdom benefits that God wants us to have. He shows us in the Bible how to get them, but those benefits are not the kingdom. The kingdom of God is not meat and drink, the Bible says, it is . . . *righteousness, and peace, and joy in the Holy Ghost* (Romans 14:17 KJV). We are to seek first the kingdom of God and His righteousness and *all these things* will be added to us. (Matthew 6:33.)

So our priorities need to stay in line with God's Word. We have to do things in God's order. And God gets weary of people who only seek His hand and never seek His face. We need to go to God not for what He can do for us, but for Who He is and because we need Him to survive every day. I have no joy, peace, nor righteousness apart from Jesus.

The kingdom of God is the realm within us. It is learning a response to daily life that differs from how the world responds, and we need to pay more attention to this inner life we have available to us through Christ. We get too concerned with what everybody thinks of us. We are too concerned with how we look, what we own, what kind of car we drive, whether we have a title that we can put on our door at our office, what kind of seat we get in the church, and what our position is in the church. We need to be much more concerned with what kinds of thoughts we have.

If you are unhappy, examine yourself and ask,

- "What's going on in me that's not pleasing to God?
- What attitudes do I have that stink in the nostrils of God?
- Am I jealous, bitter, or resentful?
- How many people am I offended with?
- How many people do I have unforgiveness against?
- How many people do I hate?
- How many people am I jealous of?"

Your unhappiness probably has nothing to do with your spouse. Discontent is most likely a result of your outlook on life.

> *It's not your circumstances that make you unhappy; it's not having things right on the inside of your heart.*

If your heart is not full of righteousness, peace, and joy in the Holy Ghost, happiness won't be found anywhere, through anyone. It's not your circumstances that make you unhappy; it's not having things right on the inside of your heart.

Jesus said we can have peace in the midst of the storm. (Matthew 8:26.) When Peter said we can have *joy unspeakable and full of glory* (1 Peter 1:8 KJV) he was in the midst of persecution from Nero's reign in Rome. Paul repeatedly spoke of his joy saying in all his troubles his joy knew no bounds. (2 Corinthians 7:4.)

As Bible teacher Jerry Savelle says, "If the devil can't steal your joy, he can't steal your goods." He can only ask you for it, and only you can give it up. I have lived the unhappy, the selfish, the self-centered, the carnal life, seeking God for what He could do for me, wanting my ministry to grow, trying to get this, trying to get that, trying to keep up with everybody else. I had a new project every week, and it was some kind of a faith project to get something else I wanted. And I finally became so fed up with being an unhappy Christian, I thought, **Dear God, I did not become a Christian so I could trade in my worldly misery for a Christian misery. Something is wrong.**

If you relate to those feelings, I must tell you there's no such thing as a drive-through breakthrough. There are no drive-through victories with God. The only way you will see changes is to learn what God's Word says and, whether you feel like it or not, start doing what it says consistently day, after day, after day, after day, after day. Improvements to your present conditions come from getting alone with God, confronting the devil yourself, and gaining victories that no devil in hell can take away from you. Truly enjoying the life God has planned for you requires maturity and self-control. You must know who you are in Christ and seek peace and joy in the Holy Ghost.

Out of my selfish, self-centered lifestyle, I began to cry out to God, "What is wrong?" God showed me many things. First, I was seeking God's hand and not His face. I needed to seek God's presence, not just what He could do for me. Then He showed me how selfish I was. The verses in James say that we have to help somebody or our religion is not pure.

The truth changed my heart. Now I just want to help people. It's the only reason I write, travel, and speak. I don't do things to impress people; I just want to please God. He keeps making our ministry bigger and bigger, but we are not trying to do things to be "big." I'm writing this book to help people.

The Lord has done such a work in my heart! I'm going to do what God has called me to do as long as I can breathe and find more people to help. If we can forget about our little aches and pains, our little personal trials and tribulations; if we can get ourselves off of our own minds and go find somebody else to help, our lives are going to get better. This is a marvelous discovery.

I can be in a position where something is going on in my life and I do not have the ability to help myself. But at the same time when I cannot help myself, God will anoint me to help others. You will find it true for yourself, too. When you can't deliver yourself, and you can't encourage yourself, you can still go encourage somebody else. Sometimes when you can't believe God for the mess you are in, you can encourage somebody else to believe God. And as you share with them, you encourage yourself to believe God.

You find it easy to encourage the downhearted by saying, "Now don't get depressed — don't get discouraged." Why does God make us like that? He has created us to give out of ourselves to other people. As we do, we are sowing seeds that we need to grow so God can bring a harvest in our own lives. As you help someone else, God will help you. Always remember that **what you make happen for someone else, God will make happen for you.**

Do we have any idea what would happen if everybody prayed every day, "God, show me somebody today that I can help"? We are missing out on joy. If we walked in this love on a daily basis, we wouldn't be fighting off grief and depression. Our love for others would shield us from the darts the enemy tries to inflict on us.

I learned all about spiritual warfare, but I still didn't have authority over the devil's fiery darts and I didn't understand what was wrong with me. I went to the seminars, bought the tapes, and screamed at the devil until I didn't have a voice left. I fasted until I almost died, prayed with groups of people, yet was left without victory. What was wrong?

I had a method but no power flowing through that method. You can have all kinds of methods, but they can become empty, dead works that wear you out and get you burned out with Christianity. People wear out because they think, **I have to say my confessions; I have to do this and I have to do that, and I have to yell at the devil** . . . They do all these things without a personal relationship with Jesus. Jesus didn't come to teach us about rules, regulations, and methods; He came to teach us how to have a personal relationship with Almighty God and then with others.

When asked which was the greatest commandment and law, Jesus replied:

You shall love the Lord your God with all your heart and with all your soul and with all your mind (intellect).

This is the great (most important, principal) and first commandment.

And a second is like it: You shall love your neighbor as [you do] yourself.

Matthew 22:37-40

In Matthew 7:12 Jesus said, *Whatever you desire that others would do to and for you, even so do also to and for them, for this (sums up) the Law and the Prophets.*

So, to experience God and His plan for our lives, we are to look for the needs of others and do what we can to serve them. Our religion is not pure if it is polluted with "self." Our self-centeredness keeps us from noticing what other people are going through. We must get our needs, wants, and desires out of the way.

The Bible says to delight in the Lord, and He will give you the desires of your heart. We don't have to chase our desires away, just our selfishness.

The Bible says plainly to delight in the Lord, and He will give you the desires of your heart. We don't have to chase our desires away, just our selfishness. Psalm 37:4,5 tells us that when we delight in the Lord, He gives us the desires and secret petitions of our hearts. When we commit our way to Him, repose the care of our load on Him — trust, lean and rely on Him with confidence in Him — He will bring to pass the desires of our hearts.

HOW TO BE RID OF STRIFE

James 4:1 asks the question, *What leads to strife (discord and feuds) and how do conflicts (quarrels and fightings) originate among you? Do they not arise from your sensual desires that are ever warring in your bodily members?* Verse 2 answers the question with, *You are jealous and covet [what others have] and your desires go unfulfilled. . . .*

What leads to strife? Jealousy and unfulfilled desires lead to strife. Churches, businesses, schools, and marriages are full of strife; brothers and sisters can't get along, and on and on. When I came across the Scripture above, I had a great deal of strife in my life. James 4 explains that conflicts and quarrels and fights start because our sensual desires are ever warring in our bodily members.

Strife gets started because of all the stuff that we want that we don't know how to get. And so we are struggling to make all these things happen. I struggled in trying to change myself, my husband, and my kids. I struggled with trying to get healed, to become more prosperous, and to get my ministry to grow. I was working on various "faith" projects all the time that I had started. I'd make all my plans then expect God to bless them.

Jesus is the Author and the Finisher of our faith, but He's not obligated to finish anything He did not author. God said if we delight in Him, He would take care of all the desires and secret petitions of our heart.

James 4:2 continues explaining the consequence of our actions when we are jealous of what others have: . . . *[So] you become murderers. [To hate is to murder as far as your hearts are concerned.] You burn with envy and anger and are not able to obtain [the gratification, the contentment, and the happiness that you seek], so you fight and war. . . .*

And then, this next simple statement from God's Word changed my life about twenty years ago. The rest of verse 2 says, . . . *You do not have, because you do not ask.*

But then verse 3 says, *[Or] you do ask [God for them] and yet fail to receive, because you ask with wrong purpose and evil, selfish motives. Your intention is [when you get what you desire] to spend it in sensual pleasures.*

So here are the reasons why we don't get the things we want: First of all, we are trying to do it ourselves instead of asking God and the result is strife in our life. Secondly, we do ask God for it, but our motive is wrong. He can't reward our wrong motives. There is a purification process that has to go on in our life.

I was trying to get all this "stuff" and make certain things happen, but I was leaving God out of the loop. All I needed to do was ask God for what I wanted, and if it was right for me, He would give it to me in His way and in His time. If it wasn't right, and I was smart, then I had better hope He wouldn't give it to me anyway. I finally found out, either God is going to get His way, or I'm going to be one miserable lady. I can save you years of agony, so listen to "Mama Joyce." If you want to have a nice life, you had better pray on a regular basis: "God, help me to stay in Your will. I don't want anything that You don't want me to have. If it's not You, God, slam the door in my face."

I love what David prayed in Psalm 26:2, *Examine me, oh Lord, and prove me; test my heart and my mind.* What would happen if we started praying that way every day? "Test me, God, prove me. Look me over, God; examine me. And if there's anything wicked in me, I want to know it." We don't need to be afraid to walk in the light of God's truth. Light exposes every bug and every rat in the room, and when you turn the light on, they all start running for some corner to hide in. That's exactly what happens when the light of God's Word is shed on us. All the little bugs and rats like to start running away until the light goes out again.

James 1:2,3 tells us to be exceedingly joyful when we fall into all kinds of diverse temptations and tests, knowing the trying of our faith works patience. But, before trials brought patience out of me, a lot of other junk came out first such as fits of anger, jealously, resentment, and my bad temper. At first I thought the Word wasn't working, but that's how the Refiner's fire works. When you apply heat, the impurities rise to the top first.

We don't know what's in us until we are tested. We don't know what kind of faith we have until it's tested. We don't know what kind of endurance, steadfastness, or faithfulness we have until it's been tried. We don't know anything about being faithful to our spouse until that spouse is failing to do a few things we want them to do.

Most people try to run away from life when it gets hard. If God puts us around something hard, it's for our benefit and our good so that we can build spiritual muscles by applying our faith in trusting Him. Many people leave a church if they don't like it. If they don't like a job, they leave. If they don't like a neighbor, they move. If they don't like a friend, if they don't like their husband, they get another one. If they don't like that one, they get another one and another one.

I thought every problem I had was Dave's fault. I thought, If he'd quit doing this and that and something else, then I'd be happy. Or, **If I didn't have to work, I'd be happy.** When I quit working and got bored, I thought, **If I could work I'd be happy. If I could go out there and be with adults all day, instead of with all these kids, then I would be happy.**

One day, Dave said, "Look, you wanted to quit working, and we let you quit working. It hurt us financially, but you quit working. Now you are not happy because you are not working. If you want to work, go back to work, but then you won't be happy, You'll want to quit working."

He continued, "Joyce, I have done everything I know to make you happy. I give up. I don't know how to make you happy. Guess what — I'm tired of trying." And then he sadly concluded, "You just about have me to the point where I can't stand you."

Now, thank God, that's been more than twenty-five years ago since I first realized that I had myself on my own mind too much. But even now I have to maintain the freedom I have gained by standing against selfish, self-centeredness, remembering to be adaptable, not to make mountains out of molehills, and countless other things. Meditate for a moment on how many marriages would be saved if people were not selfish. Perhaps you know one right now that is bordering on disaster, and the root cause is nothing other than selfishness. If so, why not give them a copy of this book and pray it will have an impact on their life. If the person you know is you, then you're in good shape because you have the answer in your hand that you have been looking for — a book filled with godly principles that will show you the way to happiness and fulfillment.

7

MAY I CHOP THAT FRUIT FOR YOU?

---

*And the harvest of righteousness (of conformity to
God's will in thought and deed) is [the fruit of the seed]
sown in peace by those who work for and make peace
[in themselves and in others, that peace which means
concord, agreement, and harmony between individuals,
with undisturbedness, in a peaceful mind free from
fears and agitating passions and moral conflicts].*
James 3:18

God's goal for our relationships with others is peace. From the
Scripture above we learn that harmony with others results from
conforming to God's will for us. God knows the healing power of a
loving act, and He calls us to minister peace in our homes before
He calls us to minister outside of our homes.

When I get up in the morning, sometimes God tells me to do
things for Dave that I don't want to do. For example, Dave likes to
eat fruit salads. He likes everything all cut up in a bowl. I don't
mind taking him an apple, an orange, and a banana, but he wants
it all cut up. Then he wants his vitamins and his orange juice and
his coffee.

A few years ago we started having a housekeeper come in
during the week. She takes care of Dave's fruit salad, vitamins,

God's goal for our relationships with others is peace.

orange juice, and coffee and she's great, but one day, when it was a holiday, I went downstairs to make coffee in the morning and I was not in the humor to do anything but get my coffee and go back to my room. I wanted to pray and be with God.

That's our problem — we are so spiritual that we just want to "be with God" but don't want to do anything Jesus tells us to do. He said that we need to serve each other. That particular holiday morning, the Holy Ghost started putting it in my heart to make that fruit salad for Dave. I got a banana and stuck it on the tray. The Holy Ghost said, "Fruit salad."

I didn't want to make the fruit salad. I **really** didn't want to make it. I even said, "I don't want to — I want to go pray." Then the Lord said to me, "Joyce, serving Dave is serving Me."

So I made the fruit salad.

And the harvest of righteousness (of conformity to God's will in thought and deed) is [the fruit of the seed] sown in peace by those who work for and make peace [in themselves and in others. . . (James 3:18). Peace is something that we sow and then work for in ourselves and in others. The reward is harmony, agreement, and a peaceful mind free from fears, agitating passions, and moral conflicts. Suddenly, in light of God's Word, making fruit salad for Dave was more than an act of conforming to God's will; it was seed that brought peace and joy in my life.

My initial bad attitude reflects the heart of many Christians who will do something in the church for somebody else as their "ministry," but if they do that same thing for someone in their family, they think they're being turned into a slave. But if ministry doesn't work at home, it's not working.

If I'm willing to do something in the church as "my ministry," but won't do it at home, then I have to question myself and find out what is making the difference. Many times at church someone is usually kind enough to tell me how wonderful I was for what I did. They clap and cheer and pat me on the back, when if I do the same thing at home, I may not even get thanked.

How much quicker are we to do something if there's a little something in it for us — a little recognition, a little bit of money, a little bit of promotion, a little bit of favor? I read a statement in a book about love that tore my life up. The author said, "If you want to measure your love life, watch and see how you treat people that can do you no earthly good. If your actions are not coming out of a right heart — if you are doing it to be seen — you have lost your reward. If you are doing it to be well thought of, you have lost your reward." He said, "Do good works in secret; do them to honor God, not to get something for yourself."

God anoints us so we can do something to make somebody else's life better. True happiness is found in the joy you feel after ministering to your spouse and family. Soon, you will want to find other hurting people with whom you can share your gifts, but in most homes today there are enough hurting people in our living rooms who desperately need us.

One morning several years ago on a Sunday, lying in bed next to Dave, I woke up and started thinking about how I could talk him out of watching the football game that day. (The devil likes to get in your brain before you are fully awake.) There I was, lying there having just woken up, planning how I could get Dave to do what I wanted. Mind you, I didn't care that he had worked all week and really liked to watch the game on Sunday. I had only myself on my mind: **I have been stuck here with these kids all week, and Dave needs to do something with me to give me a break.**

Most of us think about what we need, and seldom consider what others around us may need. Many couples are getting divorces because one or both of them feel as though the other person never thinks about his or her own needs. But if that same individual were thinking about the needs of their spouse, the way they wish their spouse was thinking of them, they would be sowing seeds that God could return in a harvest to satisfy their own needs. Why is it easier to wait for others to do the right things first before we will do likewise?

LEAD THE WAY IN LOVE

So on this particular morning, as I was lying in bed thinking about how I could get Dave to take me out to eat and get the kids to clean the house, the Holy Ghost spoke to me. He said:

"Joyce, sometimes you remind me of a little robot. You get up in the morning, and you stand by your bed, and the devil runs up to you and winds you up real tight as though you have a little metal winder on your back." I could see how I looked to the Lord as He said, "This is the way you look to me all day — you walk around like a robot, saying over and over in a voice that sounds like a robot's, 'What about me? What about me? What about me? BEEP! BEEP! What about me? What about me . . .?'"

Make a choice to quit trying to preserve yourself; just give yourself away. Just say:

God, here I am. You do what You want with me. Show me where You want me to serve.

I am fed up with thinking about myself, talking about myself, trying to provide for myself, worrying over what everybody thinks of me, what they're saying about me, why they're not doing what I want them to do for me, and why they're not getting me gifts.

I don't want to think about myself — about what's right with me, about what's wrong with me — I just want to get myself off my mind. God, if I'm going to change, You will have to change me. If I'm going to have anything, You will have to give it to me.

All I know is that I'm going to give my life from this point on to make somebody else happy, and if You can't make me happy, I'll stay miserable all my life. But I am finished with trying to do it myself.

Happiness is found in living a "giving lifestyle." Happiness is found in giving things away. Give away compliments to people who don't have any to give back to you. Give away time to people who need help. Give away love to people who have never learned to express love themselves, and especially give these things to your own family, too. Carry "seed" in your pocket all the time, and look for opportunities to bring peace where there is chaos, harmony where there is dissension, and agreement where there is contention. Make a decision to be a radical blessing to your spouse, family, and world of influence.

Be a radical blessing to your spouse, family, and world of influence.

Pray:

Lord, anoint my heart right now and break the yokes of bondage that keep me from serving others.

Help me to see that happiness will come by pouring myself out to others — not through dribbling out a few little blessings every now and then — but by pouring myself out.

Fill my mind with ways that I can be a blessing to the ones I love and the ones who need love.

I will not allow laziness to stand in my way of loving someone.

BUT WHAT IF IT *IS* THEIR FAULT?

Sometimes, the problems in your marriage may really be the fault of your spouse. You can be doing everything right and still face grief and disappointment. But, if you continue to do what is right, even if your spouse is not responding, righteousness will cultivate a harvest of blessing, and God will honor your obedience. So don't give up.

Many men and women enter marriage with serious insecurities that challenge their relationships. Having firsthand experience with these issues, I want to discuss how low self-esteem affects a marriage and how to live with an insecure person.

A pastor once came to me at a conference and said, "I don't know if you feel led to or not, but I feel it would help women if they would understand that some men have been abused, too. In many instances men have been taught that they are not supposed to cry or show emotions. How a man is raised and what happens to him in the first few years of his life can greatly affect his marriage relationship."

Of course, I had experienced this myself for years. Many times we try to deal with bad behavior without ever getting down to the real root of what the problem is. Jesus said, "I will restore your soul." Only the Word of God has the power to get on the inside of us and change us; it's not our behavior so much that needs to be changed. It's the inside of us that needs to be changed and then the changes in our behavior just follow suit.

When Dave and I were first married, I did not comprehend that the abuse that I had gone through in my past had anything to do with my current behavior. I believed that I was a new creature in Christ and that old things had passed away, and legally that's true. But experientially, newness in Christ has to be walked out in your life. Even though Jesus comes to live in your spirit, there still is a work that has to be done in your soul.

Your soul is your mind, your will, and your emotions. Your soul harbors your thinking skills where you rationalize and justify what happens to you. We are living in a society today in which, I would venture to say, the large majority of people with whom we come into contact are dysfunctional in the ability to "think through" the best way to respond to a situation. Consequently, they display dysfunctional behavior.

I define dysfunctional behavior as not functioning the way God intended for a person to function. We look at dysfunctional people and think, **What is your problem? What is wrong with you?** Then we spend our time trying to change them, or we simply reject them.

Unfortunately, many people treat marriage partners the way they do friends that they no longer want to tolerate. They simply walk away from the relationship because they have never learned a functional solution to bad behavior problems.

To bring triumph to our relationships, we must learn what the other person is thinking then find out how to show them truth that will renew their soul and help them reach their potential in God. My husband, Dave, has done that for me. I think that our life is a great example of how someone with the love of God can help another person be all that he or she can be. A loving spouse can bring their mate through to a complete place of healing and victory.

When Dave and I got married, I looked OK on the outside. I was a younger version of what I am now. I had a good job and was put in charge everywhere I worked. Being the boss is just my personality, the way God put me together for leadership. The deep problems in my soul were not obvious by just looking at me. When people are courting, they don't let those problems surface.

Dave and I had been married three weeks when he looked at me and asked, "What is wrong with you?"

With the abuse I had suffered in my childhood, and then the mistakes of my first marriage, I might have looked good on the outside, but my soul was a wreck. I didn't trust or like anybody, including myself. I had all kinds of fears. But you would never have thought that was the case because I was almost obnoxiously bold.

Most people who have been deeply hurt are unbalanced in their personalities. They're either obnoxiously aggressive, or they're obnoxiously shy and withdrawn. God wants us to have balanced personalities.

I doubt if we can comprehend how many dysfunctional, insecure people we deal with every day in society. The most dangerous thing about our dysfunctional society is that hurting people hurt other people. People don't go around hurting each other just for the fun of hurting each other. Many problems start in dysfunctional people during the years they are forming an opinion about their own self-worth.

When people with problems haven't learned how to see beyond their problems, they become dysfunctional — incapable of having healthy relationships. Those same people want normalcy as much as anyone else, but their thinking and emotional skills are not developed beyond their point of pain or the critical outlook of life that they were taught in those formative years. If there are no good role models in their life, they cannot "see" how to change.

Instead of acting on your emotions, be led by God's Spirit.

Don't give up on your mate. You can be the role model for your spouse as you submit yourself to Jesus and respond to tensions and trials the way He would respond. I am a living testimony of what God can do through a patient and loving spouse. There are millions of people who have extremely serious problems in their marriages. If you are one of them, ask God for wisdom. He will give you the grace and power to sow seeds of peace in your loved one. Don't give up on your spouse unless you absolutely know that you have a word from God to get out of the relationship. Don't act on emotions; be led by God's Spirit.

HOW TO HELP AN INSECURE PERSON

If you are living with a hurting, wounded person, I encourage you to pray and ask God for specific direction in how to help your mate through his or her insecurity to the place of confidence in your and God's love. It is possible that you are the only person in the world through whom God can truly demonstrate His unconditional love for your spouse.

Ask God to lead you to more information on how to help your mate. Get more teaching; write to my ministry for some of my tapes and learn how you can be used by God to bring healing and restoration to that other person. There is something on the inside of them that is worth going after. There is a treasure inside of that person, and it should not be thrown into a field where it might remain lost.

When Dave and I were first married, my personality was like an old ugly rock with a rough, tough exterior. I acted like I didn't need anybody — nobody was going to push me around or tell me what to do. If they didn't like me, they could just get out of my face. I had taken care of myself long enough. I believed I could continue to do so if that's what I had to do. But that wasn't what was in my heart; that was just the shield of defense that I put up for others to see.

Who would want a cold, rough stone in the house? Yet, many people are married to someone who looks and acts like an impermeable stone. And it is difficult to deal with that hardness day after day. But there is a treasure on the inside of them just like the geodes found in nature. Their exterior looks course and even brutal, but their cavities are lined with crystals and minerals that explode into beautiful colors and designs.

I believe that God gives us these rocks in nature to teach us to look beyond the surface of a thing, or a person, to see what treasure He has hidden in their design. When looking at the outside of one of these special rocks, who would ever have thought to look inside of it? That is exactly why we must stop judging people by the way they look, act, or even by what they say. We need to go a little bit deeper than how they look. Ask God to reveal the truth about them and ask to see the goodness in their heart that is worth pursuing.

Men are told in Ephesians 5 to love their wives by nurturing, nourishing, and cherishing them. This kind of love is just like Christ's love for the church that cleanses and makes us glorious and holy. The picture of this love shows that a man's love for his wife can bring her back to a place of full health.

Women are told in verse 33 to respect, reverence, and notice their husband. She is to show him regard, honor him, prefer him, venerate, and esteem him. She is to defer to him, praise him, and love and admire him exceedingly. (AMP.) Imagine what that kind of attention could do to a man with low self-esteem who had been treated ungraciously as a child. A love with that kind of strength could make him whole again.

HOW HEALTHY IS YOUR MATE?

Some people are married to a spouse who looks like an unhealthy plant. Some new growth at the top looks all right, but there is a lot of dead looking stuff on the lower branches. With some trees you think, **I don't know if this will make it or not. Maybe we'll just get rid of this one and go get us another one.**

I don't happen to have a green thumb, and if I get a plant that starts dying, I take it to one of the women in the office and ask her, "See if you can bring this thing back to life." One of the ladies there can take the plant home and in a few weeks she brings it back with it looking absolutely great. After she has nurtured it back to health, we all want it in our office again. It doesn't even look like it was ever sick after she has cared for it.

I was like a sick plant when Dave found me, but he nourished me and has been the kind of husband that the Bible tells men to be. Our relationship was God-ordained; God had a call on our lives, and He had a plan for how to get us to that calling. In looking back we can see how God had prepared Dave for our marriage since he was eighteen years old, filling him with the Holy Ghost while he was just seeking God on his own. He had a strong walk with God during those first three years of being Spirit-filled and many supernatural things happened to him.

Though he felt like that intimate relationship with God ended for a brief time while he was in the service, we both believe it was a special time of preparation in his life specifically to be able to handle me when I came along. Just as he had learned to base his relationship with God on the promise of commitment rather than feelings, he later had to demonstrate the same lesson to me. Dave taught me that faithfulness has nothing to do with feelings.

I am not trying to depict Dave as a perfect man, just as I have not been a perfect woman, but he's been patient with me and he stuck with me through the hard times. I believe that he's now reaping the benefits.

GOD'S GRACE DOES THE WORK

God does the work through us to help others. When you sow righteous seeds, you will reap rewards. Dave was used by God to sow seeds of love and acceptance in me. We don't give the credit to man, but we must understand that God works through people to reach people. He wants to use you to nurture people and help bring them back like a healthy tree planted near running water.

Part of our heritage in God is to be secure. Isaiah 54:17 tells us, *But no weapon that is formed against you shall prosper, and every tongue that shall rise up against you in judgment you shall show to be in the wrong. This [peace, righteousness, security, triumph over opposition] is the heritage of the servants of the Lord [those in whom the ideal Servant of the Lord is reproduced]. . . .*

Don't settle for anything less than your God-given, blood-bought right to be secure. Don't expect anything less for your spouse. Isaiah 61:1 says,

> *Don't settle for anything less than your God-given, blood-bought right to be secure. Don't expect anything less for your spouse.*

The Spirit of the Lord God is upon me, because the Lord has anointed and qualified me to preach the Gospel of good tidings to the meek, the poor, and afflicted; He has sent me to bind up and heal the brokenhearted, to proclaim liberty to the [physical and the spiritual] captives and the opening of the prison and of the eyes to those who are bound.

As a believer, you are anointed to bind up and heal the brokenhearted. Verses 2,3 continue:

To proclaim the acceptable year of the Lord [the year of His favor] and the day of vengeance of our God, to comfort all who mourn,

To grant [consolation and joy] to those who mourn in Zion — to give them an ornament (a garland or diadem) of beauty instead of ashes, the oil of joy instead of mourning, the garment [expressive] of praise instead of a heavy, burdened and failing spirit — that they may be called oaks of righteousness [lofty, strong, and magnificent, distinguished for uprightness, justice, and right standing with God], the planting of the Lord, that He may be glorified.

Isaiah spoke of an anointing that will come on a person to take somebody who is a broken-down mess, whose life is nothing but ashes and work with them and nurture them and nourish them until they come to the point where they are trees of righteousness, the planting of the Lord, so their lives are now giving glory to God.

I'm glad that my husband didn't give up on me. How easy it would have been for him in those first few years to just walk out, saying, "Who needs the hassle? I don't need this grief and insult." But instead of walking out on me, he would go somewhere and pray to get more of the grace of God. Then he would return and live sacrificially and wait for God to change me in honor of Dave's prayerful obedience.

REJOICE OVER SMALL CHANGES

When Elijah prophesied that God was sending rain, he became extremely excited when the report came that one little cloud was in the sky the size of a man's hand. He took that speck of a cloud in the whole expanse of the sky as evidence that God was going to do what He said He was going to do.

You may not have a full manifestation of victory in your life yet, but if you can see even just a little bit of evidence that God is working in your life, if all you can find is just one little cloud in the sky the size of your hand, then rejoice. If you have any spark of hope in you, any evidence at all that God is working in your life, in your marriage, in you, in your mate, in your financial structure, or in your children, then I beseech you in the name of Jesus, don't run away from the difficult times!

Stay steadfast and pay the price of endurance because those ashes are going to be turned into beauty. You and your loved ones will be that tree of righteousness, the planting of the Lord, and your lives will give glory to God.

God will anoint you to help other people. Jesus died on the cross so that you could have the anointing of His Holy Spirit through grace. That means you don't even have to deserve the anointing. God just loves you and the people He wants to reach through you so much that He will give you supernatural wisdom and ability to do the right thing that will bring them back to health. The only price you must pay is your willingness to die to your flesh, die to your own selfish focus, and look to see what God wants to do in the lives of others.

Dave had to be patient with me until I got enough of the Word in me, enough of God's grace on me, and enough of the Holy Ghost to be willing to die to the selfish ambitions of Joyce Meyer. God's truth and grace brought me to the place that made me willing to die to that old way of responding to situations and to begin to do things in a brand new way.

RESTORATION IS NEAR

Isaiah 61, verse 4 says, (referring to those who we've been talking about in the first three verses, whose lives have been healed with the anointing):

And they shall rebuild the ancient ruins; they shall raise up the former desolations and renew the ruined cities, the devastations of many generations.

When entering a marriage relationship, many individuals bring the devastations of previous generations with them. It is not just a little personality problem or an incompatibility problem; we war not against flesh and blood, for there are generational curses that come into the relationship that have been passed to them from generation, to generation, to generation. Psalm 23:3 (NKJV) says, *He restores my soul. . . .* Verses 1,2 state: *The LORD is my shepherd; I shall not want. . . . He leads me beside the still waters. He restores my soul.*

My soul needed to be restored after Dave and I were married. I needed to learn how to think differently. I needed to learn self-control over those negative emotions that had been passed to me from previous generations.

I needed a work to be done in my will. I was stubborn and rebellious, and God had to work with me until I could trust being submissive first to Him and then to my husband. It is easier to trust God than it is people, but God wants us to trust Him concerning

When we learn to be intimate with God, He will teach us how to have loving relationships with each other.

our relationships with other people. That is why we are to love our spouses as unto the Lord.

First we are to build a strong, dependent relationship with God and then the relationship we have with Him will affect our relationships with people in a positive and godly way. When we learn to be intimate with God, He will teach us how to have loving relationships with each other. Many people try to build relationships with people without having relationship with God. Therefore, they have no standard of what love is or should be.

The marriage relationship on earth is supposed to be an example of what our spiritual relationship is with the Lord Jesus Christ. I had prayed that God would send me somebody who would take me to church. I wanted to serve God, but I had so many problems in my soul that I couldn't seem to go to church on my own. I needed somebody to disciple me. I got a good foundation about salvation through the Protestant church we attended, but when I was baptized in the Holy Spirit, God began a restoration in my soul. I can truly stand before masses of people and testify, "He has restored my soul."

Don't abandon the promise before you see its fulfillment. When the changes start to hurt, don't run away from them because if you do, you will be running all your life. Remember, things might get worse before they get better as God works things out in your spouse. Pray all the more through these times of purifying. You are about to see gold emerge from the fire.

THE TWO SHALL BECOME ONE

God works in both partners in a marriage. I said earlier that I am not trying to portray Dave as a perfect man — he is not perfect. He certainly has faults like the rest of us. While God was working on me, He was also working on Dave. My faults were just louder than Dave's. Some people have quiet faults. For example someone might be the type who refuses to confront issues. They seem quiet, shy, withdrawn, and actually never bother anyone, but they can contribute to the breakdown of a marriage just the same as a rude, loudmouthed manipulator.

Perhaps you are like I was — your faults are loud, and it almost seems unfair that your faults are noticed all the time, while your spouse's don't seem to exist. Be encouraged: God is dealing with the quiet spouse about their faults. Also, the quiet spouse may not talk about the process as much, but God deals with all of us about our faults sooner or later.

There was a time when Dave was extremely passive, which means he did not take responsibility for some things that he needed to. He always went to work and did a good job there, but he was very nonaggressive as far as getting other things done in life. He played golf, watched sports, and was easy to get along with, but in those days it might have taken me three or four weeks to get him to hang a picture for me.

Dave has changed, and he is not that way any longer. We both had faults; they were just opposite in their nature. I talked too much; he did not talk enough to suit me. I was too aggressive; he was too passive. I had a false sense of responsibility and often made myself responsible for things that were not my problem, while Dave, at times, didn't even realize that something was his responsibility and did nothing. We are actually very different in personality and our approach to things, but God has changed us both, and the two have become one.

Be encouraged that you are not the only one who needs to change, but God will deal with you about you, not about your spouse. Do your part, and God will always do His part. Don't worry, as I did, about whether or not your spouse is listening to God. We all have choices to make, and we will all reap the fruit of them. Concentrate on making right choices yourself, and leave other people in God's hands.

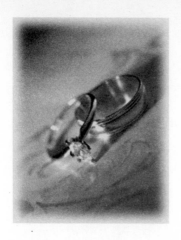

PART 2

MAKING CHOICES

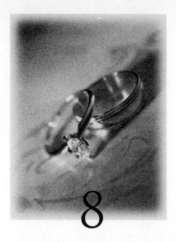

8

IS THAT YOUR DRIPPING TOWEL?

. . . Love (God's love in us) does not insist on its own rights or its own way, for it is not self-seeking; it is not touchy or fretful or resentful; it takes no account of the evil done to it [it pays no attention to a suffered wrong].
1 Corinthians 13:5

Love always makes the choice to stand firm and keep on loving. I have seen men and women make the decision to run when change starts to hurt. They run from God; they run from the person on whom they're blaming their misery; they run from themselves when there is an issue they need to work out. When they run, they take the problem with them and leave their help behind. As long as I was blaming Dave for my own unhappiness and was blaming my past, I made zero progress.

Change began in me when I made a choice to stop running away from pain. I realized that I was insecure because I was abused, but I also realized I didn't have to stay that way because Jesus loved me and had the power to change me. Truth set me free to make new choices.

The truth of God's love for me gave me the security to take responsibility for my actions. I was finally able to admit when I acted wrong and that I was sinning, then repent. All those changes took time in me, and they will take time in the person for whom you are praying. God showed me the changes I needed to make, and He will show your spouse where to start as a result of your prayers, not conversation, nagging, or temper tantrums.

HURTING PEOPLE HURT PEOPLE

I had low self-esteem; I did not like myself. I hated my personality, and I hated my voice (which I think is extremely funny because God is now blasting it all over the world). Somewhere along the line through the abuse that I had endured, I internalized the shame. I was no longer ashamed of what was happening to me; I became ashamed of me. I was hurting and, consequently, was hurting other people.

Unconditional love is the best therapy for someone who can't find any self-worth.

I believe about 85 percent of the problems that people have are related to how they feel about themselves. Your nurturing and encouragement can help them change the way they see themselves. If you keep loving them, they will begin to examine themselves to see why you find them lovable. Unconditional love is the best therapy for someone who can't find any self-worth.

When people discover that God loves them no matter what, and that you love them no matter how awful they are, a redemption process begins in their soul that only God's agape love can initiate. He loves people through you. You can help others love themselves if you make a choice to demonstrate God's love to them.

When they begin to see how much God loves them, they begin to like themselves again. When they begin to understand that they are the righteousness of God because of what Jesus has done for them, they begin to see the difference between who they **are** and what they have **done**. Once they begin to separate the two pictures and see how precious they are in God's eyes apart from what they do or have done, the revelation of love for who they are comes to them, and radical changes begin to manifest in what they do.

But as long as they think they are to **do** something right to **be** something right, then they're caught in that helpless place in which religion puts people — works, works, works. They can never work enough to deserve God's love, but that's why it is so important that someone illustrates to them that God's love is a free gift. They prove this by showing that their own love is unconditional.

If you don't know how to treat your spouse, maybe it's because you feel rotten about yourself. Maybe you need to really take a good look at how you feel about yourself. Both men and women have been abused and need a revelation of God's unconditional love for them.

A man once told me, "Your tapes have changed my life. I just got hold of 'Beauty For Ashes' a few weeks ago, and I can't believe the healing that God is doing in my life." He said, "I was abused, and this truth is changing my life." The Word of God is medicine for our souls.

PERFECT LOVE CASTS OUT FEAR

If you don't like yourself, you are never going to like anybody else, and you won't be able to help your spouse like himself or herself. You will spend all your time trying to prove your own value, and people who are self-seeking cannot be servants as Jesus was. Healing can't come to your marriage until one of you finds the Healer.

Healing comes by accepting yourself, knowing that where you are today is not where you will end up, knowing that God is perfecting you, too. If you would learn to accept the unconditional love of God, acknowledging that God doesn't love you because of what you do, you would be so full of joy that it would be easy to give unconditional love away to your spouse.

Do you understand that God can love you just because He wants to? He doesn't have to have a reason. We don't earn or deserve the love of God. God doesn't want us to impress people; He wants us to love them. In the first meeting I ever taught, I wanted to be the "woman of the hour with the message of power" so I said, "God, what do You want me to teach? What do You want me to share?"

He said, "I want you to tell my people that I love them."

I said, "Oh, God, I'm not going to go with some little John 3:16 message. Everybody knows that You love them."

He said, "No they don't. Very few of My people know that I love them. If they understood My love for them, they would act much differently than the way they do."

The first evidence of His love is that it casts out fear. When we understand how perfectly God loves us, that knowledge casts the fear, which is insecurity, out of our lives. I could never be the wife that God wanted me to be to my husband until I received the love of God. I did not love myself; I had to let God love me. It's humbling to let God love you when you know you don't deserve it.

FREELY YOU HAVE RECEIVED, FREELY GIVE

One morning, as I sat in my pajamas praying for my ministry to grow, the Lord said to me, "Joyce, I really can't do anything else in your ministry until you do what I have told you to do concerning your husband. You are not showing him proper respect. You argue with him over minor details, things you should just let go and drop. You have a willful, stubborn, rebellious attitude. I have dealt with you about it over and over again, but you just refuse to listen."

Many of us have a problem with a willful, stubborn attitude. We think we are being obedient to the Word of God, so we wonder why we are not living in the covenant blessings promised us in it. While it is true that God's love is unconditional, His covenant blessings are contingent on being "doers of the Word." It is not enough just to read the Word, or even to learn it and confess it. It is in the doing that the blessings are released.

It is in the doing of God's Word that the blessings are released.

I was having problems being submissive because I had such a strong will and was still caught in my defensive attitude from being abused as a child. But I was missing out on the blessings God was eager for me to enjoy.

After praying, I got up and went to take a shower in the new bathroom Dave had just installed off our master bedroom. Since he had not yet put up a towel rack, I laid my towel on the toilet seat and started to step into the shower.

Dave saw what I was doing and asked me, "Why did you put your towel there?"

Right away I could feel my emotions getting stirred up.

"What's wrong with putting it there?" I asked in a sarcastic tone.

As an engineer, Dave answered with typical mathematical logic. "Well, since we don't have a floor mat yet, if you put your towel in front of the shower door, when you get out you won't drip water on the carpet while reaching for it."

"Well, what difference would it make if I did get a little water on the carpet?" I asked in a huff.

Sensing the mood I was in, Dave just gave up, shrugged his shoulders and went on his way.

As it turned out, I did what Dave had suggested, but I did it by angrily slamming the towel onto the floor. I did the right thing, but I did it in the wrong attitude.

God wants us to get to the point of doing the right thing with the right attitude.

As I stepped into the shower after throwing my towel on the floor, I was filled with rage.

"For crying out loud," I ranted to myself. "I can't even take a shower in peace! Why can't I do anything without somebody trying to tell me what to do?"

In my frustration I just went on and on.

Although I was a Christian and had been in ministry preaching to others for some time, I myself lacked control over my own mind, will, and emotions. It was three full days before my soul calmed down enough for me to get victory over that bath towel!

I guess for those three days I was a noisy gong and a clanging cymbal. I certainly wasn't inspired by *spiritual devotion such as is inspired by God's love for and in us,* mentioned in 1 Corinthians 13:1. I gave up my birthright for a bath towel! But I know I was not alone in this struggle to be spiritually mature.

Love is maturity to the full degree. It is a sacrificial gift to someone else. If love doesn't require some sort of sacrifice on our part, we probably aren't loving the other person at all. If there is no sacrifice in our actions, we are most likely reacting to something nice they did for us, or simply pretending to be kind to gain some control over them. Love is almost always undeserved by the person who receives it.

Jesus said, *For if you love those who love you, what reward can you have? . . .* (Matthew 5:46). He said that we should love our enemies. How much more should we love our family? He pointed out that the Father blesses both wicked and good with sunshine and rain, and as His children we should be reflecting that same grace on both the deserving and the undeserving. In Matthew 5:48 He *reached the proper height of virtue* and calls us to maturity saying, *You, therefore, must be perfect [growing into complete maturity of godliness in mind and character, having . . . integrity], as your heavenly Father is perfect.*

If you and your mate are struggling in your marriage, I suggest that you read the first eight verses of 1 Corinthians 13 out loud together every morning. I believe if you will do it on a regular basis that you will begin to see changes in your relationship as you become grounded in God's perspective of how we are supposed to treat each other.

Verse 1 says, *If I [can] speak in the tongues of men and [even] of angels, but have not love (that reasoning, intentional, spiritual devotion, [notice this next part] such as is inspired by God's love for and in us), I am only a noisy gong or a clanging cymbal.*

If I don't have love in me, I can't give it to somebody else. That love is inspired by God's love in and for us. That is why it's impossible to love others until we know God loves us and puts love in us to give away.

Verse 2 says, *And if I have prophetic powers (the gift of interpreting the divine will and purpose), and understand all secret truths and mysteries and possess all knowledge, and if I have [sufficient] faith so that I can remove mountains, but have not love (God's love in me) I am nothing (a useless nobody).*

> *If we don't have love in us, we can't give it to somebody else. That love is inspired by God's love in and for us.*

I have God's love in me because I receive God's love on a regular basis. I now have a reservoir of love in me that I can give out to other people because I receive love from God all the time. I hope you understand when I say, "I like myself." Someone once wrote an unkind article about me, pulled that statement out of one of my tapes and used it to make me look like I was being selfish and self-centered. I don't like myself in me, but I like myself in Christ. There's a big difference in the two statements. I like the person that I am when I walk in God's love for others.

Verse 3 says, *Even if I dole out all that I have [to the poor in providing] food, and if I surrender my body to be burned or in order that I may glory, but have not love (God's love in me), I gain nothing.*

The Amplified Bible brings out truth that other versions don't communicate in quite the same way. Verse 4 reads, *Love endures long.* . . . Love doesn't write somebody off because they don't straighten up right away.

Verses 4 and 5:

Love endures long and is patient and kind; love never is envious nor boils over with jealousy, it is not boastful or vainglorious, does not display itself haughtily.

It is not conceited (arrogant and inflated with pride); it is not rude (unmannerly) and does not act unbecomingly. . . .

How would "please" and "thank you" sound in your home? Would heads turn to see who was asking? Good manners should be a normal part of our relationships.

"Honey, would you please bring me something to drink?"

"Thank you, sweetheart!"

"Would you please take out the trash?"

"I appreciate you."

Many couples give out orders to each other and to their children without ever showing any appreciation. In fact, we often treat worst the people we ought to love the most. God is never rude or demanding, and we should love others the way He demonstrates love toward us.

The rest of verse 5 says:

. . . Love (God's love in us) does not insist on its own rights or its own way, for it is not self-seeking; it is not touchy or fretful or resentful; it takes no account of the evil done to it [it pays no attention to a suffered wrong].

If you have ever acted like an emotional bag lady or bag man, who carries your collection of favorite grudges around with you every-where, I challenge you to unload your bag and leave it in the trash. If you have a habit of taking account of all the evil that's ever been done to you, just be rid of it. Leave it behind you. When you look up from reading this book, don't take those old memories with you. Leave them behind, and look at your spouse — all your family — and home through the eyes of God's love: *. . . it* [love] *takes no account of the evil done to it [it pays no attention to a suffered wrong].* Wow!

There are still times, although they are more infrequent, that I start allowing my feelings to be hurt. When this happens, God reminds me of that Scripture love *pays no attention to a suffered wrong.* I am able to respond the way the verses in 1 Corinthians 13 instruct us to do. Verses 6-8 continue:

It does not rejoice at injustice and unrighteousness, but rejoices when right and truth prevail.

Love bears up under anything and everything that comes, it is ever ready to believe the best of every person, its hopes are fadeless under all circumstances, and it endures everything [without weakening].

Love never fails [never fades out or becomes obsolete or comes to an end]. As for prophecy (the gift of interpreting the divine will and purpose), it will be fulfilled and pass away; as for tongues, they will be destroyed and cease; as for knowledge, it will pass away [it will lose all its value and be superseded by truth].

But love will never, ever, ever pass away. All things are temporal, except faith, hope, and love — these will remain. Verse 13 says the greatest of all is love. If only our love remains, shouldn't we try to make larger deposits of it wherever we can? Our ability to love others is the only success that we will carry with us into eternity.

I want to be successful at loving God, and Dave, and you. Nothing else that I will ever do will be remembered. If love isn't a part of my memoirs, there is nothing that will be worth remembering of my life here.

THEREFORE, SUBMIT YOURSELVES
TO EACH OTHER

There is a sacrifice in marriage. The husband is to love his wife *as Christ loved the church.* The wife is to love and admire her husband, exceedingly.

That is not just any old, ordinary kind of love; it is the *agape* love that we just reviewed in the eight verses of 1 Corinthians 13. The Bible says that the husband is to honor his wife as the physically weaker vessel, defending that she is not physically able to do some of the things that men do. The Bible says a man should dwell with his wife with **understanding.** Women are not like men, and men usually don't understand their wives, but God says to ask Him for wisdom, even concerning her.

Verse 4 says, *Love endures long and is patient and kind. . . . The New King James Version* says, *Love suffers long. . . .* We all need to suffer **long**, be **long**-suffering, with each other. Just the sound of the word "**long**-suffering" is strong. We don't pay enough attention to the wording in this description of love. We are supposed to suffer lo-o-o-ong, and have understanding.

Some days a woman wakes up and decides to cry all day for no reason. Her husband needs to be especially long-suffering on that day. She wants her husband to understand and just tell her every-thing is going to be all right.

We women have hormones that go in all different directions. Some mornings I get up and one goes left, one goes right, and one stays in bed. I don't know why I feel the way I feel that day but I just tell Dave, "Well, my hormones aren't all doing what they're supposed to do today, honey. So you are just going to have to be a little long-suffering today." Love gives warnings when danger is near [author's paraphrase].

First Corinthians 13:4 continues, . . . *love never is envious nor boils over with jealousy.* . . . It is a dangerous thing to be jealous of one another. When Dave and I were first married, I was used to jealousy. It was a natural part of every relationship I was ever in. Even trying to make your spouse jealous was part of the game. Dave was stable, born again, and a Spirit-filled man who wasn't interested in playing silly games with me. He wanted us to have a good marriage.

One time I was trying to make him jealous and realized that he wasn't at all concerned. Later, I said to him, "Well, you're not even jealous of me!"

He said, "Joyce, if I have to worry about whether or not you are running off with somebody else, then really, to tell you the truth, you're not worth having." He said, "I'm not about to spend all my life worrying about what you are going to do with somebody else. If you don't want me, then I'm not going to make you stay with me anyway."

Jealousy is just like a disease. It causes suspicion and vain imaginations that are not true. If you entertain jealousy as part of your relationship, you are playing with a dangerous spirit. The devil will exaggerate your concerns and hide implications in innocent circumstances as he did in the following example.

One weekend, I went to the country to visit my grandmother. When I came back home, I saw an eyebrow pencil down in one of the cold air vents in the floor of our old apartment. Having already entertained suspicion and jealously, **immediately** I thought, **He had a woman here this weekend! He had somebody here this weekend!**

I bolted to find him and started "reading" him off my list of questions: "Who did you have here this weekend?"

Puzzled, he asked, "What?"

I said, "Who stayed here with you this weekend?"

He said, "My brother stayed here with me." His little brother, Don, was about ten or twelve years old at that time. "Donny stayed here with me this weekend, Joyce. What is your problem?"

"Well, I don't suppose Donny uses an eyebrow pencil, does he? I found this eyebrow pencil! Look! Just look! I found this thing down here in this floor grate."

"I don't know how the thing got there," he said. "I'm telling you right now: I did not have a woman here!"

But my mind was convinced that he had, had a woman in that apartment while I was gone. I didn't trust him, was jealous, and suffered constant torment for about a week until Dave asked his little brother, "When you were here, did you drop anything down the vent? Or did you have anything to do with the cold air vent?"

Donny quickly admitted, "Oh, yeah, I dropped some money down there, and I got down there to find it," Then he added, "While I was looking for my money, I stirred up all kinds of stuff."

That eyebrow pencil had been there probably for years hidden under all the dirt that gets collected in something like that. When he dropped his money down there and opened it up, he stirred up all that stuff. My imaginations were just that, vain deceptions and outright lies. Don't be jealous of each other.

Rehearse the list of what love **is**, but don't focus on what it **isn't**.

Love endures long.

Love is patient.

Love is kind.

Love is never envious nor jealous.

Love is not boastful or vainglorious.

Love is not haughty.

Love is not conceited, arrogant, and inflated with pride.

Love is not rude and unmannerly nor acts unbecomingly.

Love is not insistent on its own rights or its own way.

Love is not self-seeking.

Love is not touchy or fretful or resentful.

Love takes no account of the evil done.

Love pays no attention to a suffered wrong.

Love rejoices when right and truth prevail.

Love bears up under anything and everything that comes.

Love is ever ready to believe the best of every person.

Love's hope is fadeless under all circumstances.

Love endures everything without weakening.

Love never fails.

Love never fades out.

Love never becomes obsolete.

Love abides forever.

Love is the greatest of all things.

Christ loved the church in all these ways when He was on earth. This means He loves you and me with that kind of love. He doesn't love us selfishly. He demonstrated His love for us by dying on the cross. He loves us with our needs in mind. With this understanding, the following verse should have a deeper impact on how we should treat each other.

> *Be subject to one another out of reverence for Christ (the Messiah, the Anointed One).*
>
> Ephesians 5:21

Husbands who want their wives to submit to their authority should have their wives' interests in mind when they make decisions. Decisions made based on their own selfishness are not made in keeping with the way Christ would treat us. The approach of "You have to do what I want because that's the wife's position" was never found in the attitude of Jesus toward the people in the church.

Our decisions should always have the other spouse's interests in mind. No marriage is going to be even a mediocre marriage without sacrifice. It is important to understand that true love gives of itself.

Sacrifice means you are not going to have your way all the time. This means both the husband and wife are called to love each other with unconditional agape love. There has to be sacrifice of selfish desires if couples are going to enjoy a triumphant marriage. Christ loved the church and gave Himself up for her.

Husbands are to give themselves up for their wives, and wives are to return that love as unto Christ. She should be happy to do nice things for him when he comes home just as if the Lord had returned after a long day. The husband should embrace her and reassure her of her worth and value to him just as Christ reminded us that He died so that we might live.

SET YOUR MIND ON HAVING A GOOD MARRIAGE

Every day when I get up, I purpose to have a good marriage. I'm not going to **accidentally** have a good relationship with Dave. I love to do things for Dave. He is a difficult person to buy things for because he doesn't really want anything. Dave's basically a satisfied guy. He says, "I have you, honey. What more could I want?"

Love listens to the other person and searches for clues on ways to serve, bless, and lift up that person.

I say, "Well, I know that's right. But it's your birthday, and I want to do a little something for you." Many times I have to pray and ask the Lord to give me a creative idea for a way that I can bless Dave.

Love listens to the other person and searches for clues on ways to serve, bless, and lift up that person. Listen to your spouse. Search out the needs of the one you love. God told me a long time ago, "If you will **listen** to people, they will all tell you what they want and what they need."

It comes falling out of our mouths! Listen with the attitude that you are going to be a "need-meeter."

9

I PROMISE TO
LOVE YOU, BUT . . .

*. . . but one thing I do [it is my one aspiration]: forgetting
what lies behind and straining forward to what lies ahead.*
Philippians 3:13

Forgiveness is the core ingredient to every successful relationship. So many people carry exceptions to their offer of love. "I love you, but you really hurt my feelings yesterday." Or "I love you, but I'm too tired, too busy, too distracted, too annoyed, too angry, too unhappy to be nice to you right now."

True love simply says, "I love you!" No exceptions!

The apostle Paul pointed out in Philippians 3:11-14 that to attain the spiritual and moral resurrection that lifts us out from among the dead [even while we are here in body], we must continue to forget the past and press on for the goal to win the prize to which Jesus is calling us.

We are to forget what lies behind and press on to what lies ahead. Women seem more prone to carrying grudges and remembering offenses for days, and some even remain bitter for years. Jesus called us to a higher prize that requires us to both receive forgiveness and give it to others. The Lord's prayer calls us to pray for forgiveness as we forgive others: *And forgive us our debts, as we forgive our debtors* (Matthew 6:12 KJV).

Forgiveness is the core ingredient to every successful relationship.

Each morning when we rise up, we must press toward the goal of loving others more than we did the day before. Concentrating on the reward that love brings into our lives, we need to determine our goal and say to ourselves:

I forget what lies behind me, and I press on to all the blessings that God has for my spouse and me today. I will love my spouse more today than I did yesterday. God has already forgiven me for yesterday, and I forgive my partner for any offense I may have felt before today. I will not let what happened yesterday destroy the affection and loving attention I can give to my partner today.

Be in a relationship to see how much you can give to someone, not to see how much you can get out of it. You will then be operating on godly principles of investment that will bring an abundant return because the Bible says, *Give, and it **shall** be given unto you. . .* (Luke 6:38 KJV).

The Bible never says, "See how much you can get, and then you'll be happy."

You need to be a blessing to your **family**. The family unit is the main focal point of Christianity. God's main focal point is toward your own family. He cares how you treat each other. Dave and I were talking one day about the stresses caused in families where two people living in a house are always wanting to do something different from each other at the same time.

For example, reflecting on my own determinations, I thought of the times when I finally find a few minutes to sit down and relax in front of the television. I flip through the channels to see if something decent is on to entertain my tired head, and invariably Dave will come in and somehow manage to take the remote control out of my hand. The next thing I know there's a ball game on the screen! Even though with our schedule he doesn't get to watch as many ball games as he used to watch, the first thing that Satan says to my mind is, "That is all he **ever** does!"

Be warned — the devil is an extremist! He wants to break up relationships, and he likes to use terms like "always," "ever" and "never" to do it. He whispers, "Your spouse **never** pays any attention to you. He **never** takes you out. He **always** watches football (or basketball or baseball). Even though it's not true anymore with Dave, I hear that terminology in my thoughts.

As Dave and I continued our discussion on families, I asked, "How do people get to that point where they **want** to live that life of sacrifice for the other person?"

Dave said, "I really believe that a person just has to start out doing it in obedience to the Word."

The point is, you are not going to feel like sacrificing for someone. If you **felt** like doing something, it wouldn't be a sacrifice at all. I know this isn't an easy answer, but as a person obeys the Word, the feelings of pleasure from that obedience will happen over a period of time.

I don't know anybody who just delights in letting the other person have their way. Our flesh screams at us, "But I want to do this! I don't want to do this!" We don't start out delighting in letting that other person have their way — we just practice obeying God.

As you obey God, just doing what the Word says to do, and begin to sacrifice for another person out of obedience to the Word, over a period of time you will come into such unity with the person that you will reach a place of the heart where you honestly **want** the same things. That's something that happens supernaturally in the Spirit.

And I know that's true because I know how like-minded Dave and I are now as compared to years ago. We thought differently on **everything** then. And it seems as though now we are becoming more and more and more alike. People say that when two people live together for a long time, they even start to look like each other. They start to act like the other person because they are becoming intertwined and molded into the agreement of "one person." I know that's true because of my relationship with the Lord. I started out a long time ago obeying the Word and doing what God told me to do just because it was the Word. I loved God and wanted to obey His Word.

Trust (lean on, rely on, and be confident) in the Lord and do good; so shall you dwell in the land and feed surely on His faithfulness, and truly you shall be fed.

Delight yourself also in the Lord, and He will give you the desires and secret petitions of your heart.

Commit your way to the Lord [roll and repose each care of your load on Him]; trust (lean on, rely on, and be confident) also in Him and He will bring it to pass.

Psalm 37:3-5

> *God wants us to trust His instructions on how to treat other people.*

God wants us to trust His instructions on how to treat each other. To delight in Him is to joyfully obey Him. If we do, He will give us the desires of our heart. It is not the responsibility of our spouse to give us our heart's desires; it is God Who promises to give us the secret petitions of our inner-most desires, if we love and obey Him by loving others.

There's nothing in my flesh that inspires me to give away my money or makes me want to apologize to Dave when the Lord quickens me to do so. There's nothing in my flesh that wants to forgive Dave when I think he is wrong. But God wants me to respond with love and say "no" to my flesh and "yes" to Him, even though I don't feel like it. Once I began doing what God said to do, I honestly came to the point where I wanted what God wanted. I don't even know how or when that happened.

A supernatural change takes place in us as we obey God out of respect for His Word. God does a sovereign, supernatural work in our lives as we trust Him enough to do what He says. Soon, spouses start becoming like-minded, in one accord, of one mind, having one purpose, one harmonious mind and intention, going in the same direction.

IT'S A PROMISE

Unity, to become one with each other, is God's promise to us as we obey Him. Obedience to God's directions for love is the way two people become one. The blessing that God bestows on those who are in harmony with each other through the filling of the Holy Spirit is illustrated in Acts 4:32,33.

> *Now the company of believers was of one heart and soul, and not one of them claimed that anything which he possessed was [exclusively] his own, but everything they had was in common and for the use of all.*

> *And with great strength and ability and power the apostles delivered their testimony to the resurrection of the Lord Jesus, and great grace (loving-kindness and favor and goodwill) rested richly upon them all.*

Wouldn't we all like to have loving-kindness, favor, and goodwill rest upon us? It comes from the infilling of the Holy Spirit in our lives and sharing with others what God has given us. The result is great strength, ability, and power to testify of the goodness of Jesus Christ.

It is important to understand that obedience brings the unity. . . . *a man shall leave his father and his mother and shall become united and cleave to his wife, and they shall become one flesh* (Genesis 2:24).

They become one by obediently cleaving to each other. Men are to give themselves up for their wives, love their wives and sacrifice for them. Wives are to respect, admire, notice, and obey their husbands.

It takes practice — mistakes will happen as you first begin to obey God — but resist selfishness and rebellion that are against God's plan for you. **Refuse** to give in to the devil, notice how as you persist, the two of you become one. You will soon be like two little peas in a pod!

I can see it happening between Dave and me more and more. One of us will suggest something and the other will say, "I was just thinking the same thing!" I would be thinking about something as we rushed about, too busy to mention what I needed, and five or ten minutes later, Dave would say just the thing I was thinking about. Two people become one through obeying God's Word. Systematically, over a period of time, they begin to be like-minded.

THE SACRIFICE OF LOVE

Two people become one through obeying God's Word. Systematically, over a period of time, they begin to be like-minded.

To obey God, you have to be willing to first sacrifice your personal desires, and when you do, God will give back to you more than you desired in the first place.

When Dave and I first began to travel extensively in ministry, Dave had to sacrifice a lot of golf in order to go. He enjoyed playing on a weekly league and could no longer do that, plus we usually are doing meetings on Saturdays and often were on Sundays. I know it was something he missed, but God has given him a harvest for the seeds of obedience he has sown. Not only does he have the joy of knowing he is helping people all over the world, but God arranges for him to play golf on some of the best courses in the world and often free of charge. Anything we give to God he gives back to us many times over.

Secondly, you must be willing to sacrifice your pride. In exchange, God will honor you before others. Every time I say, "I was wrong," I have to sacrifice my pride, as well as every time I apologize. I have to sacrifice my pride every time Dave tells me "no" about something, and I choose to accept his decision without making a fuss about it.

Pride is the detrimental enemy against love. Everyone is infected with pride at some point and has to learn how to take it to the altar of sacrifice. Pride separates two people who have different opinions, and who both demand to be right. But the "Love Chapter" in 1 Corinthians 13 says that love does not demand its rights. Strife only comes by pride.

Love is not self-seeking. In other words, love is willing to be wrong, even if it knows it's right. Most arguments are over insignificant things that don't make two cents worth of difference. Love gives up the right to be right. Besides, sometimes you may be wrong, even though you are adamantly sure of yourself.

Proverbs 3:7 says, *Be not wise in your own eyes. . . .* There have been times when I insisted that I knew the way to someone's house, then found out I didn't! One night when Dave and I were going out to dinner with friends, we were driving to pick them up. Dave said he didn't know how to get there, and I assured him that I knew the way.

Dave followed my instructions, but made the occasional comment, "Honey, I don't think this is the right way."

Finally, fed up with his lack of confidence in me, I said in my unmistakable "don't-mess-with-me" tone, "I know where we are going!" Then with added frustration I spurted, "You **never, never** think I'm right!" Once I had released those extreme words, more tumbled right out of my mouth, "You **never** listen to me! I know where they live! I remember! You go up this street, and you go up a hill to a cul-de-sac, and their house will be right there. Don't tell me I'm not right."

Silence filled the car and I felt warm with satisfaction knowing I had him this time. He turned the car in the direction I had insisted was right, went up the hill where we found neither a cul-de-sac nor even a house! When you are sitting in an empty field with "egg on your face" for having boasted of knowledge that you didn't have, you begin to become more open-minded to other people's ideas.

God had to let me go through several situations to help me realize that it's not worth arguing over who's right. Many times you **think** you are right, when in reality, you are not. Humility often comes only through being humiliated. These types of things were very humiliating to me, but they helped break the strong spirit of pride in my soul.

I have learned to say, "Well, honey, I think this is the way to go. But I have been wrong lots of times before. You go whichever way you feel is the wisest to go." I just pitch it back on Dave and give him a chance to show me how smart he is.

When we humble ourselves before our husbands, one of two things happens. Our opposition will soften enough to listen to us, which they will not do if we are arguing with them, so that a door can open for God to give us both true wisdom. Or if the other person is in an attitude of haughtiness that he shouldn't be in, our own humility will afford him the opportunity to make enough mistakes that he will feel free to listen when we have a suggestion.

Strife is caused by pointless arguments and ill-informed controversies. According to 2 Timothy 2:23 Paul says,

> But refuse (shut your mind against, have nothing to do with) trifling (ill-informed, unedifying, stupid) controversies over ignorant questionings, for you know that they foster strife and breed quarrels.

You can tell when a conversation is beginning to stir strife and spare yourself of many arguments. It is not difficult to discern if a conversation is agitating the other person. Or if you are starting to get mad, starting to shout or can feel all the blood rushing to your head, you should stop talking about the subject and try again later. If your husband's face is all contorted and you think, **My, he looks strange**, you are probably making him mad and should back off. That's a signal that you have said too much and that it's time to be quiet! I know that is downright, practical advice and would seem to be pretty obvious, but it is amazing how many of us just plough on through closed doors with our improper timing and wonder why the other person is irritated at us.

Sometimes when Dave and I are going somewhere, I think Dave is choosing the longer route. What sense does it make to insist that we go my way, if both ways will get us there? For example, there are two ways to reach our hardware store. When Dave drives there, I am sure he's taking the longer route and the challenge begins.

"Why are you going this way?"

"Because it's the way to the hardware store."

"Well, which one are you going to?"

"I'm going to the one in South County."

"What? That is a lot further away than the one in Lindbergh. Go to the one in Lindbergh!"

"It's not further, Joyce. South County's closer."

"No, it's not, Dave! Lindbergh is closer."

"No, it's not, Joyce."

"Well, if I got in the other car and went to the one in Lindbergh, and you went to the one in South County, and we clocked the amount of time it took us to get to each one, I'd **bet** you that I'd get there before you did!"

What difference does it make? I have learned to let the man go where he wants! If he wants to drive all over St. Louis to get one nail, let him! God has shown me the many times I question Dave's integrity on silly trivia like that. I don't like it when Dave constantly challenges me over insignificant decisions I made, yet I was trifling with him over unimportant details.

"Where are you going?" "What are you doing?" "Why are you doing that?" "Why are you doing it that way?" "Now why did you say that?"

God has been telling me, "Joyce, be still. Just be quiet. If you are trying to make your husband feel significant, a good way to do it is to not question his integrity all the time." It is an important lesson that can take some time to learn.

Dave and I had an outstanding argument about Henry Fonda that lasted for years. Dave had this little thing — he thought that every actor that came on television was Henry Fonda. We would be watching television and he would say, "Oh, that's Henry Fonda."

I'd say, "Dave, that isn't Henry Fonda."

"Yeah, it is."

"No, it's **not**."

"Yes, it **is**."

"**No-o-o**, it's not"

"**Ye-e-es**, it is."

Once we'd started that conversation, we didn't even pay attention to the rest of the movie. We would stay up half the night just to read the cast of characters so I could **prove** to him that the actor was **not** Henry Fonda. We went through that routine for a number of years! It was our favorite argument.

One night after I had been preaching a few years and had obtained a little "spiritual maturity," the Lord stopped me just as I was ready to retaliate. God said to me, "What difference does it make if it's Henry Fonda? Who cares?"

Listening to and following the Holy Spirit's advice will make your relationships rich with cohesive power.

You see, God cares about families and how we get along together. If you have never stopped to listen to the voice of God, I encourage you to ask Him for His opinion the next time you are ready to repeat a behavior that never gets you anywhere. When the Holy Spirit is in our lives, He teaches and instructs us in the will of the Father. He is full of love and grace and will give us advice that will make our relationships rich with cohesive power. The Lord may tell you **to be willing to be wrong, even if you are right.**

Sometimes even now Dave will say, "Oh, that's Henry Fonda."

When he does, I say, "M-mm, could be! I never knew he looked like that. But, who knows, maybe he had a little plastic surgery."

Far be it from me to say it isn't good old Henry. I'm just glad to have some time to sit with Dave and watch one of those old good movies again! It's amazing how much peace compliance affords you. Don't inspire trifling, ill-informed, unedifying, stupid controversies over ignorant questions that start quarrels and breed strife.

If you want to have peace in your home, you have to be willing to sacrifice your pride.

DON'T TAKE OFFENSE

The third thing you have to be willing to sacrifice is touchiness — the ability to be easily offended.

I've had to learn not to let my feelings get hurt if Dave doesn't want to do something for me. For example, when we go out to eat, after I say, "No, I don't think I want one of those," about a particular item on the menu, and Dave gets one, many times I want to eat it after all.

I'll say, "Just let me have one bite — I just want one bite."

I always get a small-sized frozen yogurt because it makes me feel as though I'm not overdoing it by eating too much. Dave usually gets the giant size, and as soon as I finish mine, I realize I can eat another small portion, only I want it out of his cup. For some reason, Dave doesn't like that. He doesn't like me eating his food.

When he stops at a drive-through, he will say, "Do you want a hamburger?"

"No, I don't want one."

"You're sure you don't want one?"

"No, really, I don't want one."

"OK, you don't want one?"

"No, I don't want one."

Then he gets his and, invariably, after I watch him and he is about halfway through, I decide I want some. I beg, "Well, could I just have one bite?" It's really all I want. If I buy a whole hamburger for the one bite I want, we would have to either throw the rest away or Dave would be tempted to overeat by taking the rest of my sandwich. It seems perfectly logical to me that he should just share one bite with me. Besides, I had seen our friends who work with us, Roxane and Paul, lovingly share food when we were with them, so I couldn't understand any harm in asking for one little bite.

Paul and Roxane have done many things for us. When our children were still at home, they took care of them when we were out of town. They help keep the ministry operating smoothly through all the things they have done for us. I have never seen any couple who is as sweet to each other as they are. Their relationship is tremendously anointed. Roxane shared with me that even when she was a little girl, she would pray that God would give her a husband to submit to. She said, "I don't even know how I knew to pray for this, but I had an intense desire to submit to a husband." And Paul is a chivalrous husband who can't stand to see a woman mistreated in any way.

Roxane is like me in that she doesn't want to order much to eat, but when she sees Paul's food she wants some of it. And Paul is really sweet about it. He just gives it to her. Paul does not seem to mind Roxane eating his food. Dave does not mind my eating his food most of the time, but there are times when he would rather that I just get what I want. We cannot expect our spouse to do what someone else's does. Dave and Paul are two totally different people with varying desires and approaches to life. Dave does not like it at all when I compare him with some other man I think is treating their wife in a way I would like to be treated. He reminds me that he does not compare me to other women and would appreciate me not comparing him to other men.

I once made a disastrous mistake and asked Dave for the last bite of his hamburger. If there is anything that is hard for a man to sacrifice, it's the last bite of his hamburger. It's easier for him to give somebody the first bite because he still has so much of it left. But when he is down to the last bite, I didn't realize before how much of a test it could be, especially for Dave.

Our exchange began as usual, with his offer, "I'm going to stop here and get a hamburger. Do you want a hamburger?"

"No, no, no. I don't want anything."

"Are you sure you don't want anything? Let me get you one."

I firmly said, "Dave, I don't want a hamburger."

He said, "I'll eat what's left."

I said, "I do not want a hamburger."

"OK."

He bought a hamburger, and I waited and waited, trying my best not to ask for a bite of that hamburger. But he got down to the last bite, and I couldn't stand it.

I asked, "Do you suppose I could have that last bite?"

He became upset with me. He huffed, "Why didn't you let me get you a hamburger?! I will buy you **all** the hamburgers you want. Why do you only want to eat mine?!"

"It's only one bite!" I defended. "You don't have to be so selfish! Maybe you need to read Mark 8:34 and forget about yourself!"

He said, "All right! Here it is."

I said, "Nope, I don't want it! I wouldn't eat that hamburger now! You couldn't pay me to eat that bite of that hamburger!"

He said, "You eat this!"

I said, "I'm not eating it!"

He said, "You eat it!"

I said, "I will not!"

"Well, I'm not eating it, so you might as well."

So I took it, shoved it in my mouth and chewed it up.

I was upset not only because Dave had hurt my feelings, but because I had compared the way he treated me to the way I saw Paul treat Roxane. I said, "Well, every time Roxane wants to eat Paul's food, he just gives it to her with no problem! I ask you for one stinkin' bite of your hamburger, and you throw a fit!" I was mad for about an hour after that last argument.

It takes a little while for the Holy Ghost to get through to us when we are enjoying our vengeance and self-pity as I was. But finally, I started feeling the presence of the Lord deep within me saying, "Joyce, you are acting ridiculous. The man told you he would buy you a whole sack of hamburgers if you want them."

Dave had offered to buy me a hamburger even if I just wanted one bite of it. He had clearly asked me in advance not to ask for his. It doesn't matter that sharing food doesn't bother Paul. As I said, everyone is different, and it does bother Dave. The person to whom you are comparing your own husband probably has some faults your husband doesn't have that would drive you crazy and be just as difficult to accept. What's the sense in pushing something on your spouse if it bothers them? Just don't do it.

FORGIVENESS RELEASES THE POWER TO HEAL

The fourth sacrifice in marriage is to give up bitterness, which leads to resentment and unforgiveness. Learn to quickly forgive others for the things they do that hurt your feelings and even for the way they behave. This is an area that people don't often think about, but sometimes we have a hard time accepting differences in our personalities and need to simply forgive when their mannerisms seem brash or abrasive to our own way of doing things.

If you like to talk and your spouse enjoys solitude, you may need to forgive him. Dave and I talk to each other, but Dave doesn't like to have nonsense conversation. When he and I were first married, I wanted to talk whether it made any sense or not.

Sometimes I would want him to just stay up all night and talk. I would begin, "Let's talk. We don't ever talk."

He'd say, "What do you want to talk about?"

"I don't know. You start."

He would sigh and say, "Joyce, what's the sense in talking if you don't have anything to say?"

"If we'd just start talking, we'd come up with something. Let's try."

Some people thrive on conversations of any kind. We just love to pick a topic and see what everyone else thinks about it. But Dave was wise and didn't want any part of pointless conversation. I learned after twelve years that talking when you have nothing to say gets you in trouble.

But I didn't know what Dave knew when we were first married, so I would get upset if he didn't want to "just talk." Whatever causes you to harbor unforgiveness, resentment, and bitterness needs to be sacrificed on the altar of love and left behind you.

Marriages are not as good as they could be when people hold onto little things that have hurt or offended them. It is difficult to completely open yourself up after being hurt because you are afraid you will be hurt again. Nobody can promise that loving someone won't hurt. In fact, you can't love without being willing to be hurt. It's not possible.

You can't have real love without operating in forgiveness. Love keeps giving the other person another chance.

You can't have real love if you are not going to operate in forgiveness. Love keeps giving the other person another chance. Love keeps trusting them over and over again, expecting them to do the right thing the next time. I realize there are big hurts and also little things we deal with daily. We need to let go of strife. Sometimes we may not even know what is agitating us, but we need to decide to let go of its irritating hold on us.

Ask the Holy Spirit to reveal what it was that caused you to feel bitterness or resentment. You may be surprised what He drags up for you, but when you see the truth, decide to let go of that grief in the Name of Jesus. Decide to forgive the person who didn't respond to you in the way you needed to be treated.

It took me several days to completely get over the bite of the hamburger. That's the truth! My feelings had been hurt because Dave didn't want me to have that bite of his hamburger. Don't trade your happiness for a bite of hamburger!

Forget what lies behind, and press on to what lies ahead.

10

LET'S
COMMUNICATE!

*The husband should give to his wife her conjugal rights
(goodwill, kindness, and what is due her as his wife),
and likewise the wife to her husband.*
1 Corinthians 7:3

Communication is more important than talk. We can say one thing but communicate something quite contrary to what we are saying though our facial expressions, body language, and actions. We can recognize the truth of these familiar expressions in support of this theory such as, "Talk is cheap," and "Actions speak louder than words." Couples need to be sensitive to what they communicate to each other through their actions.

It may seem strange to some people to realize that sex is a form of communication in marriage, but I venture to prove that sex is the highest level of communication between a husband and wife because it was designed by God to bring new life into the world. The Lord consistently compels us to choose life, and within the sexual union is the seed and the incubator for new life to continue in your relationship.

I also want to show that sex between a married couple should never be withheld from each other as an act of punishment for disagreements or wrongdoing. According to God's Word, the only reason a married couple should not unite sexually is if they both agree to devote themselves to prayer.

It may seem strange to some people to realize that sex is a form of communication in marriage.

If a woman tells her husband she loves him, but is always too tired to give him intimate attention, she is communicating to him that he is not a priority in her life. Yet, most every woman will admit to feeling insecure and lonely if her husband is not attentive to her needs. Tiredness is not an acceptable excuse for withdrawing from each other.

There must be a sacrifice of selflessness even in your sex life. The plan of God for your marriage is bigger than your "feelings." If you are too tired to enjoy your husband, you are too tired to enjoy anything else wonderful that God has planned for you.

First Corinthians 7:4,5 continues to discuss this issue:

For the wife does not have [exclusive] authority and control over her own body, but the husband [has his rights]; likewise also the husband does not have [exclusive] authority and control over his body, but the wife has her rights].

Do not refuse and deprive and defraud each other [of your due marital rights], except perhaps by mutual consent for a time, so that you may devote yourselves unhindered to prayer. But afterwards resume marital relations, lest Satan tempt you [to sin] through your lack of restraint of sexual desire.

Satan hates the purpose of sex because its ultimate expression is new life. Sexual fulfillment releases tension, is enjoyable, and brings a bond of unity that is unlike any other. It truly does minister new life. A consummated marriage may bring babies into the world, but even long after a woman is of childbearing age, the intimacy of the marriage bed continues to bring new life to her relationship and union with her husband. God is the one who put a strong sexual drive in men and women because He loves new life on every level, and He wants us to be drawn to its potential.

New life is the very thing that Satan abhors, so beware if you are caught in his temptation to lure you away from intimate time with your spouse. When I teach on this subject in my seminars, the auditorium, filled with thousands of listeners, goes suddenly still, or people begin to laugh and giggle. People get very uncomfortable when the subject is mentioned. I know for a fact that more married couples have problems in this area than those who don't, and I also believe if proper instruction came from the church, much of it could be avoided. Of course we should approach the subject respectfully, handling it with great propriety, but to ignore it is a big mistake.

At one of my meetings, a lady stopped me before I went to the platform and asked, "Are you going to teach on sex, communication, and money tonight?"

I said, "I'm going to try to."

She said, "You may need to call out the vice squad."

Sex is obviously the least talked about yet the greatest threat to the success of our marriages. When we have our audience complete questionnaires we get the same response everywhere — sex, communication, and money are the greatest sources of stress in marriages. Oddly enough, these three great obstacles to relationships are intertwined with each other and are doorways to the greatest areas of blessing that God designed for us.

If you are too upset with your spouse to make love to him, it is probably more important to lovingly offer yourself to him at that time than ever before. The act of sharing what God has encouraged you to give and what Satan is tempting you to withhold is to resist the devil and draw near to God. Obedience is a powerful weapon against the tempter. When the two of you come together as an act of obedience to God's plan for your life, you are telling the devil that you are keeping your promise to each other and you are ignoring his attempts to steal your power of agreement with each other.

Now some readers are cheering me on, but others need to stop and think about this for a moment. Let the truth of God's plan for men and women settle in on you. Didn't He say, "be fruitful, multiply, and fill the earth, and subdue it?" So what is the devil going to try to stop you from doing? He's trying to stop you from God's command of blessing in your marriage.

First Corinthians 7:4 says that a married man and woman's bodies do not belong to themselves, but to each other. They each have rights that should be yielded to the other. This verse is telling married couples that they have equal rights to each other, and should not withhold loving attention to the other or Satan will have free reign to tempt them to sin. Continual rejection to this intimate expression of love will tear down the self-esteem and sense of self-worth of the spouse who is being turned away.

A woman once told me that her husband was leaving her after twenty plus years of marriage. I know and love this woman. She had been sick for a long time and just hadn't felt good. She wasn't so sick that she couldn't motivate herself to get up and accomplish things, but she was consistently "worn out." Consequently, she completely abandoned her husband sexually because she didn't feel good. Unfortunately, if abstinence in marriage becomes habitual it is sometimes difficult to approach each other again.

> There are times when circumstances may preoccupy the attention of a spouse, but even through those times affection can be communicated.

Obviously there are times when a person is genuinely tired or under extenuating circumstances that may preoccupy the attention of a spouse, but even through those times affection can be communicated. But if the excuse of tiredness is used too often, a person is asking for trouble. Many times, however, a woman will say "no" to her husband just because she doesn't **feel** like she wants to stop what she is doing and spend time with him. If a woman (or man) frequently refuses this focused time with their spouse, they need to realize that they are being selfish.

More understanding needs to be gained in the area of marital sex. Couples need to give tender attention to each other out of respect for the needs of their spouse, without making ridiculous demands, realizing that not all people are alike. Some have stronger desires than others do, and it is important to remember that God designed this sexual drive. To consistently reject your partner in this area will quickly tear down their feelings of attractiveness and desirability. It damages self-worth.

Hebrews 13:4 says,

Let marriage be held in honor (esteemed worthy, precious, of great price, and especially dear) in all things. And thus let the marriage bed be undefiled (kept undishonored); for God will judge and punish the unchaste [all guilty of sexual vice] and adulterous.

Marriage is no longer being held in honor by the world, and that same deception is seeping into the church. But the Bible says to hold your marriage in honor. Esteem your marriage partner as worthy, precious, and of great price. Consider your relationship as especially dear in all things and let the marriage bed be kept pure. For God will judge and punish the unchaste — all guilty of sexual vice — and the adulterous.

This doesn't mean that we can't be forgiven for sin, but sin brings its own punishment. The more we live a holy life, the happier we are going to be and the more we are going to enjoy God's blessings. There is nothing worse than an internal heaviness from knowing that we are not living right before God and from being in bondage to something that we neither want nor from which we can get free.

I have heard a good number of people teach on this Scripture and say that because the marriage bed is undefiled, a married couple can do anything that they agree together to do and it's all right under the guise of marriage because this Scripture says the marriage bed is undefiled. But *Strong's Exhaustive Concordance* brings out the meaning of "undefiled" as "unsoiled" and "pure."[1] This expresses the proper translation of this verse as saying that the marriage bed **is** pure, and it is to be **kept** pure.

I don't agree with the teaching I have heard stating that a married couple can do anything that they want to do or that anything that feels good is all right between them because they are married. I believe that there is a knowledge on the inside of us of what is holy and what is not. God gives us wisdom for what is natural and what is not. The Bible tells us to stay away from unnatural acts and perversions.

Pornography, for example, is definitely a perversion. Those who feast their eyes on it will come in to bondage to it. There are certain triggers that Satan uses to set up the spirits that can gain strongholds in a person. Playing with these temptations is like playing with a loaded gun. No one can afford to play games with things that have been strongholds in their lives.

If people have been caught up in adultery, it did not just happen overnight. They didn't just wake up one morning determined to be in an adulterous affair. The idea of it started in their mind long before they acted out their fantasy. Initial compromise was made over little things that they knew they shouldn't do. Perhaps they had lunch with somebody when they knew they shouldn't have gone to lunch together. Perhaps they took somebody home or picked someone up for work without telling their spouse and soon found it difficult to explain.

The more difficult it became to tell the truth, the more the person entertained the idea that something more was in fact happening besides an innocent ride. Perhaps they got into a personal, private conversation with someone that they shouldn't have had. In our ministry we are extremely careful and possibly even go overboard about not opening any doors for anything like this to take place.

No one should consider themselves exempt from this temptation. The devil hates marriage and will pursue the fruitful and happy unions of productive, life-giving couples. It is better to be extreme in protecting our marriages than to be too loose and ask for problems. When things come into our minds that shouldn't be there, we need to cut them off because if we play the mind game, we are inviting the next step of temptation. James 1:14,15 defines the destructive path of temptation:

> But every person is tempted when he is drawn away, enticed and baited by his own evil desire (lust, passions).
> Then the evil desire, when it has conceived, gives birth to sin, and sin, when it is fully matured, brings forth death.

You have to discipline yourself when the warfare first begins in your mind. The battle is won or lost by what you decide to do at the point of temptation in the mind. James explains that first the evil desire is conceived. If entertained, it causes you to act in sin, and sin in its full maturity will bring death. Death will come to your marriage, your hopes, and eventually your life if you continue to give in to temptation.

Your eyes are the window to your soul. What you see is what you start to think about. I know that most people will admit that movies can and do impact our lives. I now know to turn off certain types of movies, but when television first started showing movies filled with pornographic scenes, it took many of us by surprise. We weren't expecting the producers to give such a graphic display. We were caught up in our interest of the story when suddenly there was a pornographic scene that we allowed ourselves to watch. Then at times when we didn't want to see that scene again, flashbacks came, and sometimes for months, or even a year later, we still saw flashbacks to suggestive portrayals of temptation.

When we open our eyes to blatant temptation, we invite the vision of its maturity into our soul and place it where the enemy can use it against us whenever he wants to. Safeguards need to be placed in our life. Some magazines, and even advertisements that come to your home, can be filled with images to inspire lust in your heart. Even advertisements from department stores are full of women and men half clothed. Life-sized billboards of a man or a woman in skimpy underwear line our streets.

While we cannot stop temptation from coming to us, we can ask God to give us power over the temptations to keep us from taking the next step that leads to sin. We may have to plead the Blood of Jesus over our soul to even ride up and down the street! It is a mistake to think we can resist temptation on our own. We need to ask God to keep our minds cleansed and give us the power to live holy lives because the devil is out to destroy marriages and homes.

We need to work at keeping the marriage bed undefiled because Satan will certainly use all the junk that is out there to destroy our blessings. Married couples should protect their freedom and liberty to enjoy each other, and be quick to ask God for help in times of weakness to temptation. Keep in mind that every good gift and every perfect gift is from God. (James 1:17.)

I love and enjoy my husband. We have a good time together. Coming from an abusive background, I wasn't always at ease with my own sexuality. I share this only because I know a number of people admit to the same "hang-ups" that I had, and these obstacles are a threat to God's plan for our relationships. I believe that my own honesty will help others break loose from their own bondages.

I was rigid, didn't want any lights on, and wasn't going to open my eyes. I had real problems because of the way that I had been treated before I married Dave. I had enough sense to sexually submit to my husband, which I think was good. Somehow I knew that continued rejection could cause temptation in a man to go find somebody else, and, of course, I didn't want that. But I never really enjoyed our sex life because I had been hurt and wounded so bad.

People have asked me to teach on this subject, but I always felt like I wasn't qualified to teach on sex because I'd had some problems myself. But the Holy Spirit spoke in preparation for the teaching in this book. This is what I felt like the Lord said to me, "Most people have problems in this area. There's more people that have problems with this than there are people who are free."

The largest number of people in prayer lines are there because of marriage problems. There are only a precious few marriages where both partners are totally free, where their marriage is sin free, and they have holiness in their marriage. Too few couples are liberated to enjoy each other.

Most of the time, one or both of the partners has some kind of problem that neither of them wants to talk about. It is not easy to teach on such a private subject before thousands of people who have different convictions in this area. But I felt like the Lord told me, "You had problems and most of your audience still have problems. No one is better qualified to teach someone with problems than a person who has had the same problems and come out of them."

When our friend Roxane married Paul, she had never been abused. She never had any serious problems. She grew up in a right situation and yet she still admitted that she had to tell herself, "Roxane, this is OK. There's nothing wrong with sex. The devil tries to present sex as dirty, but sex was God's idea."

Unless perverted outside of marriage, sexuality is to be holy, fun, and wholesome. It's a stress reliever that brings two people into a closeness that cannot be found in any other way except through a right relationship in a marriage union.

> *Unless perverted outside of marriage, sexuality is to be holy, fun, and wholesome.*

If the devil works so hard at perverting something, it's because he knows how much power there is in a good sex life. That is why he works so hard at trying to pervert it and tear apart couples who are committed to each other. He knows what the Word says. He heard Jesus say, *"Again, I tell you that if two of you on earth agree about anything you ask for, it will be done for you by my Father in heaven"* (Matthew 18:19 NIV).

Agreement is a powerful weapon of spiritual warfare against the devil. Two people who are in agreement can cause miracles to happen. If a husband and wife are in agreement, the devil comprehends the damage they could do to his own plan to steal the blessings of God from them. The devil wants to destroy and pervert sex inside of marriage; he wants to distract couples away from the bond of agreement that this act was intended to bring between them. Many couples disagree about — and even during — sex. But God's purpose and His truth need to be brought back into focus. A right godly sexual relationship between two married people is beautiful, and it is a weapon against the devil's plot to destroy.

Sometimes you may even argue over what is right to do and what is not right. One partner may want to do something with which the other one does not feel comfortable. How do you handle that? First, let me say that I certainly don't have all the answers, nor do I consider myself an expert, but I will share what I believe God has shown me.

I don't believe it is wise to try to force your marriage partner to go against their conscience. I realize there are probably some people, usually women, who are extremely shy and overly conscience-stricken in this area. If that is the case, forcing them to something with which they are not comfortable is not the answer. Proper education will help; prayer will help; patience will help — force will only make it worse.

I cannot give you a list of "do's" and "do not's," but I would hope that an honest consideration of body parts would educate us concerning what they are and are not to be used for. Each couple must follow their own convictions in these areas. We are to avoid all evil and perversion. Sex is a natural act; nobody has to be taught how to do it, not even animals. Let nature take its course, and enjoy each other.

A GODLY ATTITUDE IS A WEAPON OF WARFARE

Being abused like I was, I didn't have a very good attitude towards sex. And even though my physical body would respond fairly well, my mind, my mentality didn't want anything to do with it. There were times when Dave and I might be lying in bed and he would say, "You don't ever approach me."

I would endure whatever I needed to, but I didn't participate. I just sort of lay there like a dead fish. I had the attitude of "Here I am; do whatever you have to do, but don't expect me to get involved." Unfortunately, many women have this attitude towards sex, and it is causing a problem in their marriages.

God wants you to enjoy sex and view it a precious thing between a husband and his wife. I have learned that even when I am too tired to enjoy the sex act, I can still greatly enjoy being close to my husband and giving him pleasure. It is holy in God's sight.

At a point of frustration, not wanting to continue to push my husband away, I asked the Lord, "When am I going to get anything out of this?"

He replied, "When you decide to put something into it." It's amazing how good God's answers are to the questions we take to

Him. I wasn't expecting that answer, but that was what He told me. "When you decide to put something into it."

Passivity robs us of many things, including pleasure in our marriage union. We put off doing the right thing because it seems too hard or because we get embarrassed. We put off assertiveness in our marriage relationship because we were abused. We put it off because we've had problems in the past and we will not take the time to focus on getting well. We will not get free until we obey God and do what He is telling us to do.

Because of being forced into sex when I was young, if Dave ever encouraged me to make love when I didn't want to, I believed he was "forcing me." Dave would never force me, but any playful attempt on his part to persuade me to change my mind after I had said "no" would make me almost violently mad. I would snap at him with, "Stop trying to make me do stuff I don't want to do."

I would get really upset, until God revealed to me that my emotional reaction was toward my past and that I needed to let that old stuff die out. God encouraged me to do what I knew I should do, and not what I felt like doing. I had to let my flesh be crucified in Christ and accept God's truth in my life.

When you obey God's Word no matter how difficult, you will begin to enjoy a release from the past and a new expectancy for the future.

When you see what the Word says and do what God is saying, no matter how hard it is, you will begin to enjoy a release from the past and a new expectancy for the future. There were many times when I let my husband make love to me simply out of obedience to God, and though Dave didn't know it, tears were running down my face. I was in agony from trying to obey God and get rid of the bondage in my soul from the problems that I had when I was growing up.

There were times when I hurt so bad emotionally in my soul that I have laid on my office floor and held onto the legs of the furniture in my room to keep from running away from God. But obedience brings victory and reward, and I am now here, a living witness, proof that it pays off to do things God's way.

I am the proof that if you are willing to do things God's way, not only will you be joyous and happy, not only will you be free and have a successful marriage, but God can use your testimony just like He is using us to reach out and set multiplied others free. He will use the right relationship that you have with Him and with each other to bring life into the world.

Make the choice to enjoy life. Make the choice to live God's plan. He will dry every tear in our eyes and bring joy in the morning when we are obedient to His ways.

Most likely, your flesh will feel the pain while you are getting free of old ways of thinking. But hold to something that will keep you from running away from God. God wouldn't let me continue to mistreat Dave while I was in the process of changing and renewing my mind.

Some people who were abused and mistreated by people in their past retaliate on their current partner when it was not their fault. My father was very controlling and manipulative, and he would get violent if I showed any dislike for what he was doing. To survive his abuse, I had to pretend that it was happening to somebody else.

I had taught myself not to mentally participate in the sex act. Having developed the habit of fantasizing that it wasn't happening to me was the only way I knew to engage myself in intimate moments with Dave. I, Joyce Meyer, couldn't get involved. I had to pretend like it was somebody else.

As I grew in knowledge of the Word, God began to convict me to make the choice to choose life. In one way, getting free is hard, but in another way, it is easy because God has a personalized, individual plan for everyone. God knows infinitely the problems that each person faces and though everyone's problems are different, God knows what it will take to get over them.

The Holy Spirit is ready to help those who call upon the Lord. If you will simply and systematically agree to obey God, He will walk you out of every bondage that you have and take you into a life of freedom. But if you choose not to obey God, you will never get out of bondage because you can't get in enough prayer lines and you can't get enough counseling to ever be set free.

If you will simply and systematically obey God, He will walk you out of every bondage into a life of freedom.

You have to be willing to listen to God for direction on what you should do to restore life in your marriage. Shutting out His voice is adversely affecting your marriage if you are bringing unholy fantasies into that marriage bed, and your mind needs to be renewed. God will bring the healing, but the choice to resist temptations is yours.

When you ask God to set you free, He will start showing you little changes that you can handle a little bit at a time. But you will never get free unless you are willing to do what He tells you to do each step of the way.

For example, once I stopped fantasizing that I was not even in the room with Dave, the Lord would quicken me with new suggestions that sound funny to me now, but were major obstacles to overcome at the time. I always kept my eyes shut all the time so I wouldn't see anything. I remember clearly when the Holy Ghost said to me, "It's time to open your eyes." That step of obedience was hard for me.

I struggled with obedience when the Lord first said, "Now, you approach Dave. You go and let Dave know that you want to make love." Buried way back in the back of my mind was, **this whole act is not right.** I was still believing that angels and the Holy Ghost and everybody else went and hid when we made love.

We get funny ideas about sex, but I learned to pray my way through them. I learned to obey God even though tears were running down my cheeks. Once in a while Dave would catch me crying and say, "What's wrong?" I would tell him I was just trying to obey God but was having a hard time doing so. Dave respected my willingness to do whatever I needed to do to be set free.

I remember when the Lord said, "Now, why don't you leave the lights on tonight." And so I would obey God, one thing after another — I chose to obey God. God has walked me out of that bondage and into victory and into freedom to enjoy my sex life.

I'm not positive that I'll ever be 100 percent the way that I could have been had I not been abused. There are scars from abuse, and I don't know that I can ever completely relate to what would be 100 percent normal. But I know that I am forever pressing on to that place of victory. I have enough freedom that even if I still find some problems, I'm freer than most people who have never even been abused.

LOVE IS A WEAPON IN WARFARE

I believe that sex between a man and a woman who are married and love each other — that is, sex — in God's order, is spiritual warfare. I don't know that I can fully explain all that I believe the Lord has shown me concerning this, but I know what I have learned through personal experience. He has shown me several times how making love to my husband can prevent spiritual attacks that are formed against us. I have seen it happen enough that I'm getting the fear of God on me about it. Once you get the fear of God on you about something, it is easier to obey God because you are also afraid of disobeying.

There are times when I had a desire for Dave, but because of the poor attitude that I have had toward sex, I would ignore the prompting and decide that it was "too much trouble" to take time to be with him. Women probably relate to this response more than men, but God had to show me that my attitude was wrong, and obedience to this prompting was not too much trouble, but that yielding to that drive would save us trouble through what was coming toward us.

When the desire to be with my husband is present, the Lord is letting me know that there is a need for Dave and me to come together. When I don't respond to this leading, I have felt the Lord say to me, "If you don't listen to Me, you are going to have trouble." I can make all kinds of excuses, "Oh, God, I don't want to tonight.

I'm tired; I need to go to sleep. I'm this, I'm that, I'm something else." But the Lord will gently prompt me with warnings not to deprive myself from Dave at that time. But recently, not too many months prior to this teaching, I can recall two specific times I chose to ignore clear instruction from the voice of God and refused to obey His leading.

The very next day, on both occasions where I specifically felt the Lord had spoken to me in advance, something happened that was an obvious attack from the enemy. One time we got in an argument and the other time the devil just launched a blatant attack in our household. I don't even remember all the particulars, but God reminded me of what He had said to me the night before saying, "I told you."

Why is it that sex is spiritual warfare?

There's something powerful in that coming together. It reseals the marriage covenant and closes the door on the devil. The devil is full of hatred toward proper lovemaking between a married couple who love each other. Their union is a holy and a beautiful thing that drives the devil backward from any progress he might have been making to separate them.

The lovemaking of a married couple is a holy and beautiful thing that drives backward any progress the devil might have made toward separating them.

That is as much as God has shown me so far. When we obey God we may not see the fiery darts that were shot at us, but disobedience pays a great price. I have seen the misery that results from ignoring the gentle leading of God, so I'm beginning to get the fear of God on me in a positive and uplifting way concerning this. It is natural to go our own way, but supernatural power to thwart the enemy comes into our life when we follow God in His way.

We don't always have to know the "why" behind everything that God leads us to do; what we are to do is obey. I have had times, and you probably have also, when I have felt led to pray about a certain situation or for someone, and because I did not think it was a good time, ignored the leading of the Holy Spirit. I discovered later when trouble came in that area that I missed an opportunity to divert an attack from Satan upon me or someone else I knew.

Some may think it is wrong to speak of sex and prayer in the same breath, but we must remember that God originated sex and the normal desires that come with it. It is man who has perverted sex and made it seem ugly and unholy. The book of Proverbs lists several things that are said to be *too wonderful* (to explain), and one of them is . . . *the way of a man with a maid* (Proverbs 30:18,19). We of course should discuss the subject with great respect and propriety for it is truly a mysterious secret that was birthed in the heart of God.

HOLY MATRIMONY

Through obedience we can bring holiness back into our marriages and return to God's original plan for husbands and wives. When you study covenants that God blessed throughout the Bible, you will see that a godly promise was always sealed with the shedding of blood. There is a blood covenant that takes place between a man and woman when they first consummate their marriage. The woman's hymen is broken during the first time she has intercourse and blood is shed to seal the vow of purity between them. How precious it is for a woman to be a virgin on her wedding day and be able to stand before her husband and her Lord with evidence of the shed blood to prove her faithfulness.

I wasn't a virgin when I married Dave, but those who suffered abuse and previous broken marriages, as I did, can come under the same covenant promise through the shed Blood of Jesus. We who suffered bad choices and impositions can stand before the Lord and our husbands and say, "Not by my might or power, but by the Spirit of the Lord, I make a covenant with you as we enter holy matrimony in the eyes of God." (See Zechariah 4:6.)

We can pray Psalm 54:1 (NIV):

Save me, O God, by your name; vindicate me by your might.

The Blood of Jesus cleanses us of all sin and His Name empowers us to live a justified life in God. There is still a shedding of blood that makes a covenant between marriage partners and God's blessing.

When a covenant is made, it is a promise to share ownership of all that one possesses with the other one. With God in this promise our inheritance is rich. When non-believers look upon such a marriage and see the glory of God's presence uniting the two believers, they will be drawn to the light that surrounds that blessed couple. People will say, "My, what a good God you serve. How can we know Him, too?"

No wonder the devil tries to pervert this covenant plan of God.

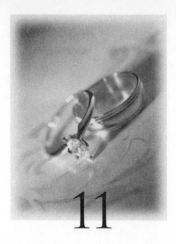

11

IS THERE A NICER WAY
TO SAY THAT?

The words of the wicked lie in wait for blood,
but the speech of the upright rescues them.
Proverbs 12:6 NIV

Verbal communication is important between two people who are trying to build a strong relationship. If people don't develop good communication skills, problems can be provoked through simple misunderstandings between couples. There are various types of communication that need to be developed between couples to establish healthy relationships.

Some communication is simply for the purpose of sharing information that both parties need to know. Clear information saves a lot of confusion and a lot of misunderstanding. We ask our employees all the time to communicate, communicate, communicate. It's amazing what a mess can take place in an office when somebody doesn't bother to tell somebody else what they were doing or what they weren't going to do. The same need for communicating information is needed for responsibilities that are shared at home.

Some people seem to live in their own little world, unaware of the need to pass information on to others. Perhaps they don't realize how much information affects the plans of other people with whom they live and work, but it is selfish to continue to ignore the need for information that others have. Clear communication keeps down confusion and many misunderstandings.

How difficult is it for a wife to simply say, "Oh, honey, did you remember that Johnny's ball game is tonight and that we need to be there at six o'clock?" That is far better than to wait until a father gets home from work only to find that he has to rush off suddenly, when he may have anticipated a chance to relax or had planned to finish some work after dinner. It is even worse for him to come home late and find that his wife and child are gone and he can't recall where either of them might be.

Communication includes the art of leaving little reminders here and there to help others achieve the goals that are important to them. Reminders are always more pleasant than regrets of missing important deadlines.

"Remember now, you need to go to the bank today."

"Remember now, I need you to do this."

"Now, remember, I'm going to be half an hour late getting home tonight so . . ."

"Remember, it's our anniversary this Friday and we are going out to dinner . . ."

> *Just a few informative, little words of communication can do a great work in building a healthy relationship.*

Just a few informative, little words of communication can do a great work in building a healthy relationship.

Presumption and assumption cause strife in marriage. Which of the following two statements is the nicer way of sharing information?

"Oh, I almost forgot to tell you, I am going to go out with the guys tonight. I was sure you wouldn't mind." Or, "The guys would like to go bowling tonight if it won't interfere with any plans we have. Is there anything you were wanting to do or is it OK to tell them to count me in?" While the first approach might hurt her feelings, the second approach is so considerate it might even inspire her to change her plans if she sees that another night will still work for what she had planned.

THE FELLOWSHIP OF COMMUNICATION

Some communication simply enhances fellowship and takes place by just talking together. When you share both your most intimate hopes and hesitations with each other, you build a mutual trust and admiration that bond you together. You don't have an agenda or talk about anything intense; you just need time for a friendly exchange of ideas and conversation. Sharing information is more like talking **at** each other, while fellowship is talking **to** each other.

Couples need to appropriate time on a regular basis to sit down and share some face-to-face fellowship when they can converse with each other without distractions. What they share with each other doesn't have to be any great earthshaking news. But the gift of undivided attention fills the craving left by loneliness that two people living in the same house can sometimes feel.

Sometimes I'll tell Dave, "Just come in here, and sit down with me while we have a cup of coffee." Or, when we have both been busy all morning and have been apart from each other I will find him and say, "Let's take a break and go get a coffee." Dave and I are together all the time, working at the same place, traveling together, and yet we still need to spend time just talking together. We understand the difference in talking at each other and talking to each other. Sometimes we need to communicate just for the fellowship.

If you really want to have good lines of communication to remain open between you and your spouse, then take an interest in your mate's interests. Adapting to whatever your spouse is interested in is a way to build fellowship and find common topics to "just talk" about together. I believe that if you show an interest as unto the Lord that God will give you a true desire for it.

One of my daughters goes to the car races with her husband. This is not a sport she would naturally love. But she's adapted to what her husband likes to do and even looks forward to spending this kind of time with her husband. My other daughter works out at the gym with her husband because that was something that he enjoyed when they first married.

I used to get unhappy because I thought Dave never wanted to "just talk." I would pout about it and rehearse, "We don't ever talk. We don't ever talk." The Lord interrupted me one day, saying, "You don't ever want to talk to Dave about anything he's interested in. You only want people to talk to you about what you are interested in. That's selfishness."

Dave loves sports, and I don't know anything about sports. I adapted and learned to play golf, and I like saying that I'm even pretty good at it, too. Years ago, Dave taught me how to play right. I have a pretty good golf swing and enjoy a decent chance to keep up with the guys. I learned that I enjoyed what Dave was interested in after all. If you are willing to adapt to something, God can cause you to enjoy the very thing you thought you were not interested in.

I adapted to golf, but I honestly can't handle football. I tried, but I cannot keep track of who has the ball. It takes forever to get two inches down the field! They throw the ball to somebody, pile on top of each other, and then go through the whole thing again. Believing that I am finally getting the idea of the game, I start rooting for someone and Dave says, "He doesn't even have the ball!" At that point, I go find a good book to read while Dave watches the rest of the game.

Sometimes I listen to my husband when he talks to our friend Paul or son David. They just converse on and on, and I think, **Well, why don't you ever talk to me?** But if I want him to talk to me, then I have to be willing to talk about some of the things he's interested in and not just expect him to talk only about the things that interest me.

Recently I have started asking Dave a few questions about the sports he enjoys. I don't have to ask many questions before he is willing to talk to me for a long time. I can provoke a lot of conversation with just one simple question such as, "When does the baseball season begin?" Ask God to show you what your partner is interested in and how to ask questions to show your interest in your partner. You will be sowing good seeds that will cause your spouse to want to talk to you about things that interest you.

Besides, listening and sharing interests is a way of showing respect. Respect your spouse enough to take an interest in what they enjoy as a loving act of giving yourself away to them. When you converse for fellowship, both talking and listening are required. Practice giving your spouse your undivided attention as often as you can. Talk about things he is interested in.

PROBLEM-SOLVING SKILLS

Don't use this time of fellowship to challenge and provoke your partner. Galatians 5:26 says not to challenge and provoke others. The quickest way to close communication lines with someone is to challenge them.

We have a young grandson who is at the stage of growth when he challenges almost everything anyone says. He frequently says to another who is talking to him, "No, **that is not the way it is!**" That kind of a challenge is irritating even coming from a child, so imagine how irritating it is from an adult who is supposed to know better and be educated in how to treat other people.

There are times to challenge a person or to offer a differing opinion, but it certainly should not be done frequently or over insignificant matters.

As I mentioned earlier, communication consists of more than words. Voice tone, facial expressions, and body language reinforce the emphasis we place on what we say. I read once that 37 percent of communication is words and 63 percent is voice tone, facial expression, and body language. In reference again to our sexual relationship, for example, when Dave playfully comments that we need to find time to be alone together, I might say yes but convey through my body language that I wanted nothing to do with his suggestion by showing no further interest.

> *Communication consists of more than words. Voice tone, facial expressions, and body language reinforce the emphasis we place on what we say.*

One of the main reasons why people don't communicate well is because they have had bad experiences when trying to express their point. Many times those unsuccessful experiences have resulted from poor timing and insensitivity to God's leading. Learn to wait until you sense the presence of God preparing the heart of the person with whom you need to communicate.

Timing is extremely important in good communication.

Timing is extremely important in good communication. If you start talking to someone who sighs and looks away it is fair to assume they don't want to hear what you have to say or they are too distracted to pay attention to you at that time. We can cause ourselves trouble by not picking the right time to speak.

Ecclesiastes 3:7 says there's a time to speak and a time to be silent. There's a time to talk about a problem and there's a time to leave it alone. That doesn't mean that you should **never** talk about it, but you should look for the right time to discuss the topic on your heart if you want it to be received with a fair evaluation.

THE TIME FOR SILENCE

• Keep silent when you are angry.

I have learned the best time to discuss a problem is not when I'm mad. When anger is present is not a good time to try to work out a solution to a problem.

• Keep silent when you are tired.

The best time to try to discuss a problem is not when everybody's tired and worn out.

• Keep silent when you are under unusual duress.

The best time to try to discuss a problem is not when there's already stress coming at you from five or six other areas.

Choose a time when you feel the leading of the Holy Ghost opening the moment to express your needs. I have always been the kind of person who wants to settle an issue as soon as I notice it. I don't have any problem confronting people about our differences. My problem has always been in trying to wait for God's timing to solve a problem.

I have been in trouble enough times from communicating the wrong way at the wrong time that I am now choosing to wisely plan confrontation instead of quickly reacting as soon as I see the need of it. In the past, as soon as a problem appeared I would want to sit down and talk about it right then and there. I wanted to get the issue out in the open, get it over with, talk about it, and not let anyone leave until the problem was solved. I have finally learned to pray first, saying, "God, is this the right time?" A lot of times He will say, "No." I still react to the shock of having to wait until God says, "Now you can say it."

People who are quick to confront others get themselves into a lot of trouble by just barreling into issues without waiting for God's timing. Those people with a strong personality are not inclined to put up with very much. If anything happens around you that doesn't seem right, or just, or fair, or the way it should be, they immediately jump to make everything right again. They tell everybody the right way something ought to be done. Problems result when all of this is done without God's leading.

A TIME TO SPEAK UP

Some people are such peace lovers that they will do anything to keep from causing a disturbance, even by allowing things to continue that they know God is telling them to confront. These individuals are like lambs who would rather resist any and all disputes. These lambs are so laid back and passive in their nature that the Holy Ghost has to prompt them to take a stand.

Then there are individuals who tear into confrontation with lion-like ferocity. These "lions" are the people who counter others in fleshly zeal, and woe be it if they decide to confront one of the timid lambs who are too shy or fear-based to defend themselves in danger. The lions actually stalk out their next victim of dissent.

Examine yourself to see if you are a lion or a lamb. If you generally don't want to discuss things and you don't want to deal with issues, then you are going to have to obediently speak up if God says to, whether you want to or not. If you automatically confront, then you will have to practice leaving things alone until God tells you if or when to pick them up again. Some people have to be pushed forward by the Holy Spirit, and then lion personalities, like me, have to be pulled backward.

Nearly half of the people in any given conference respond when I ask people to raise their hands if they are laid back individuals who would rather forget about problems than to deal with anything that might lead to an argument. The other half admit that they are more likely to jump right into the situation without a second thought. Of course, with half a room full of people who love confrontation and half a room full of those who despise it, many of them are married to each other.

Tragedy comes when one person always wants to confront and the other one is afraid of confrontation. Then the one who wants to talk all the time complains to the one who doesn't, "You never talk to me." The one who doesn't talk thinks it is because the other one never shuts up! What we all need is balance and a commitment to be Spirit-led, not flesh-led.

Everyone needs to confront issues in their life and yet neither lions nor lambs emulate Christ's example of making peace if they are out of balance. We are to be imitators of God as a light for unbelievers to see their way to the kingdom of God because they desire the life we live. One of the hardest characteristics of Jesus to imitate is His ability to be that lion-hearted Lamb. When confrontation was needed, Jesus always firmly followed through with love.

I want to have the humility that is manifested in Christ. We are to imitate His gentleness and meekness and still deal with certainty with whatever needs to be solved. As the leaders of a large ministry, we have to deal with conflicting situations all the time. I used to wish we could have at least one week where we didn't have to **deal** with something. Dave and I finally understand that we will always have to deal with things, but we want to confront issues in a godly way.

Conflict is part of everyone's life. How we deal with conflict is important. The more I have studied the Word, the more I have understood why Jesus is called the Lion of the tribe of Judah. It means that He had a strength that was characteristic to a lion that caused Him to deal with things in a majestic way, and yet He's also called the Lamb of God.

The characteristics of the lion are totally different from those of the lamb, yet the Lord is recognized as having both qualities. Someone gave us a picture of a lion and a lamb lying down together, and it reminds me that I'm supposed to be a good, godly mixture of both qualities. I never had any trouble with the lion part, but I had a lot of trouble with the lamb part. When we need to communicate with someone, especially concerning confrontational issues, we should first pray for God's grace and mercy to anoint us as lion-hearted lambs. Then we should wait until we have balance in our perspective and approach.

Hasty words spoken without giving any thought to them often cause tremendous trouble. Ecclesiastes 5:2 says, *Be not rash with your mouth, and let not your heart be hasty to utter a word before God.* . . . I believe we should not only be careful with our words to people, but also with our thoughts before God. There have

> *Hasty words spoken without giving any thought to them often cause tremendous trouble.*

been many times when I have thought out how I would handle a situation, and God has let me know that is not how He wants me to handle it. We should form a habit of asking the Lord what He would do before we do any speaking or planning about confrontation.

It is very easy to jump to conclusions, but Paul said in 1 Corinthians 4:5, *So do not make any hasty or premature judgments before the time when the Lord comes [again], for He will both bring to light the secret things that are [now hidden] in darkness and disclose and expose the [secret] aims (motives and purposes) of hearts.* . . . We should give God time to "come" into a situation with His wisdom and knowledge before we hastily make our own decisions. Only the Lord knows what is in a person's heart, and He judges according to that, not only according to what He sees and hears. Abiding by these principles has helped me in a major way in my relationship with Dave and, I am sure, prevented countless arguments.

The Bible says, *Be well balanced (temperate, sober of mind), be vigilant and cautious at all times; for that enemy of yours, the devil roams around like a lion roaring [in fierce hunger], seeking someone to seize upon and devour* (1 Peter 5:8). If we are not well balanced, our adversary, the devil, may find an opportunity to devour us.

Jesus demonstrated the balance between a lion and a lamb that we too need to emulate. In Revelation 5:5, Jesus is depicted as the Lion of Judah, *Then one of the elders [of the heavenly Sanhedrin] said to me, Stop weeping! See the Lion of the tribe of Judah, the Root, (Source) of David, has won (has overcome and conquered)! He can open the scroll and break its seven seals.*

Then in verse 6, the very next verse the Word refers to Jesus as the Lamb, saying, *And there between the throne and the four living creatures (ones, beings) and among the elders [of the heavenly Sanhedrin] I saw a Lamb standing, as though it had been slain, with seven horns and seven eyes, which are the seven Spirits of God [the sevenfold Holy Spirit] Who have been sent [on duty far and wide] into all the earth.*

Throughout the New Testament, we see Jesus acting in two contrasting ways. He confronted the moneychangers in the temple, overthrowing their tables and firmly demonstrating God's will to all those who watched Him. *He said to them, "The Scripture says, My house shall be called a house of prayer; but you have made it a den of robbers"* (Matthew 21:13). Yet in other places, we see Jesus standing falsely accused, without speaking one word in His own defense.

So what are we to learn from His communication patterns? He was a lion when He needed to be and yet always a lamb — He never sinned or failed to be excellent in speech. It's a challenge not to defend yourself when someone comes against you. It's difficult to ignore insults and shun retaliation.

Isaiah 53:7, says of Jesus, *He was oppressed, [yet when] He was afflicted, He was submissive and He opened not His mouth; like a lamb that is led to the slaughter, and as a sheep before her shearers is dumb, so He opened not His mouth.*

Sometimes I find that one of the hardest things God has asked us to do is to be Christ-like in our communication with others. When somebody is rude and tells you off, mistreats or insults you, it is hard to just stand there and look at them with godly love and just wait on God.

Thank God, He gives us the power to change and to become like Christ. I still feel the reaction of my old nature sometimes, but more and more I am learning self-control. The key to improvement is to learn to confront when God says to confront and to leave an issue alone when God says to leave it alone.

> *Learn to confront when God says to confront and to leave an issue alone when God says to leave it alone.*

Our old nature reacts to conflict with:

"Let me straighten you out!"

"You are not going to treat me that way."

"I don't have to put up with that."

"Who do you think you are?"

"Who do you think you're talking to?"

Sometimes we even throw Scripture at them: "Touch not God's anointed." (1 Samuel 26:23.) But when Jesus was afflicted, He was submissive. God did not release Him to say anything, so He kept His mouth shut and took the blame for us.

Matthew 18:15 depicts that, "If your brother offends you, go to him privately and show him his fault." Confrontation is not a public affair. Most of the time confrontation should be done privately.

Galatians 6, verses 1-5, explains how to approach confrontation through the love of God. Realizing that we have plenty of faults of our own, we are to be humble about the fact that we too can fall into the same faults that we want to criticize others for having. We are to be gentle in our approach with the purpose to build the other person's understanding of God's intense love for them, not to tear down his or her self-esteem. Read these verses while carefully giving thought to the way you have handled confrontations in the past or have planned to do so in the future.

Brethren, if any person is overtaken in misconduct or sin of any sort, you who are spiritual [who are responsive to and controlled by the Spirit] should set him right and restore and reinstate him, without any sense of superiority and with all gentleness, keeping an attentive eye on yourself, lest you should be tempted also.

Bear (endure, carry) one another's burdens and troublesome moral faults, and in this way fulfill and observe perfectly the law of Christ (the Messiah) and complete what is lacking [in your obedience to it].

For if any person thinks himself to be somebody [too important to condescend to shoulder another's load] when he is nobody [of superiority except in his own estimation], he deceives and deludes and cheats himself.

But let every person carefully scrutinize and examine and test his own conduct and his own work. He can then have the personal satisfaction and joy of doing something commendable [in itself alone] without [resorting to] boastful comparison with his neighbor.

For every person will have to bear (be equal to understanding and calmly receive) his own [little] load [of oppressive faults].

Before confronting each other, we have learned to pray and wait for God to confirm the need and the timing. Then, a key to godly confrontation when we feel that we are to bring something to each other's attention is to begin by saying, "Look, I know that I have plenty of faults myself. I know that I do plenty wrong myself. But this is something that I believe God wants me to share with you." Humility and love express conflict in a totally different way than when we arrogantly stand before somebody with our list of everything that's wrong with them.

12

YOU NEED
WHAT?

. . . For whatever a man sows,
that and that only is what he will reap.
For he who sows to his own flesh (lower nature, sensuality)
will from the flesh reap decay and ruin and destruction, but
he who sows to the Spirit will from the Spirit reap eternal life.
Galatians 6:7,8

Everyone needs stability emotionally, spiritually, mentally, and even verbally. We want to be assured that words spoken are sincere, that they will be followed through with action when needed. Words spoken are promises, and promises should not be broken. Our spouses need the same reassurance that we desire. The Spirit of God has promised to return to us whatever we sow in other people's lives. The desire to be involved with stable people is fulfilled when we give to others what we expect them to give to us. A stable foundation in our life and surroundings gives us confidence to face the trials that come against us.

My husband has always been very stable; therefore, I always know I can count on him in times of difficulty to remain the same as he is in good times. His moods do not fluctuate — neither do his decisions or confession. I grew up in a very unstable environment, and Dave's stability is part of what God has used to bring healing to

---

my life. When we become like God in our actions toward others, then He can use us to bring to them healing and restoration. Jesus is the same, yesterday, today, and forever (Hebrews 13:8); He is the Rock on which we firmly stand (see Psalm 62:1,2,5-7) — we should all strive for that same stability to manifest through us. Stability releases a sense of security, something everyone needs and desires, especially women.

We are encouraged by God's Word to look for every occasion and opportunity to do good to all people (this includes our mates), not only by being useful and profitable to them, but also by doing what is for their spiritual good and advantage. We are to be especially mindful to those in the family of God with us. (Galatians 6:10.)

The sacrifice we are called to through marriage has a promise of great return attached to our obedience to it. For some reason women always enjoy hearing what the Bible says men are supposed to do for their wives. Likewise, men sit up straight and pay close attention when I talk to women about the way they should treat their husbands. But God's Word validates that if we each continue doing right, He will reward us by a harvest of righteousness from all the seeds we planted first. So we should listen to what God tells us individually rather than pay so much attention to how our spouse is supposed to treat us.

One of the basic needs of women is security, while men instinctively need significance.

Bottom line, one of the basic needs of women is security, while men instinctively need significance. Both of these needs can be more readily fulfilled by their spouses than by themselves. A woman seeks security to know that her needs will be taken care of financially, physically, and through whatever surprises might come her way. One day, the electricity suddenly went out in one portion of our house. It makes me feel secure to know that Dave will take care of those things I would not know how to correct.

The main thing that a man wants out of a marriage relationship is significance. He wants to feel important, and this basic desire is influenced by God. It is not wrong for a man to want significance in his life.

Let's read 1 Peter 3:1:

In like manner, you married women, be submissive to your own husbands [subordinate yourselves as being secondary to and dependent on them, and adapt yourselves to them], so that even if any do not obey the Word [of God], they may be won over not by discussion but by the [godly] lives of their wives.

I used to work at trying to win over Dave with my words. As I realized through the Word that a lot of discussions would not change Dave, I learned to pay more attention to trying to make my own behavior more godly. Instead of changing Dave, I was to reinforce his sense of significance.

That's exactly what the Word says, that a woman should respect and reverence her husband. In other words, everything that a woman does should make her husband feel as though he is the most important thing in her whole life. That need is built into the heart and godly ego of men. If a wife can make her husband feel his importance in her life, it seems to supercharge him to want to find ways to take care of her needs.

Satan does not want couples to reinforce each other in a marriage. He whispers deception into the hearts of wives, "Don't submit; you deserve to have things your own way. Don't give in or adapt to him. Look at your husband who is doing his own thing all the time. He doesn't even know what 'cleave' means. He married you, threw you in a house with a couple of kids and then took off. He's gone all the time doing his own thing."

When a woman listens to the devil, she has been set up for a fight as soon as her husband comes home. She fights all evening, goes to sleep mad, and sometimes the fight continues for years. As she remains open to the devil's lies, she finds it more difficult to talk to her husband and misses out on the relationship that God intended her to have.

God wants to help couples with marriage problems and work with those who have good marriages to make them even better. How married couples treat each other is important to God. Men are to love their wives and treat them with respect. He is to be considerate of her needs and to think about what she needs and what she might want. Wives are to make their husbands feel significant. They are to make their husbands feel important and treat them the way they in turn want to be treated.

Do we want our marriages to be triumphs or tragedies? If you want to be the queen in your home, treat your husband like the king. If men want to be the king in their homes, they should treat their wives like queens. Obviously, Satan's desire is that they all become tragedies. But I believe we can prevent tragedy and find healing for the differences that work to destroy us.

Most people get married without knowing what God expects them to do for their spouses. Many individuals have never read what God's Word has to say about filling the needs of each other in marriage. Their marriage may have been inspired by some physical or emotional attraction to the other person, then they "tie the knot" and Satan quickly begins to use their ignorance of God's intentions against them.

We usually follow the examples that have been placed in front of us prior to our own marriage and, in many cases, that example has been a bad one. If a young man has never witnessed his father giving affection to his mother, chances are he won't know how to give it to his wife. If she, on the other hand, grew up in a family in which the father gave a lot of affection to her mother, she will naturally expect the same. She will be quite devastated when she does not get it.

As I already mentioned, my father always got his own way through becoming angry and staying that way until everyone submitted to him. Because the way my father acted was the only way I had seen people get what they wanted, I followed that example until I learned to pray and trust God to bring into my life what He knew was right for me.

We can only do what we know to do. The Bible says that people perish for a lack of knowledge. (Hosea 4:6.) Many marriages are perishing because people are not educated in how to gain and maintain good, godly relationships.

With all the information available today anyone can get educated in any subject. All they need to do is apply themselves to studying in the particular area needed. We can't blame anyone else for our failures if we lazily refuse to do our part. Whatever your particular problem is, turn it into a college course. Study, ponder, pray, reflect,

Many marriages are perishing because people are not educated in how to gain and maintain good, godly relationships.

think, read, search until you have all the answers you need for victory. Don't sit by idly while Satan destroys your marriage. Stand your ground and fight for what is yours.

Often people marry hoping that the other person can make them happy. But marriage must be looked at from the viewpoint of giving, not getting. When each partner fully gives themselves over to thinking about what they can do for their partner, then in that process of giving, they will get everything that they want in return and more besides.

The Bible says, . . . *It is more blessed to give than to receive* (Acts 20:35 KJV). It takes most of our lifetime to get around to believing that. We stay busy trying to get somebody to do something for us, don't we?

You may have noticed that I keep saying the same thing in different parts of the book about having a mindset to do for others instead of always expecting them to do for you. I am saying it over and over in various ways because it is probably the single most important principle that contributes to making any relationship work. It takes us right back to what we have called the "golden rule" in God's Word — *Do to others as you would have them do to you* (Luke 6:31 NIV).

The world does to others whatever they want to do to them, and obviously the world's ways are not working. Give away what you would want, and you will always be amply supplied.

Hebrews 13, verse 4, says, *Let marriage be held in honor (esteemed worthy, precious, of great price, and especially dear) in all things. . . .* Many couples in the world aren't even getting married anymore; they just live together thinking that if it doesn't work out, they won't have to spend the money to get a divorce.

There are actually generations of people who have never heard that God said it was wrong for unmarried men and women to live together. They have never even heard that marriage in God's eyes is an honorable institution where He can bless them and make something of eternal benefit happen between them. I hear people talking openly about living together with no shame or embarrassment about it at all. They have convinced themselves that it makes more sense to try living together first to see if they like it before making a real commitment. That theory may make sense to the human mind, but God does not approve of it, and anything He does not approve of ultimately will not work.

To God, marriage is a covenant — a covenant relationship. And in God's eyes, covenants are not ever to be broken. Coming into a covenant relationship with somebody literally means that everything you have available becomes theirs and everything they have becomes yours.

As believers in Christ, we have a covenant relationship with God, and we need what He has! I didn't have much to offer God, but God gave me enough of His strength to make up for all of my weaknesses. Likewise, the marriage is to visibly reflect the benefits of our invisible covenant with God. So, the first blessing of a good marriage begins with honoring the marriage relationship and being willing to give what we have to our spouse.

Born again and Spirit-filled people are getting divorced after many years of marriage. After I learned of at least twenty of these situations happening within a year's time, I asked the Lord, "What is going on? These are people who know the Word! They know that divorce is not Your will for them! And yet they're just doing it anyway! What is going on, God?"

I heard the Lord speak to me in my heart, and I don't think I have ever heard Him sound like this. His voice was sad, and He said, "Joyce, My people are not using wisdom." The Lord preached a whole message to me in that one sentence.

Honor is missing in our society today. Even thirty years ago, men put high regard in honor. If something wasn't honorable, you just didn't do it. Godly principles are being stripped from society.

There are generations of people who have never been taught the importance of keeping their word. But those of us who have the privilege of being in a relationship with Jesus Christ and have understood the Word of God, can learn and do what is right. We can have wonderful, strong, and powerful marriages. But we must use wisdom.

Satan always begins tempting somebody by lying to them. He begins through little suggestions — a little temptation here and a little temptation there. But if the temptations are entertained, they will progress into real sins. I remember a young girl who worked for us in the very early days of our ministry. She had problems with insecurity and, though we didn't know it at the time, she had occasionally become inappropriately involved with men. She started bringing donuts to one of the married men who worked for us. Every morning she continued to give him this special attention.

It didn't take me very long before I said, "Hold it! If that man needs a donut, his wife can send him to work with donuts. He doesn't need you carrying him donuts. If you are going to bring donuts, you bring them for everybody at the office and not just for one man!"

The man, of course, liked the attention she was giving him. Evil spirits work on people through little flirtations. They say, "I'm going to make you feel good about yourself." But we are called to use wisdom! Don't think that you can play with fire and not get burned! If we need to be built up, we should go to our spouse for reinforcement and resist security and significance from other sources.

If your spouse will not or does not know how to reinforce and encourage you, then get what you need from God or your mother or another friend, but under no circumstances should anyone allow themselves to be drawn into Satan's trap of adultery. We all know countless people who have been caught up in an adulterous affair who always say, "I never meant for this to happen." If they never meant for it to happen, then why did it? It happened because one thing led to another and, before they knew what was happening, it was too late. Their emotions were in control instead of the wisdom of God.

When we follow wisdom, our lives are blessed, and when we don't, they are destroyed. That is the bottom line, and I am a bottom-line person. I have found living that way is much better than living with my head in the clouds somewhere, not facing the reality that will eventually chase me down and force me into a confrontation anyway.

> *When we follow wisdom, our lives are blessed, and when we don't, they are destroyed.*

Some people may not even know that the devil is real! Twenty-five years ago I didn't understand the reality of the devil as my enemy. I didn't know about demon principalities and powers. I didn't know that there were spirits that would get on people and try to lure other people into sinful relationships.

We must use wisdom against the enemy. Nothing will change without wisdom. We use wisdom in our ministry that some people say is a little strict, but we do not let one of our male and female employees get in the car and go somewhere together. If they have to go somewhere on business, we will spend the money to take somebody else off their job and put them in the car with them, rather than let the two of them go together.

When I'm out preaching in different places, Dave will not let another man pick me up at the hotel unless a woman is with him. It's not because Dave doesn't trust me. We just don't feel that traveling alone is wisdom, even if it is simply to avoid the appearance of evil to someone who may see us and wonder why we were together.

There are countless ways we can avoid evil simply by using wisdom. I recall one time when a male friend of Dave's started telling me how pretty he thought I was and how he wished his wife looked like me. I immediately sensed trouble! So instead of hiding it from my husband and secretly enjoying this man's compliments thinking they wouldn't hurt anything, I went to Dave and told him what was said and that I did not feel comfortable with it. We decided to pray and then if it ever happened again, Dave would talk to him. The prayer worked, and we never had another incident. Obviously Satan knew from my reaction it was not going to work, so he aborted his plan. We need to be smart enough to abort Satan's plan, rather than allowing him to abort God's plan for our life by drawing us into sinful relationships that can only end in disaster.

We need to be smart enough to abort Satan's plan, rather than allowing him to abort God's plan for our life.

Let me emphasize one more time: **You cannot play with fire and not get burned.**

GIVE YOUR SPOUSE SECURITY

If, for example, you and your spouse are in relationship with another couple and your personality and the other man's personality match up well, you may just like to talk when you get together as a foursome. But if you find yourself not wanting to spend a lot of time with the others and prefer to sit apart by yourselves to talk, you may be headed for trouble. Be careful! I'm not saying that you can't talk to anybody — just don't get out of balance.

A good marriage does not just happen. I don't care how wildly in love you were when you got married, if you don't continue to work at your marriage, by paying attention to the needs of your spouse on a regular basis, your marriage will get in trouble. Your relationship will get stagnant. You'll get tired of each other. You will lose the excitement in your marriage, blaming your spouse when all along you were neglecting him.

Marriages decay and fall apart, but it doesn't happen overnight. It's almost always a result of people just not using wisdom. You won't have a good marriage if you don't spend time together. If you don't learn how to respect one another and care for each other's basic needs, you will definitely have serious problems.

There's no better relationship between people than through a great marriage, but there's no greater pain in a relationship than the disappointment found in a bad marriage. Do whatever you can do to make your marriage not just passable, but excellent. God's blessing on marriage is that through trying to make your partner happy, you will end up being happy yourself.

Proverbs, chapter 7, shows that wisdom is to learn what the Word says to do, then do it. If we are having problems in our marriage, wisdom says that nothing will change if we don't change our approach to it. Wisdom may tell us to stop doing some things that we are doing, and to start doing some things we don't want to do. We have to be willing to change.

I heard a great definition for insanity — it is when we do the same thing, the same way, expecting different results. Going to a marriage seminar or simply reading a book will not change one thing in your home if God convicts you of disobedience in an area and you don't change what you are doing.

Learn to respond quickly if God prompts you with:

"Hey, that point is for you!"

"Your problem is a poor attitude!"

"You are in rebellion!"

"You are not spending enough time with your spouse."

The Word is like the prod of the shepherd's staff. When the sheep get out of line, the shepherd comes along and taps the lamb to get her back in line. That's exactly what the Word does to us. God's Spirit keeps us in line with the Word of God. Know what to do and then know to do it.

It might interest you to know that while I was doing the final edit on this book, which required me to read it, I was convicted by my own book of a few things I teach others that I have let slip myself. They are things that I know to do, but have gotten lazy in doing them. We all need the prod of God's Word to keep us on the narrow path that leads to life. It had been a long time since I had played golf with Dave because I have been busy, but after reading this book I decided to rearrange my schedule and make having fun with my husband a priority.

When I asked Dave if he wanted me to play golf with him the next day, his eyes lit up, and he sounded very pleased and excited. Because I have sown seed with the intention of making him happy, I already know that he will go out of his way to make me even happier than I already am.

Follow the leading and promptings of the Holy Spirit — He is always trying to lead you into blessings.

Follow the leading and promptings of the Holy Spirit — He is always trying to lead you into blessings.

When God speaks, it is natural to look for an easy way out other than to sacrifice self-will and pride to obey. We cry in panic saying, "I don't want to suffer. I don't want to be uncomfortable. I don't want to have to give anything up. I just want my marriage to be better. Gee, I hope I can find a prayer line where someone is laying on hands to make marriages better."

But you can have hands laid on you until you don't have any hair left on your head, and nothing is going to change if you don't go home and make some changes!

Read Proverbs 7:1-5,

My son, keep my words; lay up within you my commandments [for use when needed] and treasure them.

Keep my commandments and live, and keep my law and teaching as the apple (the pupil) of your eye.

Bind them on your fingers; write them on the tablet of your heart.

Say to skillful and godly Wisdom, You are my sister, and regard understanding or insight as your intimate friend—

That they may keep you from the loose woman, from the adventuress who flatters with and makes smooth her words.

We are to keep wisdom around us all the time, embracing it as a sister and seeking understanding or insight as an intimate friend. Wisdom promises to keep us from loose people who are intent on bringing destruction to our lives.

Verse 21 speaks of the recognizable patterns of temptation: *With much justifying and enticing argument she persuades him, with the allurements of her lips she leads him [to overcome his conscience and his fears] and forces him along.*

How many people could stay out of trouble if they just paid attention to their conscience? We know this "loose woman" is specifically speaking about a woman trying to draw a man into sexual sin, but I believe it can also represent other things, like the temptation to sit around and watch too many television shows when your conscience is telling you to turn the television off and spend some time with your family. Sometimes we force our spouses into temptations by leaving them alone to find their own excitement and to cheer themselves up without our help.

God gives wisdom to anyone who asks for it. He will put in our heart a consciousness of what is right. To have good marriages, we have to do what our heart tells us, not just what we want all the time.

Proverbs 7:22-27 continues to explain the destructive goal of temptation.

> *Suddenly he [yields and] follows her reluctantly like an ox moving to the slaughter, like one in fetters going to the correction [to be given] to a fool or like a dog enticed by food to the muzzle*
>
> *Till a dart [of passion] pierces and inflames his vitals; then like a bird fluttering straight into the net [he hastens], not knowing that it will cost him his life.*
>
> *Listen to me now therefore, O you sons, and be attentive to the words of my mouth.*
>
> *Let not your heart incline toward her ways, do not stray into her paths.*
>
> *For she has cast down many wounded; indeed, all her slain are a mighty host.*
>
> *Her house is the way to Sheol (Hades, the place of the dead), going down to the chambers of death.*

Temptation plays on those who are already wounded. If someone isn't getting his needs met at home, he is more likely to be played upon by the temptress. Notice that the victim is reluctant to follow, and if not diverted from her lead, temptation will lead a man to death. Obviously the "loose woman" could also be a "loose man." This message is for men, women, young, and old. No one is beyond temptation.

Marriages need protection. It won't work to think, **Well, we are married so, that's it. He's stuck with me and I can act any way I want and look any way I want because he is committed to marriage.**

If a wounded man whose needs have been ignored goes off to work, there will be somebody out there with that seductive spirit on them, who will try to entice him into a trap. So use wisdom. Don't let your husband be like an ox led to the slaughter. Hopefully godly men will be smart enough to not let a loose woman steal their life, but some men need their wives to build up their defenses from such temptations. Likewise, wives need to be built up against this trap, too.

RESIST THE DEVIL

Married people need to flee from flirtations as quickly as possible. Even if someone is in need of compliments, it is dangerous to receive them from the wrong source. We must avoid and stay away from evil, asking God to strengthen us in all the areas where we are weak. We must **resist** the devil, and when we do, he will flee. The way we resist the devil is through submission to God. (James 4:7.) There are many voices in the world, but the one we must follow is God's. Not only will the devil try to lead us astray through wrong thoughts and emotions, but he will use people, sometimes even good friends, to bring temptation into our lives.

The voice of people can be strong, but we must choose to be God-pleasers, not man-pleasers. You might have a single friend who wants you to go somewhere with her where she can meet a man, but it would be a place your spouse would not be pleased to find you. You will have to

The way we avoid living in regret later is by making right choices now.

disappoint your friend and do what you know is right. Consistently doing this in all things is the way to stay out of trouble. Follow wisdom; follow peace — if you do, you will like where the path leads you. If you don't, you will regret it in the end. The way we avoid living in regret later is by making right choices now.

God deals with His children. When we have problems in our marriages, I believe that He shows things that we need to do differently. He writes His instructions on our hearts and we know what we should be doing or what we should stop doing.

The beginning of wisdom, the Bible says, is the reverential fear and awe of God. We need more reverential fear and awe of God so that when God tells us something, we understand that He's telling us for our own good. When I ask for a show of hands in my seminars for those who can admit that God has told them to do something that they haven't been obedient to, 75 percent of the people lift up their hands. They already know what God's told them but they haven't done it.

> *This one principle can change your life: Know what to do, then do it!*

What help is there for those who refuse to obey God? If we are not going to do what God tells us to do, then nothing is going to change in our circumstances. **Knowing** what to do and not doing it is not wisdom. This one principle can change your life. You have to know what to do, then do it!

Beginning in Haggai 1:2, we see a group of people whom God had told eighteen years previously to rebuild His house. They still had not been obedient to what He had told them to do; yet they didn't understand why their lives were in a mess. They wondered where the blessing of God was.

After reminding them of their disobedience to His instruction, the Lord said them in verses 4-6:

> *Is it time for you yourselves to dwell in your paneled houses while this house [of the Lord] lies in ruins? [Now therefore thus says the Lord of hosts: Consider your ways and set your mind on what has come to you.]*
>
> *You have sown much, but you have reaped little; you eat, but you do not have enough; you drink, but you do not have your fill; you clothe yourselves, but no one is warm; and he who earns wages has earned them to put them in a bag with holes in it.*

Does this sound like anybody you know? How often have you heard someone say, "I just don't understand what's going on, God. I just don't understand."

Verse 7 brings the answer:

Thus says the Lord of hosts: Consider your ways (your previous and present conduct) and how you have fared.

In other words, if we are not satisfied with what is going on in our lives right now, maybe we should look back and let God show us how the way we have conducted ourselves has affected what is happening to us now. We must be willing to change our ways if we want to receive His blessing. If we are willing to change from the previous and present conduct that is holding back God's blessings, we can have greater victories than what we have ever had before.

Many Christians, who spend a great deal of their time trying to be happy, wonder why they are not being blessed. They believe the devil is trying to keep blessings from them. They think more spiritual warfare is needed for blessings to break through for them. Spiritual warfare is very important, but warfare without obedience isn't going to do any good!

SUBMIT TO GOD

The Bible says, "Submit yourself to God, resist the devil, and he will flee." (See James 4:7.) A lot of people are trying to resist the devil, but they still are not submitting to God! How can people keep the devil out of their marriages if they won't do what God's told them to do? If God puts on my heart, "Go and apologize to Dave," then I need to be quick to obey. The Holy Ghost is not going to let me have peace until I obey His voice, "Apologize to Dave. Apologize to Dave. Go and apologize to Dave."

God wants to build security and significance in couples. He knows love never fails, and His Spirit consistently prods us to do what love would do. The Word of God **shows** me what to do! The Word of God shows me how to have a great, wonderful life, but I have to do it.

We don't sleep well when we are stubborn and bullheaded. On nights that I refuse to apologize to Dave and go to bed mad at him, I have found that I can sleep on the outside seam of the mattress to distance myself from his presence! I was angry, and I did not want him to touch me. I can remember being freezing cold all night, but stubbornly refusing to ask him for any of the covers. In fact, at those times I felt that I would never speak to him again as long as I lived. (Does this scenario sound familiar?)

Yet, while I sleep the Holy Spirit is still waiting to encourage me to do the right thing. In the middle of my sleepless night, I hear His voice, "You should have apologized to Dave. You didn't apologize."

I finally get to the point where I can't live under that kind of pressure, so I say, "OK, God, tell me what You want me to do. I'll just go do it. Let's get it over with." I understand that nothing is going to change if I don't do it.

Ephesians 4:26 says, *When angry, do not sin; do not ever let your wrath (your exasperation, your fury or indignation) last until the sun goes down.* Anger is an emotion that rises up sometimes before we know what is going on. I have discovered that I cannot always prevent it from coming, but I can deny its right to remain.

Make peace. Be a peacemaker. Swallow your pride and apologize. We have everything we need in the Word of God to help us live great lives! The Word is a lamp to our feet and a light to our path. (Psalm 119:105.)

HOW TO BUILD SELF-ESTEEM IN YOUR MATE

In order to build His house according to His plans, God will ask you to build up and edify your spouse. Wives are called to respect, honor, and submit to their husbands in order to build him up and esteem him in the Lord. Husbands are to love their wives as Christ loved the church in order to establish her sense of value. Christ loved the church so much He gave Himself up for her. When God's couples are built up in their sense of self-worth and value, they will proceed to fulfill God's plan to multiply through godly offspring and subdue the earth through the work of their hands.

Both the husband and wife need to sacrifice their self-will in order to obey God's command for their homes. How can anyone believe that someone loves them if they never see sacrifice on their behalf? If a spouse always has to have it their way or no way, how would the other partner ever feel loved? Both sides must make sacrifice to demonstrate their love to the other.

Love must be demonstrated by what we do. To avoid strife we must constantly forgive and let go of the offenses that happened that day. To stay focused on each other's needs is a sacrifice but it is also the secret to great happiness and blessings in God. The alternative is to be selfish, demand your own way, and wonder why your marriage needs repair.

The Holy Ghost has your desires in mind when He tells you to demonstrate love towards someone. A lot of times I have felt prompted, "Just do it; just do it."

I would argue, "Well, God, You are always saying something to me. When are You going say something to Dave?!!" I felt as though I was the only one who was ever corrected. If God wasn't dealing with Dave, too, I couldn't stand it! A couple of times I even went to Dave and I said, "Dave, is God dealing with you about anything?"

Invariably, Dave would shrug and say, "No, nothing that I can think of."

One time God dealt very strongly with me about showing Dave respect, yet I felt as though there were plenty of times that Dave wasn't respectful to me! If I interrupted Dave when he was talking, the Holy Ghost would say, "That is disrespectful." I would think in retaliation, **Well, he interrupts me when I'm talking! Why can he be rude and I can't be rude?!**

It's a flesh burner when God wants you to stop doing something that the other person is doing, too. But we are each responsible to do what God shows us to do. He wants us to pour ourselves out for the other, like two liquids poured into the same glass that cannot be separated again. Do the hard things now, and your reward will surely come later.

Marriage began with sacrifice. Genesis 2:24 says, *Therefore a man shall leave his father and his mother and shall become united and cleave to his wife, and they shall become one flesh.* Right away couples have to "give up" their dependence on their parents. That doesn't mean they can't have a good relationship with Mom and Dad, but it does mean that if they don't leave their parents and cleave to each other, they will have problems.

My understanding of the word "cleave" means to be glued to; cemented together; to associate with a person so as to accompany him or to be on his side; to go where another goes; to be attached; devoted to; to hang upon and express love. It depicts permanent adhesion, or a welding together. If we are permanently welded to someone, doesn't it seem wise to nurture that person's self-image so we can better enjoy our "attachment" to them?

> *For no man ever hated his own flesh, but nourishes and carefully protects and cherishes it, as Christ does the church.*
>
> Ephesians 5:29

The irony in being one is that if we build up our spouse we are in fact being good to ourselves.

13

SO WHAT WILL
THIS COST ME?

*By this we come to know (progressively to recognize,
to perceive, to understand) the [essential] love: that
He laid down His [own] life for us; and we ought to lay
[our] lives down for [those who are] our brothers [in Him].*
1 John 3:16

Love has a price, but loving people is the only thing that will
bring true happiness to our lives. I bought every book on love that
I could find and they were all alike. They told me what love is
supposed to be, but not one of them mentioned that love would
hurt. Love requires sacrifice and because we are inherently self-
centered, no one particularly enjoys sacrifice. While loving people
outside of our immediate family calls for intermittent sacrifice, the
daily event of loving a spouse leaves little time for self-seeking.
There is no greater way to show your love than to sacrifice
something you want with a good attitude.

First Corinthians 7:32,33 explains that while single people can
be anxious about the things of the Lord — how they may please
Him — a married man (or woman) is anxious about worldly matters
and how he or she might please the spouse. There are people who
have the gift to be single, but the biggest majority of people want

to get married. Paul taught in 1 Corinthians 7:36 that there is nothing wrong with marriage.

He said, "If you can't control your passions, then get married," but he pointed out that marriage brought anxiety and distressing cares that single people don't have. A married person is drawn in diverging directions; their devotion to God and devotion to their married partner can cause divided interests. If you are married then you must have concern for your mate.

THE SACRIFICE OF PERSONAL FREEDOM

Love requires a sacrifice of a certain amount of personal freedom. If you promise to love someone, you will no longer be able to only please yourself. You will no longer be able to watch just what you want to watch on television, or go just where you want to go, always eat where you want to eat, or buy anything you want to buy.

There are many opportunities every day to sacrifice for our mates, but we often fail the test. It is obviously a struggle to believe it is more blessed to give than to receive. Instead most of us fight to get our own way because we haven't learned how to give, but giving contributes to the success of a relationship.

If our attitude is to bless others, then the blessings of God will chase us down the street and overtake us. What would happen in a marriage relationship if couples would actually compete to see who could do the most for the other one? We would no longer linger in bed in the morning thinking, **If I lie here five more minutes, he will get up and make the coffee.** Some of us would have to lie there 100 years before our husband would go make the coffee!

The reality is that we will never stop wrestling with our self-serving flesh. Every single day we will have to fight to overcome self-centeredness. How many times a day do we pass up opportunities to sacrifice something for our partners? Most of us try every which way to get out of doing anything other than what serves our own interests. Selfishness is ruining marriages.

THE SACRIFICE OF TIME

Time is another sacrifice a married person must make. To have a good marriage, we have to invest quality time in our relationship, or else it will never flourish. What does not grow will stagnate and eventually die. I have read that people need twelve loving, meaningful touches every day to live out life to their fullest expectancy. The best part of hugging someone is that we invariably get hugged back. The principle of sowing and reaping is built in to the act of a loving touch. Reaching out to others helps replenish our own life support.

Just think, hugging your husband will add years to his life, and yours! Hugging only takes a little bit of time. Don't be surprised if the Holy Ghost reminds you to hug your husband before he goes out the door in the morning. Even if he is all the way out to the car when the Holy Ghost reminds you, go and hug him. You should chase him down and plant a loving hug around him.

If you are praying about your marriage relationship, I believe the Holy Ghost will speak to husbands saying, "You didn't kiss your wife. You didn't hug your wife. You didn't even say anything to her this morning."

He will argue against the idea of turning around and going back into the house, thinking that he doesn't have time. Besides he has to stop for coffee and a cinnamon roll for his morning "buzz." And just when he starts the car there you will be, shouting, "Wait, wait, wait, wait, wait, wait — come back — come back — come back. You didn't kiss me."

I have literally chased Dave down the driveway to be obedient to the voice of God. Dave would defend himself, "Well, I kissed you when I got up."

"I don't care if you kissed me when you got up. This is another event — now you're leaving. Kiss me again."

Women especially need these twelve loving touches every day — not pinches — touches. A wife wants to be loved, and some wives need to step forward and receive the hugs and attention that they need from their husbands. Let your husband know that you want your hugs each day. If your spouse has shown affection in the past and your response has not let him know that you liked it, he may have quit showing the affection. Be responsive; don't act like a dead log when shown affection. I personally know that I despise giving someone a hug who just stands there and does not reciprocate at all.

Take time to think about your mate and how you might bless him. What do you think would happen if, just once everyday, you asked God the question, "OK, God, what can I do to bless my mate today?" I challenge you to pray this prayer everyday,

Lord, show me something I can do for my partner today, just to be a blessing to him.

Marriages would flourish and love would grow if every married person would ask God for that help. God may tell a husband to call his wife just to tell her he loves her. What would his day be like if his wife called him, out of the blue, and said, "I just want to tell you I think you're great." Imagine the points that would be scored between that couple who consistently found ways to build each other up.

Galatians 6:10 says, . . . *Be mindful to be a blessing.* . . . We are to fill our minds with ways to be a blessing. You may even have to sacrifice the last bite of your hamburger, some of the fudge on your ice cream, or the cherry in your limeade just to be a blessing to your mate.

THE SACRIFICE OF COMFORT

Married people have to sacrifice both physical and emotional comfort, too. A display of emotions may be uncomfortable for some, especially men, but you may have to show your spouse how you feel emotionally sometimes. Admitting the emotional needs that you have is to make yourself vulnerable to the trust of your spouse. It may be a sacrifice to open yourself in this way.

Give hugs and compliments, and say, "I love you. You're beautiful." Tell your husband, "You're handsome. You're important to me.

I appreciate you." If you can't say it face-to-face, start by writing it in a card. If endearments are hard to say out loud, find other ways to express them, but start communicating.

Physical comfort must sometimes be sacrificed for a good relationship. Men may have to give their wives their coat when it's cold. They may have to run through the rain to get the car from the parking lot for her so she does not get wet. A husband may have to drive his wife to the door of a building so she doesn't have to walk through the sub-zero temperatures as he does.

He may have to wait for her to try on twenty-five outfits and then watch her buy the first one she put on. Men learn that shopping is an emotional experience for women. Men go out and they want to conquer the mall. Women go to enjoy the mall, but we'll talk more about that Chapter 18.

SWALLOW YOUR PRIDE

There is no room for pride in a healthy relationship. The words "I'm sorry" need to be easy to say even when you really don't think you were wrong. The Bible says in Romans 12:16 that we should live in harmony with one another and not be haughty or high-minded.

Forget having a good relationship if you are not willing to say, "I was wrong." Why do we have such a hard time with admitting that we were wrong about something? Those are hard words to say, especially when we are upset. But blessings will come if we swallow that pride and let humility rule instead.

John 13:1 says, *[Now] before the Passover Feast began, Jesus knew (was fully aware) that the time had come for Him to leave this world and return to the Father. And as He had loved those who were His own in the world, He loved them to the last and to the highest degree.*

The highest degree that you can love somebody is to sacrifice yourself. *For God so greatly loved and dearly prized the world that He [even] gave His only begotten (unique) Son. . .* (John 3:16). We know that Jesus gave up His own self for us. The Bible says that men should love their wives as Christ loved the church, which was to the highest degree of self-sacrifice.

John 13 continues with the story of how Jesus washed the feet of his disciples, an act of servanthood, to show them how very much He loved them. He, fully knowing Who He was, being the Greatest of all, became the Servant of all. Pride never kept the Lord from showing His love for us. To be a servant, as He called us to do, requires that we sacrifice self-will.

Simon Peter resisted the Lord when He came to wash his feet saying, "Lord, are my feet to be washed by You? [Is it for You to wash my feet?]" Imagine for a moment how you would feel if Jesus came and said, "Sit down — I want to wash your feet." Wouldn't you feel hesitant, as Peter did, thinking that you should be the one who was washing the Lord's feet, instead of Him washing yours?

But Jesus said to Peter, *You do not understand now what I am doing, but you will understand later on* (John 13:7).

Peter replied, *You shall never wash my feet!* (verse 8).

And Jesus answered him, *Unless I wash you, you have no part with (in) Me [you have no share in companionship with Me]* (verse 8).

He was saying that unless we serve each other we have no true part in each other. If you love someone to the highest degree you will be willing to serve them.

We are all to be sensitive to the other person's needs, even in little things.

When Jesus finished washing their feet He said in verses 12 through 14,

. . . Do you understand what I have done to you?

You call Me the Teacher (Master) and the Lord, and you are right in doing so, for that is what I am.

If I then, your Lord and Teacher (Master), have washed your feet, you ought [it is your duty, you are under obligation, you owe it] to wash one another's feet.

We are not to seek to be served, but to serve. That means that I should do things for Dave that normally I might not want to do. That means he will do things for me that he doesn't necessarily want to do. We are all to be sensitive to the other person's needs, even in little things.

A FRESH START

In the mornings, I like fresh orange juice with grapefruit juice in it. I used to make the juice by squeezing the fruit by hand rather than just drinking bottled or canned juice. One morning we had a lot to do, and I grabbed a can of juice to pour it into a glass.

When Dave came into the kitchen, he said, "Don't you want some fresh squeezed juice?"

I told him that I had thought of it, but I had so much to do that morning.

He said, "I don't mind making it — I would love to do it for you."

Those are the moments that make a marriage good.

Have you ever heard the expression that "sex begins at breakfast?" Considerate exchanges throughout the day do much to build a relationship. A woman finds her greatest satisfaction through attentive affection from her husband while a good sexual relationship is of great importance to a man. When a husband shows affection to his wife, she is emotionally drawn to her sexual relationship with him. By filling her needs, she in turn fills his needs.

But so often, a husband doesn't understand how difficult it is for his wife to be physically drawn to him without the emotional attachment that is nurtured by affection. When no affection leads to no sex, and no sex leads to no affection, the couple stagnate in a war zone all because the woman doesn't **feel** loved. Bottom line, love is what we do for each other.

Bottom line, love is what we do for each other.

If you ask God, He will give you creative ideas on how to bless your mate. The cost of showing loving attention is minimal to the cost of letting your relationship fall apart. Great relationships are missed just because people are too lazy to do something nice for their spouses. We have to fight against our selfishness when we don't want to get up and move on the suggestions that God gives to us. Small gestures can add up to big differences. We need to learn to be servants to one another.

If you ask God, He will give you creative ideas on how to bless your mate.

One night, I hurriedly went to get myself something to drink, wanting to get back to what I was doing, when I knew I should ask Dave if he wanted something, too. God didn't have to say, "Joyce, ask Dave if he wants a soda." I knew in my heart I should ask him. Our selfish nature wants to take care of only ourselves. But it's all those little things that build strong relationships and satisfy the Lord's instruction to "wash each other's feet."

It's humbling to say, "I'm willing to serve you. I want to serve you." But humility is required when entering into a marriage relationship. Partners are called to sacrifice and serve each other. It's sacrifice and service, sacrifice and service, and then more sacrifice and service. If there hasn't been any sacrifice or service between you and your spouse, then start doing little gestures of love to demonstrate thoughtfulness. Don't start with the attitude of, "Well, what are you doing for me? You should get me something. Why don't you do something for me?" That would not be operating in godly principles.

After telling Simon Peter that he should wash the feet of others, just as He had done for Peter, he continued in John 13:15-17,

> *For I have given you this as an example, so that you should do [in your turn] what I have done to you.*
>
> *I assure you, most solemnly I tell you, A servant is not greater than his master, and no one who is sent is superior to the one who sent him.*
>
> *If you know these things, blessed and happy and to be envied are you if you practice them [if you act accordingly and really do them].*

If we study the Word of God, then do the things that God has already put on our hearts to do we will be blessed, happy, and even envied. We can have good marriages, but we have to be willing to sacrifice and serve. It isn't "Happy are ye if you **hear** it," but, "happy are ye if ye **do it**."

PUTTING DOWN THE MONEY

To have the right perspective toward money, we need to know what the Bible says about its importance. First of all we can see that most women were born to shop! That's why Adam had a job before he ever met Eve. God put him in the garden and told him to tend and take care of it. Once Adam had established himself at his job, God told him He was going to give him a helpmate. So Adam got a wife and she was called a female because there was a **fee** for having her.

Seriously, money and financial management is a major area where married people have to make sacrifices. A married person is no longer free to spend a paycheck on whatever he or she wants to buy. I believe it is safe to assume that every married couple has argued over their finances.

Not having enough money can put a tremendous amount of pressure on a marriage. Likewise, having too much money without knowledge of how to handle it, can also put tremendous pressure on a marriage. Money is important, but according to the Bible we have to be very careful that we don't love money.

To test yourself on whether money is too important, consider how you act if something of yours gets damaged. Do you get upset if your car gets a little dent in it? First Timothy 6:10 says, *For the love of money is a root of all evils; it is through this craving that some have been led astray and have wandered from the faith and pierced themselves through with many acute [mental] pangs.*

If **all** evil is rooted in the love of money, then we should understand why it is so important to get a godly perspective on how to handle it. We need to re-evaluate ourselves on a regular basis to determine if the love of money is taking root in us. No matter how godly we are, there is a temptation to let the things that are important to the world become overly important to us.

- Jesus was betrayed because of the love of money.
- Ananias and Saphhira lied about their money and fell dead.

- Demetrius caused a rebellion against the apostle Paul because of the loss of his money that was derived from the worship of the goddess Diana.
- Jezebel tried to kill Elijah because of the revenue she lost when her prophets were destroyed.
- For money men sell their souls; women sell their bodies.
- Governments fall when its leaders are corrupted by money.
- Men worry about money, kill for it, commit crimes, and go to prison because of it.
- Families are destroyed from the stress of having too much or not enough of it.

God places an importance on money throughout the Bible and while it has an important role in a godly home, it should never rule the believer's household. As Christians, we are in the world, but not of it. Matthew 6:24 says we can't serve God with all of our heart if we love money or the things that money can buy.

The Bible says in Matthew 6:33, . . . *seek (aim at and strive after) first of all His kingdom and His righteousness (His way of doing and being right), and then all of these things taken together will be given you besides.* If we seek God first, He promises to take care of all the things we need.

Philippians 1:10 encourages us to learn to sense what is vital in our lives.

So that you may surely learn to sense what is vital, and approve and prize what is excellent and of real value [recognizing the highest and the best, and distinguishing the moral differences], and that you may be untainted and pure and unerring and blameless [so that with hearts sincere and certain and unsullied, you may approach] the day of Christ [not stumbling nor causing others to stumble].

We should know what is important and place value on what is truly excellent. Parents often spend too much time trying to make money and ignore their families for years and years. Suddenly the children are grown and they find they don't have a relationship with them. Value was misplaced on providing things for their

Joyce as a young girl (Age 6) with
her mother

Dave Meyer in grade school

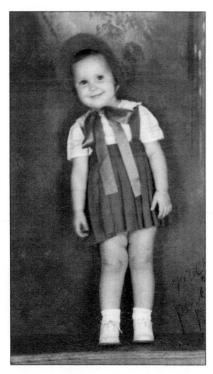

Joyce at Age 3

Dave (Age 20) serving in the United States
Army

Dave (Age 20) sharpening
his basketball skills

Dave and Joyce pose in church for their
wedding Photo in January of 1967

Dave and Joyce cut the first slice of their
wedding cake at their wedding reception

Dave and Joyce affectionately feed each other
wedding cake in front of their beautiful wedding
reception spread

Joyce throwing wedding bouquet at her
wedding reception in January of 1967

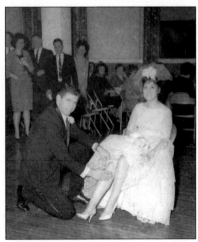

Joyce and Dave preparing for the traditional
"throwing of the garter"

Dave with oldest son, one-year-old David

Joyce in St. Louis, Missouri, with her three children, David (Age 6), Laura (Age 4) and Sandy (Age 2)

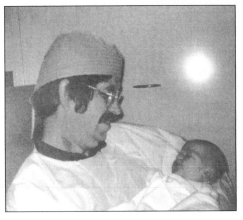

Dave in delivery room holding their youngest son Daniel

Dave and Joyce happily pose for a picture in the early 1980's

Joyce during her early ministry years

Dave and Joyce proudly display her products from the tape tables during the early years of ministry

Joyce answering her own mail in the early years of ministry

Joyce is awarded an honorary doctorate from Oral Roberts University (Tulsa, Oklahoma, 1998)

Dave and Joyce review the early stages of new building plans for the ministry

Dave and Joyce in the late 1990's

children, when above all else was the higher prize of being with them. This used to be a problem primarily for fathers, but since we have so many mothers working outside the home, they have to be careful to avoid this same regret.

Priorities are displaced if dad is working two jobs or frequently working overtime, more than what is necessary, just for the sake of having more things. A job may require someone to work overtime for a season, or a temporary second job can take care of some special need in the family, but if that job becomes a regular habit and the parent is away from the home on a regular basis, an unwanted price will be paid.

Many children are being raised by people other than their own family members. I went to work when I still had a small child so we could buy a house. My children went from baby-sitter to baby-sitter, but because of the Word that we have in us now, it seems that our family has recovered from that time. I'm just saying that knowing what I do now, I don't think it was the best choice for me to work so much outside of our home. I believe that if you have to do it, God will cover you and your children. But, parents who have small children should try to be at home with them as much as possible.

God's anointing can come on any situation. He can take something that could be a disaster otherwise and make it work out. God will cover the home of a single parent who has to work. But I believe there is a difference between **having** to work and simply **wanting** to work for love of what the extra money will buy. Prayerfully consider what you may be giving up for what you are getting.

Many families are already structured around two incomes, but be aware that even some wealthy people are still miserable because money does not make people happy. Couples who choose to keep both incomes need to work together at home, too. Laundry and household duties need to be shared by both the husband and wife in order to keep building a good relationship. It is difficult for a woman to manage both an external job and the internal responsibilities of home without help from the husband and children. Be willing to help each other through these stressful times. You may even need to humble yourself and ask for help if your spouse hasn't noticed your stress.

I am sure many people reading this book are working mothers or even men who are holding several jobs trying to provide for the family. I certainly don't desire to place condemnation or guilty feelings on anyone. I simply encourage you to make sure your family needs the money more than they need you. If working too much is creating a stressful atmosphere in your home, the choice to work part time might be a solution. Dave and I had years of both, years when I worked and years when I did not. I am sure our children preferred the years when I did not. Some of the years when I did not work were definitely much harder financially, but as I look back, those were the years when I really learned how to trust God for a miracle supply. Whatever you do, as long as you are being led by the Holy Spirit everything will work out fine.

PEACE IS GAINED THROUGH RIGHTEOUSNESS

The satisfaction that we are all looking for is found inside of us through knowing who we are in Christ.

Christians have righteousness, peace, and joy available to them through the Holy Spirit. The satisfaction that we are all looking for is found inside of us through knowing who we are in Christ. Happiness comes from being able to get up in the morning liking yourself and going to bed at night still liking yourself, without living under a cloud of guilt and condemnation. Peace is the reward of righteousness not of money. You can have all kinds of **things**, but if you don't have peace, you won't have joy.

People need right relationships more than they need money. If people are going to spend their lives climbing the ladder of success, they need to be sure their ladder is leaning against the right building. It is sad when people spend their lives working to acquire things at the expense of their families, only to get to that top position and find it is one of the loneliest places they could be. It is tragic to spend your life chasing something you didn't want after all.

First Timothy 6:17 says, *As for the rich in this world, charge them not to be proud and arrogant and contemptuous of others, nor set their hopes on uncertain riches, but on God, Who richly and ceaselessly provides us with everything, for [our] enjoyment.*

God abundantly gives us all things to enjoy. There is balance only if we enjoy things without putting them before the needs of the people in our lives. While we are not to love money, we are not to think we can't enjoy ourselves. My husband and I have more **things** right now than we have ever had in our whole lives. We have a lovely house, and we drive nice cars. We don't live in extravagance, but we do live in excellence.

We have given thought to what we really want. Many times the things we think we want are the same things we don't want to take care of. Ask God for wisdom when making decisions on whether or not to buy something that requires a lot of your time and attention.

God provided us with friends who have offered to let us stay at their vacation property any time we feel the need to get away. We know people who are willing to take us boating if we have the time to do so. God wants us to have fun, but fun doesn't have to drive us to the love of money. If we will make decisions according to the Word of God, while trying to honor God in our lives, I believe that God will supernaturally provide many things for us that we could have struggled to have had. God has performed tremendous miracles in our lives because we chose Him over things.

SWEET CONTENTMENT

Some couples need to learn how to enjoy what they already have. And some even need to ask God to show them how to go spend some of their money on themselves. We can get fearful of money even when we have plenty. God, not money, has to be our security.

Revelation 18:10 says that Babylon, the great city of power, will fall in one hour. Babylon really represents the whole financial system in the world. We can all see there are problems in the world structure. While I don't mean to sound negative, we must put our hope and confidence in God, no matter what happens to the economy. By developing our faith now, we know that God will take care of us and meet our needs just as He did in the wilderness for the children of Israel.

One of the ways that we try to build our faith is to look at the nice things we have but realize how much of it we could live without. It pleases me to think about how pretty our home is, but I know that if we had to live in a two- or three-room apartment again, I would be just as happy because my joy is coming from the inside of me and not from things that I have.

In Numbers 18, verses 20 and 24, God told the priestly tribe of Levi that He alone was their inheritance. The Word says, . . . *[They have homes and cities and pasturage to use but not to possess as their personal inheritance.]* (verse 24). We find balance in realizing that everything we have is on loan from God. He's given it to us to use, but we are neither to possess it, nor let it possess us.

The minute we start grasping at things that become too important to us, God will start shaking them from our hand. If we will let go when He shakes it, and say, "OK, You're right, God, I am getting too attached to this, or I am starting to like this too much, or I am depending on this too much," then most of the time He lets us keep it. But if we grasp too tightly and it becomes too important to our sense of security and our joy depends on it, then God will take it away from us.

I'm glad that God looks after me that way. I've given God permission to bring to my attention the things that are getting in the way of my total dependence upon Him. I encourage everyone to submit themselves to God in this way. Sometimes things begin to mean more to us than they should. Everything that God gives us should be held loosely in our hands, so that He has no trouble getting it from us if He wants it. God will give us all kinds of things to use and enjoy, but He will not let them possess us.

Balance is one of the keynotes of our ministry and it has brought favor into our lives. First Corinthians 7:31 teaches us to continue to be close to God through all conditions of life, even, . . . *those who deal with this world [overusing the enjoyments of this life] as though they were not absorbed by it and as if they had no dealings with it. . . . We need the Holy Spirit to keep us free from all anxiety and distressing care in order to promote and secure our undistracted devotion to the Lord. (Verses 32-35.)*

This means that even if we are in the busy, decision-making process of building a new house, we are not to get absorbed by it. We are to continue to walk with God as if nothing else is happening. I use this example because of an interesting experience we had when we bought our last house. People kept asking me if I was excited about our new house and I honestly wasn't. I had a joy because I knew it was something God was giving me.

For years I had prayed to have a quiet place to study since our house was on a highway where the noise of traffic disturbed my desire to sit outside and meditate on the things of God. There were no trees at our previous house to remind me of the natural things God had made. So for years I hoped for a different house.

Now God has given us a house with a little lake and all kinds of trees surrounding it in a beautiful setting. I have a comfortable feeling down inside because God has given us this desire of my heart, but my emotions aren't caught up in it. When we first moved in there, I walked around for days saying, "Thank You, God, we really appreciate this." But my greater joy was still in the fact that I knew Him, and not from what He had given us.

There is nothing wrong with having things, but if you have things to be happy, you will never be satisfied.

There is nothing wrong with having things, but if you have things to be happy, you will never be satisfied. If you must have that new house to be happy, if you must have that new car to be happy, if you must have that new furniture to be happy, if you must have that new dress to be happy, you will be looking for happiness your whole life.

HAPPINESS COMES TO THOSE WHO GIVE

Finally, and even foremost, if you want God to bless your finances, you must operate on God's financial plan. The Bible says that believers should tithe by giving a tenth of their income to the Lord. Malachi, chapter 3 is clear on this subject. There are some who argue that instruction from the Old Testament does not apply to believers today, but the New Testament never does away with anything in the Old Testament. Jesus came to fulfill the law and to give us the grace to keep it. God did not do away with the Ten Commandments, but He did give us the grace to keep them through Jesus Christ.

The Bible clearly teaches us that we should tithe and give offerings besides. If you are not tithing and giving offerings you are missing out on God's best for your life. Because Dave always knew to tithe, we have been tithing ever since we got married. In all the years we have been married, through raising four children, Dave has only been out of work for a total of five days and we have always had the money to pay our bills on time. God has always blessed our finances, and I am thankful that Dave knew to tithe when we got married.

Don't let the devil deceive you into thinking that you cannot tithe. He wants to rob you of your inheritance as a believer, and one of the easiest ways to do so is by causing you to either love or fear money so that you hoard it or crave it. James 1:22 says that if you hear the Word, but don't do what you know is right, then you are deceiving yourself by reasoning that is contrary to the truth.

If your marriage is struggling because of finances, ask God to loose you from whatever bondage keeps you from tithing. Be honest with God and tell Him, "I'm not tithing because of this, or I'm not doing it because I'm afraid to, or it is because I don't want to." By being honest with God and asking Him to establish you in His truth you allow God to help you out of the financial rut you are in.

Malachi 3:10,11 says,

Bring all the tithes (the whole tenth of your income) into the storehouse, that there may be food in My house, and prove Me now by it, says the Lord of hosts, if I will not open the windows of heaven for you and pour you out a blessing, that there shall not be room enough to receive it.

And I will rebuke the devourer [insects and plagues] for your sakes and he shall not destroy the fruits of your ground, neither shall your vine drop its fruit before the time in the field, says the Lord of hosts.

God doesn't need our money, but He does want us to be givers. He knew that there would be great temptation to love money, which is the root of all evil. Proving our willingness to let go of its security opens the floodgates of heaven to pour out blessings upon us. It is so important that we as believers stay in a giving attitude because love gives to others. *For God so loved the world, that he gave. . .* (John 3:16 KJV).

If we won't give our money, there is no hope of ever giving ourselves. If we can get to the point where we can give money away when God says to give it, we are finally growing out of our habit of selfish, self-centered living. Giving our money is an outward work of love, and love is spiritual warfare against the devourer.

Sometimes one partner in a marriage believes in and desires to tithe and the other one does not. Many women ask, "What am I supposed to do if my husband refuses to allow me to tithe?" First let me say that God does not rejoice in things given under compulsion or force. I doubt that He would want a tithe on a family income from someone who does not mix their faith with their giving. God asks us to give for our benefit, not His. He wants us to sow seed so He can bring a tremendous harvest. He is not trying to take something away from us; He is trying to get something to us. We must first be of a willing heart and then our actions are acceptable. Even if a person does not want to give their money away, but they are willing to do so in order to obey God, that is a starting place. Eventually their heart will change.

If a man is married to a woman who does not want to tithe, he would normally have liberty to do so anyway since he is the head of the household. If a woman is married to a man who does not want to tithe, then she should certainly not do it behind his back. She can give from what she has as her own, or what she has control of, or earns. If the man allows the woman to take care of the finances and he basically does not care what she does, then I believe she is free to follow her heart. Very few men would totally forbid their wives to give anything at all, but if you happen to be one of the few, then give of your time, talents, or other things that your husband has no control over. Pray for his heart to soften. Even if he cannot believe in the principle of sowing and reaping yet, pray that he will give you permission to tithe. Then you can release your faith for your family's finances to be blessed. One thing is for sure, God sees your heart, and He will take care of you if your heart is where it should be.

God is working amazing financial miracles for us so that we can operate the world ministry that we now have. But even in the earlier years of our life, when we went through hard times financially, we still sowed the tithe. We just had enough to pay our bills and then we had to believe God for everything else that came in. When I look back, some of those leaner times hold my best memories and were the most fun times for us.

I had a little prayer book that I kept and one time I wrote down, **"Dear Father, I need twelve new dishtowels and I don't have the money to buy them. Please provide those dishtowels."**

One day, a friend of mine rang the doorbell and said, "I hope you don't think I am totally insane, but I believe God told me to bring you a dozen dishtowels."

The excitement of God hit me and I almost knocked her over as I screamed with delight and shouted, "That's God!" Who gets that excited over dishtowels these days? But excitement comes into your life when you begin to live God's way.

If you need financial miracles, don't be afraid to obey God concerning your finances. Begin proving God's power to bless you by tithing, then beyond that develops a giving lifestyle. As a couple, Dave and I are both trying to live a lifestyle of giving and we enjoy giving away more every year. As we obey God and give when He leads us to do so, somebody always gives back to us and keeps us in that realm of exciting miracles. We actually search for ways to give. We don't wait for some great feeling to come over us; we give on purpose and with purpose. As a result, our joy and prosperity is always increasing.

14

PASS THE
BAND-AIDS®, PLEASE

We who are strong [in our convictions and of robust faith]
ought to bear with the failings and the frailties and the
tender scruples of the weak; [we ought to help carry the
doubts and qualms of others] and not to please ourselves.
Let each one of us make it a practice to please (make happy)
his neighbor for his good and for his true welfare, to edify him
[to strengthen him and build him up spiritually].
Romans 15:1,2

When you read the Word of God, and it says to make your neighbor happy, to edify him and build him up spiritually, do your thoughts lead you to the people next door? Did it even occur to you that this word might be in regard to how you should treat your spouse? The word "neighbor" in Greek, according to *Strong's Exhaustive Concordance* implies one who is "near," or "close by."[1] *Merriam-Webster's Collegiate® Dictionary* explains a neighbor as "one living or located near another."[2]

For some reason, it seems easier to obey the Word if it doesn't mean our immediate family, but nearly every home has someone within it who needs healing over a past hurt. In these last few chapters, we have looked at our opportunities to either build up or tear down our partners in various areas of our marriage relationship.

Another choice we can make is whether or not we are willing to bring healing to past hurts with which our mate may be dealing.

Of course, God leads us to choose life by following the example of Christ Who did not choose to please Himself and gave no thought to His own interests, but took on Himself the reproaches and abuses of those who reproached and abused us so that we might be healed. Those of us who are free are now called upon to bear up others who are weak in faith.

Men and women are very different, but it helps to understand that God made us different on purpose. Don't confuse weaknesses with differences. We are to help build up frailties but we are not called to change our differences. It certainly is not God's plan for us to try to make our partners be like us. But we are in each other's lives to help build each other up to become all that God had in mind for us to be.

Dave and I suffered many, many heartaches from trying to change our differences instead of trying to build each other up in what we were to become in the Lord. God will almost always put you with somebody who is different from you, but that is part of His plan so that together we complement each other with our strengths and learn to depend on each other for areas in which we are weaker.

God's ways are not our ways and we don't always understand His plans. Almost every couple starts out thinking that they must change each other to become compatible, when acceptance is the key to harmony in marriage. If the Lord received us with unconditional love, how much more should we embrace each other with the same patience? But instead we easily fall back into our prideful thinking that we alone are right and everyone should do as we do.

God's ways are not our ways and we don't always understand His plans.

There were many things that I thought Dave should and shouldn't do. I wanted him to be more outgoing, but he was not outgoing. I wanted him to be a social butterfly. He was not a social butterfly. I wanted Dave to preach. He's not called to preach, at least not right now. I did not want him to watch as much football as he watched. I didn't want him to like sports. I didn't want him to play golf. I wanted him to sit down every night and just look at me and talk and talk and talk. There were many things that I wanted him to want.

Dave liked his job and was a great provider. He went to work every day, always came home with the money, and took real good care of us, but he had no great ambitions to advance on his job. They offered him promotions, but he knew that it would require him being out of town a lot and he didn't want that. He just wanted to be happy and have us all live a happy life.

Many times I tried to push him to be something more saying he ought to have more goals. Then when we started actively serving God together, I began to appreciate his differences and how much his approach to life had done to bring God's healing for my past hurts. If Dave had not been born again and Spirit-filled, I don't believe he could ever have stood me. As I said before, by the time Dave found me, I had so many wounds and hurts from both my childhood and earlier marriage that I was in a really serious condition. As I already stated, my previous husband had relationships with other women and did things that finally sent him to prison.

It is often difficult for people to go forward in new relationships when they are loaded up with deep wounds and hurts from past situations and abuses. Whether they suffered emotional abuse, physical abuse, or verbal abuse, they need healing to overcome their trained suspicions and defenses. If a person was repeatedly talked down to as a child by his parents or teachers, that person is going to have problems with insecurity. He will need more tender loving care than somebody who was lovingly reinforced as a child.

We need to know about each other and care about what kind of background our spouses came from. Understanding the past may help you to understand some of the things that are happening now. Many people admit to some thing in their past that they know is still crippling them emotionally. They need godly understanding to be able to go on past these things before they can properly relate to people.

> *Jesus is in the healing business — we don't have to live all our lives in bondage to our past.*

Jesus is in the healing business — we don't have to live all our lives in bondage to our past. I used to think, I would never change. I believed that once those kind of things happened to you, you could never get over it. But if you are willing to let God work with you, He will help you.

HEALING OLD WOUNDS

If your partner needs healing, it will come even more quickly if you will help. If you will try to put yourself in their place, you will see ways to help. Just take an hour and sit down sometime, and in your wildest imagination consider what it would be like to go through what your spouse has tried to share with you that they went through.

Romans 15:5,6 gives instruction on how we can help:

Now may the God Who gives the power of patient endurance (steadfastness) and Who supplies encouragement, grant you to live in such mutual harmony and such full sympathy with one another, in accord with Christ Jesus,

That together you may [unanimously] with united hearts and one voice, praise and glorify the God and Father of our Lord Jesus Christ (the Messiah).

God will give us the power of patient endurance and supply us with encouragement so that we can live in harmony and in sympathy with one another. Dave's father died from drinking, but Dave had a godly mother and it saved him a lot of the problems that he could have had. But Dave went through many years of being passive to avoid conflict with his father. Now, he is not like that any more, but he didn't deal with certain responsibilities for a time. As I mentioned previously, Dave went to work and he did his job, and he took care of all that, but beyond that, getting him to move was difficult. If he had a golf match, he could remember to call everybody in town, could come home and tell me every ball that he hit, even every ball that everyone else hit, his score, and their score, but he couldn't remember to hang the picture or mail the bills. That kind of stuff used to easily anger me.

I thought Dave just didn't want to do the things I wanted him to do. He is healed from passivity now, but God has shown me that Dave got into that behavior pattern by looking at his role models. Children learn from what they see their parents doing and Dave saw his passive father sitting on the sidelines and basically doing nothing. Even though Dave never had a temptation to drink, he still followed his father's example and dismissed most all of his responsibilities around the home.

When Dave made the decision to change that type of behavior, it took him a long time to make new habits. But I respect him for the work that he has let God do in his life. The devil had us in a trap because I wanted to control everything anyway, and Dave's passive nature just fed my controlling spirit. Dave and I both needed healing from situations of our past, and while God was working on our deliverance, the devil used our weaknesses against each other.

The Bible tells us to bear one another up in our weaknesses. To build each other up requires godly sympathy and understanding. What you don't understand about each other or even about yourselves, get busy and find out. Why do certain behavior patterns develop in people's lives? We need to care enough about each other to get involved and find out how to help our partner.

Dave and I enjoy reading books by author Gary Smalley, who has many helpful titles available on interpersonal relationships. In one of his lessons, Gary uses the example of a plant which he called "Ivy." He said if he married Ivy and she had a lot of brown leaves it might not be his fault that she had the brown leaves. She might be browning out from things that happened to her long before he met her. But, he continued, now that he was married to Ivy her brown leaves were his responsibility and he must find a way to give her the nutrients she needs to become vibrant and healthy again.

Even though we may not have caused poor behavior patterns in our mate, God has put us in their life to be a help to them. God already determined that there are things we can't do alone. God repeatedly calls us to love each other and bear one another's griefs and burdens. Galatians 6:2 says,

> Bear (endure, carry) one another's burdens and troublesome moral faults, and in this way fulfill and observe perfectly the law of Christ the (Messiah) and complete what is lacking [in your obedience to it].

Dave and I struggled for a long time because we didn't understand this important role we were to play in each other's life. God has brought you to this page and place in time to give you knowledge and understanding so that your marriage might become a picture of his plan for the world. We are a privileged people to know the things that God has revealed.

Doctors' offices are filled with people wanting to know how to relate to their spouses and how to be healed from those things that bind them. God's Word gives clear instruction, and God anoints His Word with the power to be fruitful if we will simply do as He says to do.

Dave used to ask me, "Why do you act like that?"

I didn't know why I behaved the way I did. Then I would ask him, "Well, why do you act like that? If you wouldn't do that, I wouldn't do this."

And he replied, "Well, if you'd do this, I wouldn't do that! If you would quit griping all the time, I wouldn't stay on the golf course."

I would say, "Well, if you would stay home, I would quit griping."

How often have you had a similar conversation? I am trying to illustrate and impart understanding of how hurting people hurt people. If you are hurting each other in your relationship, it is probably because there is a hurt inside of you that hasn't been healed. Some way, somehow, you have been hurt yourself somewhere, and you need to get with God and let Him bring you the healing that you need in order to go forward.

Dave brought healing to me by showing me unconditional love for years and years and years. I had never lived around this kind of love before. All the love that I ever received in my whole life was conditional. If I did what someone wanted then I could get what I needed.

Conditional love fills you with rejection if you don't perform exactly right all the time. Many people have trouble in their relationships because it is the only kind of love they know about. Even if you didn't come out of an abusive situation and saw only conditional love from your parents, it has the same effect. How many of us were raised to believe that Mom and Dad would only be happy with us if we got all A's on our report cards and other things like that which placed conditions on love given?

Destructive behavior problems result from a feeling of insecurity and insignificance, but God is in the healing business. If you recognize these problems in your marriage, then ask God to help. You can't keep sweeping these things under the rug, hoping they will go away on their own. You have to deal with these issues in your life.

Determine in your heart that whatever help your spouse needs, you will give it to them. If there is anything hurting you, try to explain what it is and ask for help. Rededicate your love to each other by learning how to cherish and nurture each other. Once you understand what needs to be changed, ask for and grant patience when it is needed. Honesty is the turning point of recovery. Admit when you are not real sure how to do something, but let your mate know that you are going to try to either help them or make changes yourself.

If either of you are hiding in the television set, or spending too much time at something that keeps you separated from each other, don't make excuses; find out why this distance is developing between you. Search for balance. It's OK to have outside interests, but you must have time for each other or you will continue to wound each other in addition to the hurts you received in your past.

HEALING SELF-INFLICTED WOUNDS

Some of the wounds that couples suffer from have nothing to do with their past. There can be offenses that the two of you have inflicted upon each other that need to be treated and healed. Years of harsh words can wound relationships. Adulterous situations where one partner or the other has been unfaithful can leave lingering traces of distrust. You may believe that you forgave the situation and are moving on, but something still isn't right between you.

We need to begin exhorting each other in love to bring all the healing that is needed in every situation.

Maybe you are just now realizing that in all the years you have been married, you have not talked to your partner in a way that has been edifying or encouraging to them. Hebrews 3:13 (KJV) says, *But exhort one another **daily**, while it is called To day; lest any of you be hardened through the deceitfulness of sin.* It's not enough to just stop speaking harshly; we need to begin exhorting each other in love to bring all the healing that is needed in every situation.

There are things we need to do in our relationships on a daily basis that will bring healing from the hurts that are still binding and wounding us. First of all, we need to stop throwing the past up to each other. We need to stop operating with one another based on past experience. When we keep the past before us, we are retreating instead of advancing.

Some couples destroy each other by not letting each other change. The past is constantly referred to even years later, showing that grudges have taken a deep root in the heart of the offended spouse. Even if the offender is sorry, the other will not let him move on toward new behavior. Love does not take account of the evil done to it. Have you been a good accountant, keeping a running total on all offenses? Philippians 3:12-14 (NIV) needs to be pinned to our bathroom mirrors as a reminder of our goal:

> *Not that I have already obtained all this, or have already been made perfect, but I press on to take hold of that for which Christ Jesus took hold of me.*
>
> *Brothers, I do not consider myself yet to have taken hold of it. But one thing I do: Forgetting what is behind and straining toward what is ahead,*

I press on toward the goal to win the prize for which God has called me heavenward in Christ Jesus.

I firmly believe that one of the greatest benefits that we have as believers is found in 2 Corinthians 5:17 (KJV): *Therefore if any man be in Christ, he is a new creature: old things are passed away; behold, all things are become new.* I don't think our renewal just happens the day we are born again and suddenly all traces of past hurts no longer exist because we are a new creature. But I do believe that every day old things can pass away and all things can become brand new. I believe every single day that we need to do what the apostle Paul teaches in Philippians and let go of those things which are behind us and press on to those things that are ahead.

FIND WHAT NEEDS TO BE LET GO

If you are concerned about your relationship and you want to bring healing to the wounds you have inflicted upon each other, you will need to talk to one another. Find out what is separating you and communicate how you feel. When you start communicating about what has hurt you and how it has made you feel, you can expect your defensive nature to flare up. But you can displace new offenses by expressing your love and concern for the other person.

If your partner gets the courage to admit what is bothering them, you may want to retaliate instead of accepting responsibility for the offense. These are important moments to stay focused on the needs of the other person instead of on yourself. If you shut your spouse down now, they might not open up again.

It requires great maturity to be able to listen to your spouse's honesty and consider words without getting hurt again. Dave and I have been married for years, and we are only beginning to be able to talk about our hurts and wounds with this new level of maturity. But the good news is that it is possible and it is necessary.

Perhaps once every couple of months the two of you could go out to dinner and practice your healing skills on each other. Through confrontation skills, you bring correction. Through healing skills, you let old wounds be medicated so they will no longer infect your relationship.

You could begin by saying, "I want you to share with me openly and honestly, and tell me if there things that I'm doing that are bothering you or hurting you because I love you and I don't want to hurt you anymore. If I'm doing things that are hurting our relationship, then please tell me about it."

A healthy way to respond is to say, "When you do _____, it makes me feel _____. I wish you would _____."

Can you imagine what a difference it would make in your relationship if you could simply take turns expressing your needs to each other?

A good response to that new information is to simply say, "Thank you for telling me how you feel. I am glad you trust me enough to tell me that, and I want to make the changes that you need. I will prayerfully try to respond to your needs the way Jesus would."

Can you imagine what a difference that would make in your relationships if you could simply take turns expressing your needs to each other?

I could say, "Dave, is there anything I'm doing that really bothers you? What area would you like to see me come up higher in so I can be a better wife."

If he knew it was safe to be honest with me, he could use this privilege to say, "Well, Joyce, it really bothers me when I try to correct you about little things around the house, like not hanging up a towel over the sink. We bought this house and God has given me the logic to see some of the things that we can do and take better care of it, and I feel like every time I suggest one of those things to you, you think I am 'nit picky' and don't regard my idea as important. But it's important to me."

That was bugging him, and it bothered him more than a little bit. I had no idea it was starting to eat at him, but I could tell he was starting to get unhappy.

And he said, "When I ask you to do something, I wish you would respect me enough to just say, 'Sure, honey. If that's something that you don't want me to do, I'll be more than happy to do that for you,' and not make me feel like a moron every time I mention something like that." His honesty was hard to swallow, but by my receiving it, our relationship improved.

A lot of healing comes through understanding and giving value and honor to a person who is worthy of esteem. But when people are full of insecurities, they cannot be corrected. When you ask for honesty, and your spouse gives you their wish list, remember that the Bible says that only a fool hates correction. Be thankful if your spouse tells you ways to improve your relationship. Hopefully, they will give you the same opportunity you are giving them.

I don't recommend giving a lifetime list at one time. Pray and start with the most important one or two things that are on your heart. Be sure to keep voice tones gentle and keep a smile or pleasant look on your face. Voice tones and body language will determine partially whether or not the conversation remains peaceful.

A pastor told me once about a young man who worked for him, who was a master at taking correction. He told me the following story, "This guy is unbelievable. I called him into my office to chew him out about something that he did wrong, and he sat across from my desk and looked me in the eye and said, 'Oh, Pastor, thank you. Thank you for correcting me. I am so glad that you love me enough to take the time to do this and to tell me what I'm doing wrong. Because God put me here to help you, and if I'm not doing it the way that you want it done, then I want it changed. And I'm happy that you're talking to me.'"

Then he added, "Sometimes I call him in there to chew him out, and am dreading it, but by the time he leaves, I'm feeling good about doing it." That may sound a little bit extreme, but wouldn't it be great if every confrontation was soothed over with such a healing response? It is hard to bring things into the place of unity if every request for somebody to do something a different way results in a war.

Our own pride and insecurity make it difficult for us to receive correction. If someone tries to tell another person they are doing something wrong and that person already struggles with a lack of self-worth, then their fears are reestablished and they become defensive. The solution is not to avoid correction, but to affirm each other in love when we present our suggestions. If you are struggling in this area, I encourage you to read my book titled *The Root of Rejection* in which I have expounded upon the Scriptures you can lean on to build yourself up to a healthy, godly state again and find freedom from rejection.

It is good to recognize this need in yourself, and admit to your spouse when you need affirmation or encouragement. Trust your spouse enough to admit the fears and doubts that you have about yourself. When you understand each other's insecurities, you can learn how to strengthen them. These meaningful moments of honesty can enhance relationships with lasting reinforcement.

A person who is still dealing with a shame-based nature already feels wrong because wrong things have happened to them. Extra care may need to be given by saying to them, "Honey, you know I love you; you are great, and most everything you do is right . . ." Don't just start in with your list of what is wrong. Even partners with a healthy sense of self-esteem should be treated with thoughtfulness and honor. Be loving, kind, gentle, and humble as you focus on building up your wounded spouse.

Dave and I were not always good at confrontational issues. If we got into something and confrontation was starting, Dave would just get up and walk away from it. If I followed him around the house long enough, he would finally get in the car and just leave.

I asked him once, "Why can't we talk about this?"

And finally, he said, "Because **we** aren't talking. **You** are talking and I'm listening. You're good with words and I'm not. You're manipulating me and I don't like it."

Dave does have a much harder time expressing what he wants to say, while I can talk anybody into a corner and convince them of my point. So when you do sit down and try to communicate with somebody, you need to lay down some ground rules to create a safe place for confrontation. But don't give up until you find a way to communicate your needs and find out what your spouse is needing.

And above all things have fervent charity among yourselves:
for charity shall cover the multitude of sins.

1 Peter 4:8 KJV

Love may be blind to someone's faults, but insecurity is overcome by true admiration. Building a strong relationship requires a lot of forgiveness. The Bible has a lot to say about forgiveness; for example, we know our prayers won't be answered if we don't forgive others. If we are going to live peacefully with anybody we must be quick to forgive and not easily offended.

There are just things that your partner will do that you are not going to like, and there are things you will do that will irritate those who live with you. Your spouse will say things and do things that you don't want said or done and you will simply have to let it go and proceed through the day about your business. Even some of the bigger hurts that people have done to you need to be forgiven.

But the other key to building a solid relationship is repentance. For love to abound between two people, nothing brings healing faster than to simply say, "Honey, I was wrong, and I shouldn't have treated you that way, and I'm sorry. Will you please forgive me?" Luke 17:3 says,

Pay attention and always be on your guard [looking out for
one another]. If your brother sins (misses the mark), solemnly
tell him so and reprove him, and if he repents (feels sorry for
having sinned), forgive him.

If Dave and I have had a problem, it is my responsibility before God to always forgive him. But Scriptures also say that if your brother *repents,* forgive him. I have seen situations where one spouse has done something wrong and is obviously sorry, but the other partner will not let it go. But Luke 17:4 says that if your brother repents, you must forgive him.

And even if he sins against you seven times in a day, and turns
to you seven times and says, I repent [I am sorry], you must
forgive him (give up resentment and consider the offense as
recalled and annulled).

You need to forgive. God is your Vindicator — let Him do His job.

What if someone hurts you and does not repent? I don't believe they can receive forgiveness if they are not repentant, but you still need to forgive. You need to forgive for yourself but also in order to release God to work in the heart of the other person. Don't put the person in prison by holding an offense against them until you feel they have paid their debt. (See Matthew 18:28-35.) God is your Vindicator — let Him do His job.

The offended party that is hurt has a responsibility to forgive, but the offending party has a responsibility to repent. If they don't repent, then that situation is not truly reconciled; it's buried in the subconscious and leaves an open wound there.

Many people are very unhappy and even physically sick due to unconfessed and hidden sin in their heart. We recently had a young man come to us who had done something dishonest when he worked for us. We felt he had stolen some money, but he adamantly insisted that he had not. When he confessed and I asked him if he had felt guilty all that time, he shared that he actually had buried the sin so far down in his subconscious that he did not even remember doing it. He said he had even convinced himself that he had not done it. It only surfaced through some counseling he was getting to help uncover the root of his extreme passivity.

A person's sin always finds them out one way or another. If someone has wronged you and they won't admit it, that unconfessed sin will continue hurting them in one way or another until that open wound is cleaned out and healed.

When we teach on confrontation in seminars, Dave often points out that the confrontation is not designed to place blame somewhere. Its purpose is to find a solution that will bring healing and not more pain. Some wounds take time to heal and as we make changes, we need to be patient while waiting to see the results we want. Love never fails, and healing can be found in a loving environment filled with acceptance and forgiveness.

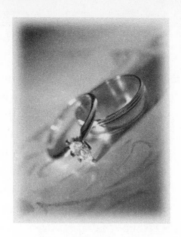

PART 3

THE FRUIT OF MARRIAGE

15

WHY ARE YOU SO
DIFFERENT FROM ME?

Through skillful and godly Wisdom is a house
(a life, a home, a family) built, and by understanding
it is established [on a sound and good foundation].
Proverbs 24:3

The Word says that understanding establishes a home, a family, and a life. I enjoyed a major breakthrough in my relationship with Dave when I discovered that people have different personalities. This knowledge helped me to understand why we will seldom approach decisions the same way. However, these differences don't have to keep us from agreement with each other. In fact, diversity is an important part of God's plan.

I don't want to spend a lot of time on the subject of diverse personalities because there are so many books and studies available that will help you discover your own personality preferences and how they differ from your partner's. Two of my favorite books on this subject that I encourage everyone to read because they have taught me a great deal are *Your Personality Tree* by Florence Littauer and *Spirit-Controlled Temperament* by Tim LaHaye. Much of what I will share here is a summary of the wisdom Florence Littauer offers in her book, but I cannot cover in a brief chapter the great detail that is provided by her extensive studies.

I believe it is so important to understand that these differences are God-given and are what are intended to make us strong as a family unit. Without that understanding, we can let these differences tear us apart instead of strengthening our family unit and corporate body as they were meant to do.

Our individual temperaments reveal how we approach life in general. One of these tests that we enjoy working with in our seminars measures whether you are a sunny-sanguine, methodical-melancholy, controlling-choleric or a peaceful-phlegmatic personality. When couples both take these tests at our weekend advances, partners invariably discover that they are married to someone who is not at all like themselves.

> When you understand that people are different by God's design, you will see why you can't change people or become like them.

I want to call your attention to the significance that these differences have and help you to understand why the person you are married to is probably not like you. When you understand that people are different by God's design, you will see why you can't change people or become like them. But, we can still be in agreement with each other, even though we have strong personality differences.

Occasionally, both husband and wife have the same test results, and if they both happen to have easygoing personalities, that's not much of a problem. But if they are both in the strong-willed category, then they could have a tendency to knock heads a lot. An examination of a few Scriptures will help you see God's bigger picture when He decided to make us all be different from each other.

There are also tests that can help you understand which of the motivational gifts you are most drawn to.[1] These spiritual gifts facilitate your distinctive service in the body of Christ. Learning to understand the differences that motivate people will help you to know how to deal with the person you are married to as well as all the other people that you come into contact with in your daily life.

For example, Romans 12:6-8,10 explains the various spiritual gifts that we might have. While each of us can operate in all these gifts if the Holy Spirit chooses to use us, we are usually more gifted in one or two of these gifts over the others.

Having gifts (faculties, talents, qualities) that differ according to the grace given us, let us use them: [He whose gift is] prophecy, [let him prophesy] according to the proportion of his faith;

[He whose gift is] practical service, let him give himself to serving; he who teaches, to his teaching.

He who exhorts (encourages), to his exhortation; he who contributes, let him do it in simplicity and liberality; he who gives aid and superintends, with zeal and singleness of mind; he who does acts of mercy, with genuine cheerfulness and joyful eagerness.

Love one another with brotherly affection [as members of one family], giving precedence and showing honor to one another.

Notice that even though we have different gifts to drive us, we are to love each other and give precedence to one another. Whatever gift we have, we should do the best service with it that we know how to do. While we should honor others, we should never try to be **like** someone else. God has the big picture and best knows how to distribute these gifts to fill the needs at hand. Many people have spent years of frustration because they could not understand why they couldn't do something that their spouse could do.

I went through a lot of frustration in the earlier years of my life because I wanted to be like other people I knew. I'm happy now to be who I am. And I'm glad that I don't have to look at my husband any more and say, "Why aren't I like Dave? Why can't I be as easygoing as Dave is? Why do I have to want things a certain way? Why can't I just say, 'Oh, well, it's OK with me. Whatever — it's fine'?"

I tried to be like my artistic neighbor who did crafts, grew tomatoes, made plant hangers, and sewed her kids' clothes, but I couldn't sit still long enough for any of those things. I did talk Dave into growing tomatoes one year. That is more my style; I'm bossy, so I got him to do it, and he is easygoing so he did it. He didn't want the tomatoes any more than I did, but he did it to keep peace.

He grew the tomatoes and the first year the bugs ate them. We tried it again the second year and the bugs came again. Then I thought, **Why in the world would anybody want to do this when you can go to the grocery store and buy canned tomatoes, three cans for a dollar on sale** (in 1981)? It was no longer logical for me, but I tried to do that because my neighbor did that.

I even bought a sewing machine and took sewing lessons. I about drove myself crazy sitting down in the basement sewing, ripping out seams, and putting in hems. After all that work, one arm would turn out shorter than the other one. I hated it, but kept trying to be like my friend.

Now I think that it is great that my neighbor liked to do all those things. I'm thankful for the people who grow tomatoes. If nobody grew tomatoes, we wouldn't even have canned tomatoes in the store that people like me could go buy. But I'll probably never grow another tomato as long as I live.

I'm happy to tell you that I'm free from sewing and growing tomatoes. It's important to enjoy who you are because self-assurance affects your marriage. If you don't like yourself, you won't be likable and you won't like anyone else.

If you have not accepted yourself and resist God's design for you, you can **forget** getting along with that person you are married to. For years, I struggled to walk in love and get along with people. Finally God showed me that I had not received His love for me because I was still mad at myself for all the things in my past. I came to understand that if I did not receive God's love for me, then I could never love myself, and if I never loved myself, I could certainly never love anybody else because I didn't have any love in me to give away.

Insecurity is the deep root of most problems in marriages. If you can be at peace with yourself enough to like yourself, you can look outward to loving others. I'm not promoting self-love that is self-seeking or has a self-centered focus, but each individual should realize what his or her own strengths, as well as weaknesses, are. I know what my weaknesses are and I can face myself squarely now. I don't feel bad about myself because of them.

Self-acceptance isn't the same as a haughty attitude. I understand that everyone has weaknesses, and we are to build each other up if we are strong in an area where another person is weak. God never intended us to be self-sufficient and independent. Remember that He was the One Who said we shouldn't be alone. Our ministry gifts and diverse personalities are designed to complement each other. Our

Our diverse ministry gifts and personality types are designed to complement each other. Our talents are given to us for service to others.

talents are not in us for self-admiration but for service to others.

Dave has a phlegmatic personality; he is so easygoing he never makes waves along his journey. As a choleric, I make waves everywhere I go. If something isn't right, individuals with my personality type will try to change it. Dave's easygoing nature makes his weaknesses less visible than mine because I am always right in the middle of things, trying to move them and make things happen. We all have weaknesses and in that we are all alike.

We all have strengths, too. Dave is strong at things in which I am pitifully weak. There are areas in which I am strong and he is weak. The point is, until you get rooted in self-acceptance you are not going to get along with people. As long as you are trying to change everybody around you and mold them into your idea of what you think they ought to be, your war will continue.

Only God can get inside of a person and change them from the inside out. Dave was smart enough to know that he had to wait on God to make those changes in my life that were causing so much unhappiness. You can still tell somebody that you need them to stop doing something or start doing something else, but a person can't change just because you want them to.

Romans 12:3 says, *For by the grace (unmerited favor of God) given to me I warn everyone among you not to estimate and think of himself more highly than he ought.* . . . This is a good Scripture that every person ought to have rooted in their soul. Be careful how you think about yourself. Be careful about those haughty thoughts that say, "Well, I can do this. Why can't you?" Verse 3 continues,

. . . [not to have an exaggerated opinion of his own importance], but to rate his ability with sober judgment, each one according to the degree of faith apportioned by God to him.

This means that whatever strengths we have, we got them from God. Whatever grace we have to do things a certain way, we got it from God. If another person doesn't have those strengths, we need to bear with their failings and their shortcomings and be merciful to them and have understanding for them instead of getting a haughty attitude that makes us feel like we are better than the other person because we can do what they can't.

We need to understand that some people are more talented than other people. Some preachers can preach and sing. They make records and have beautiful voices. They can come in, lead worship, play four or five musical instruments, and preach besides. Sometimes I feel like all I can do is preach. I can't sing; in fact the technicians turn my microphone off when the singing starts. There was a time in my life when that bothered me.

I thought, **Why can't I do that?** Or, **Why can't I have these certain gifts?** We all struggle with being satisfied with who we are, but we must understand that God gives the gifts.

Some five, some two, some one. He gives gifts to people according to how He has built them, according to what God knows that they can handle, and according to the need of the people with whom they will come in contact. It's God's business how He makes us. Maybe God knows that if I could preach and sing, I'd get into pride. Maybe with my personality it's better for me if I can only preach and not sing. I use a lot of ministry examples because that's what I spend all my time doing, but you can certainly apply this to any area of your life that you choose to.

What was wrong with me that I couldn't do all that my neighbor could do? If I would sew a button on Dave's shirt, it would probably fall off the next day, so Dave puts his own buttons on his own shirt. I just don't do those kinds of things well at all, but I do what I am called to do well, so I have learned to enjoy my calling. I am not trying to do something that I'm not anointed and equipped to do. The good news is I don't have to feel bad about myself anymore because I can't do all those other things and wonder what is wrong with me.

First Corinthians 4:7 clearly warns us not to boast of our own gifts and talents: . . . *What have you that was not given to you? If then you received it [from someone], why do you boast as if you had not received [but had gained it by your own efforts]?* I like this Scripture. It is thought provoking to search for some quality in our lives that we did not receive. If we did receive it then why would we glory as if praise was due to us for our gift?

Dave doesn't preach and I'm gifted to do so. What sense would it make for Dave to go around hating himself all of his life because he can't preach? In the beginning of our ministry, a pastor stopped us at the door of the church and said, "Brother Dave, the Lord has revealed to me that you ought to be leading that Bible study in your home and not your wife."

So we went home, thinking we needed to try to do that. Dave tried to preach and I tried to shut up, and both efforts were equally hard. God had not equipped us to do what this other person thought we ought to do. Dave has a good, balanced attitude toward our ministry now. His isn't submitting to me, his wife, but he does submit to the gift in me and I submit to him as his wife.

Dave recognizes that God has put this gift in me, and he finally got to the point with me where he said, "Go for it. Do everything that God's put in you. Be all you can be, and I'm going to back you up 100 percent because God has given me to you to help you and keep you in balance and make sure that you don't get in trouble while you're out there doing it. And I'm going to be your covering."

God gave me the gift to communicate His Word, and I can't glory in the fact that I do the preaching part of our ministry because I didn't go after it or earn it. We have a good thing going here that is helping hundreds of thousands of people, but we could all have been cheated out of God's blessing and remained miserable our whole lives if Dave would have kept trying to preach and if I would have tried to be quiet. We didn't conform to society; we submitted to God's plan for our individual lives.

I encourage you to be all that you can be, but do not despise yourself if you can't be something that somebody else can and don't despise others who are not like you. Jesus puts up with all of our weaknesses. He is long-suffering and patient with us. When we make mistakes, He doesn't clam up and refuse to talk to us. The Bible teaches us to be like Jesus in the way we treat others. We are to be tolerant towards others through their weaknesses and faults. Every person has weaknesses. We will never find the perfect church, the perfect pastor, or the perfect spouse.

When you are married to somebody long enough, and your love has grown, you may get to the point where you think your spouse is perfect after all. I think my husband is nearly perfect. But I know the weaknesses that he has, and I accept them and he accepts a lot of mine, so I don't keep inventory on his weaknesses. You can enjoy the strengths that a person has instead of focusing on his weaknesses all the time.

To assist in recognizing strengths and weaknesses in other people, a study has been done on four major personality types. Usually, a person fits one of these descriptions or a blend of two. See if you recognize you and your spouse in these models. In general, a choleric wants to control, phlegmatic wants to watch, sanguine wants to have fun, and a melancholy wants to have peace and order and perfection. Being a choleric, myself, I frequently compare the other traits against my own personality to illustrate the differences we share.

SUNNY SANGUINE

The sanguine normally loves to talk and is highly motivated by "fun." These personality types believe life was meant to be enjoyed, and they are not too interested in hard labor if fun is not incorporated in the task somehow.

Sanguines are never bored because everything about life fascinates them. They can be interested in a bug, a thread, or a fly. After a few minutes of studying it, they can tell you a big long story about it.

Sanguines are always ready to start a new day unbefuddled by yesterday's problems. They are fearless and full of optimism for tomorrow.

My daughter, Sandra, is a sparky sanguine. She greets us every morning with a song or bubbly conversation. When I get out of bed, I don't even want anybody **talking** to me, let alone **singing** at me! There is nothing wrong with singing, but my choleric nature wants it quiet in the morning.

When you are a certain way, then people who are different can irritate you if you don't understand the difference in their nature. The girl that used to live next door to me was a sanguine. She and I were good friends, and I remember how she would often point out something I had not even noticed. One time she said, "Oh, did you see that cat over there in that tree?" She went on to explain that it was a certain kind of unusual cat and seemed quite amused to see it in the tree. I didn't even see the tree let alone the cat because trees and cats aren't interesting to me.

Cholerics, like me, only pay attention to what's important to them, only what helps them accomplish **their** goal. They don't care about anything else. I am so single minded on this ministry that God has to pull me up short every once in a while and say, "You need to get your mind on something else for a while." I am driven by what God has given me to do, and so I spend all my energies on this goal, and of course I want everybody around me to do it, too. Cats and trees don't impact my goal so I don't even see them.

Now that I understand personality types, I am better about paying attention to sanguines who want to give me all the details of a story, but there was a time I easily frustrated the sanguines in my life as much as they were frustrating me. While the choleric wonders why the sanguine can't just tell the point and finish the story, the sanguine would rather not tell the story at all if they can't tell you all those wonderful details.

Once you understand that just because a person is different from you, it doesn't mean there is something wrong with them, you will start to enjoy their differences.

If you understand that just because a person is different from you, it doesn't mean there is something wrong with them, you will start to enjoy their differences.

Sanguines are great company if you want to start a new project because they are easily inspired to try new plans. They may find it difficult to stay with the task to the end, but they will certainly charm you by their sincere affection that they have for people. Sanguines like to be with people, and they will often hold on to you to keep you from getting away from them.

In these studies it is nearly as fun to look at weaknesses as it is to look at strengths because these tendencies are typical now to groups of personality types rather than faults of an individual. While we do not have to feel badly about these weaknesses, we must face them if we want to change.

The sanguine can easily get distracted from intended goals because of her fun-seeking nature. Her spontaneity can leave her disorganized and unfulfilled. She may have high goals for the day. First she is going to attack the pile of laundry, then the dishes. After cleaning the house, she will go to the bank and the grocery store. Her melancholy husband even listed her priorities for her before he left for work.

She was going to have a productive day. But you have to remember that sanguines are not excited about work. When her friend calls and says, "Hey! How about going to garage sales?", she is off in a flash! When her husband asks why none of the errands were accomplished by the end of the day, she honestly doesn't know. The sanguines have to work at self-discipline in order to live up to potential. The good thing about their weakness is they don't care that they aren't living up to their potential so they just keep enjoying life.

A sanguine often marries a melancholy. The melancholy is more the depressed, deep type, and the bubbly sanguine balances him out even though one is in the basement all the time and the other one is on the roof. The sanguine fits the cliché, "He never gets ulcers; he just gives them to everyone else."

METHODICAL MELANCHOLY

The melancholy has by far the most sensitive nature of all the temperaments. Most of the geniuses come out of the melancholy temperament. Einstein and Michelangelo were both melancholies. Michelangelo studied the human anatomy and prepared for months before he painted the Sistine Chapel. If a sanguine were going to paint the ceiling of the Sistine Chapel, he would do it with a can of spray paint. Even then, he would probably leave his paint down on the floor and have to crawl back down from the ceiling to get it.

Whatever God has called us to be, He equips us with the abilities and the personality needed to accomplish that task. He wanted Michelangelo to paint that ceiling; it was part of God's plan for him, so He equipped him with the ability to plan out and think through all that needed to be depicted in his art. The whole point is we are all supposed to work together to facilitate each other's gifts for the glory of God. When I look at our ministry, it is phenomenal to see how each individual is equipped with just exactly what they need for their part. I couldn't do this without them, and yet, they couldn't do what they are doing without me.

> *Whatever God has called us to be, He equips us with the abilities and the personality needed to accomplish that task.*

Melancholy temperaments are creative thinkers who appreciate life's true values and excel in the arts. They enjoy perfection and lift the standard of excellence often with higher expectations than most of us can achieve.

One woman said that she was married to a perfect melancholy, who was so neat and orderly that when he put his shoes in the closet, he actually tied the strings in bows and put them all in a nice and neat row together. Our friend and ministry associate Roxane is a melancholy, and when she heard that story, she said,

"You know, I don't tie the strings, but I do put all the strings inside my shoes when I line them up in the closet."

The melancholy's tendency is to set goals of perfection that he cannot reach, which causes him to spend a great deal of time internalizing what went wrong. He will sit around for days and think about how he can change it. He tries to sort out what is wrong with himself that keeps him from the perfection that he deeply desires. Consequently, he searches for details that most of us find tedious.

Whenever a project is suggested by a choleric or a sanguine temperament, Mr. Melancholy can analyze it in a few moments and pick out every potential problem that they will encounter. They always point out the problems but those problems are real issues for them. Anything out of order genuinely bothers them.

It was so hard for me and the melancholy personalities who worked for me until I learned what was happening between us. I'm real positive and goal oriented. When I dream up a project, there is nothing that is too hard for me to plow through and make work. I present my idea with a hip, hip, hooray, and those melancholies quickly sink into deep introspection. I'm shocked when they don't meet me with enthusiasm, but now I understand that they are processing the details involved in my idea and will most likely be the ones to come forward with a working design in a few hours.

My phlegmatic husband can look at me with a blank face and honestly feel no excitement whatsoever. The melancholies are quickly telling me every little thing that is wrong with my plan, but thank goodness for those sanguines. They are my best cheerleaders if it sounds like fun. As long as it is exciting, they don't care. They nod their head in agreement, encouraging me to keep talking. But now that I understand their personalities, I can affectionately accept each one of those people for where they are.

You have to understand that a melancholy can't help seeing those problems any more than I can help not seeing them. When a melancholy enters a room he sees what is wrong with it, seldom what is right with it. The list of vocations given for this temperament includes mathematics, science, diagnostic medicine, architecture, philosophy, writing, and other exacting vocations.

The melancholy temperaments are naturally faithful to their friends and easily lay aside their own interests to serve those people they love. They are usually uncomfortable when the attention is on them, and they often choose a profession that improves the quality of life for others.

While a pure melancholy reserves his opinions until asked, a melancholy-choleric will quickly volunteer everything he thinks. And you can trust that he has been thinking about everything; yes, any topic, in great detail, and his answer will be worth listening to because it has been carefully analyzed. Most everyone swings to a second nature that causes a unique blend of tendencies. A melancholy-phlegmatic would operate differently from a melancholy-choleric.

The melancholy has many weaknesses that I won't cover in detail, but their greatest strength and their greatest weakness is that they are extremely sensitive. If you are hurting, the melancholy knows it and empathizes for your hurt. However, the weak side of that is that they get upset if you don't understand their needs, and they don't expect to have to tell you what they are. Because they are so sensitive, they feel like that everybody else ought to be that way, too. They don't understand why others aren't sensitive, too.

Melancholies are creative, orderly, and organized, but their detrimental weakness is self-centeredness, which makes them hard to please. Too much self-examination can stop them from accomplishing what they start out to do. If you just think about your imperfections all the time, you will be paralyzed and drained of energy.

The melancholy can overcome his weakness by becoming more outwardly focused. His self-centered viewpoint will destroy him if left to entertain itself. He can never be as perfect as he wants to be, so he must turn his strengths toward helping others enjoy the finer things of life.

CONTROLLING CHOLERIC

The choleric is determined, confident, and aggressive when it comes to accomplishing his goals. Consequently, being this personality myself, I know that it is difficult for this strong personality to learn how to trust God. To totally trust God, you have to stop trusting yourself, leaning on yourself, and relying on yourself, and self-efficiency is not easy for the choleric to give up.

The choleric has a plan and is in constant movement toward that plan. He is single-minded towards that purpose and believes his ideas are better than anyone else's. The choleric might not necessarily have as good a plan as the melancholy, but the choleric will usually succeed because of his dogged determination and unwillingness to give up. Adversity spurs him on and makes him more determined to be first at the finish line. The determination in the choleric is one of his greatest strengths. I like the Scripture that says, "Put your hand to the plow and don't look back."

The choleric temperament is given over almost exclusively to the practical aspects of life. We are often complimented that our teaching is so "practical." Now you can see that practicality is part of my personality; I'm almost purely choleric. If something is not useful, I don't want to mess with it.

The choleric is happy when busy with some worthwhile well-organized project. Cholerics make quick, intuitive decisions based on their "gut feeling" of what seemed right or wrong. If you have an emergency, one of the best personalities to have on the scene is the choleric. They just jump up right away and do something.

I like the example I read illustrating what these four personalities would do in a fire.

"If the barn caught on fire, the melancholy would rub her brow and say, 'I'm afraid the barn is going to burn to the ground.' The phlegmatic would wonder, **What should we do?** The choleric would immediately organize a bucket brigade, and the sanguine would say, 'Oh, great! Now we can toast marshmallows.'"

The choleric has a strong leadership tendency, with good judgment of people and tends to dominate a group. He has an optimistic, pioneering spirit and will abandon comfort for adventure. In other words, the bulldog tenacity of this temperament won't let go until he gets what he went after. When I have opposition on something I know is of God, the challenge just cheers me on. A choleric doesn't see obstacles but simply stays focused on the goals.

Some of the choleric's weaknesses are very serious. He is often quick to anger, hard, impetuous, and erroneously self-sufficient. The choleric can seem void of emotion and compassion and often has a serious emotional deficiency. This point has driven me to my face to seek God to work His compassion and concern on the inside of me that I knew that I was supposed to feel and didn't.

In the beginning of this ministry, somebody could come up and tell me an awful story and I would just look at them, not feeling anything. I literally went before God asking, "What is my problem?" I prayed and prayed and cried out to God about this. I fasted and prayed and cried out to God again — and God changed me in that area.

Now when people tell me things, it will touch me so deeply that I truly hurt for them. I have a deep concern now for people's needs, so our weaknesses can be changed through prayer. The Holy Spirit can take a thick-skinned choleric and cause him to lay down his life to help people reach their best in God. Nothing is too hard for God.

All the personality types have weaknesses, but our weaknesses can be changed through prayer.

The study showing that many angry cholerics became the world's most depraved criminals and dictators didn't make me feel real good about myself. Melancholies will feel better about themselves knowing they aren't the worst of the bunch after all. Their depression isn't nearly as bad as where I could have ended up. But God got hold of me before my personality led me to destruction, and I am preaching the Gospel for Jesus Christ.

The choleric's ability to act quickly can lead him to impetuous decisions that he later regrets, but his stubborn pride tenaciously sees him through. He doesn't always enjoy his achievements because he is already working on the next frontier. It is both difficult to apologize or show approval, which causes great damage in any relationship that he wants to keep. When empowered by the love of God, the choleric's confidence and determination can move mountains that few others would try to even climb. He is strong willed and a worker.

PEACEFUL PHLEGMATIC

I heard one lady teaching on the personality types who said, "We always save the phlegmatics till last because of all the personalities, if you don't get around to them, they won't care."

If you run out of time, the melancholy might get depressed, the choleric will get mad, and the sanguine will have an emotional fit and chase you around all night wanting to know what you would have said to them. But the phlegmatic will sleep well that night whether you talked about him or not. They may think the whole topic is pointless anyway.

As I have already said, my husband is phlegmatic (bless his darling heart). I tried so hard to change him before I learned about these personality traits because I was honestly convinced that the man was only half-alive. I was always zipping around the house doing all these exciting things, working on goals and having visions, telling him we ought to do this or that. Dave's standard answer was always, "We'll see."

This is one guy who does not need to hear any message about waiting on God. He knows how to wait on God. I started telling Dave what I believed God wanted me to do a long time ago, and he would say, "Joyce, you are always running out ahead of God." I said, "Yeah, and if God wanted you to do anything, you would be twenty blocks behind." The phlegmatic has no enthusiasm about anything, so that's the way we started.

Dave was in the background doing nothing and I was way out in front doing it all. I have the utmost respect for my husband and in no way am I trying to insult him, but he will tell you that this is the truth about our personalities. We have a great marriage now and can see God's perfect plan for knitting us together. We both have changed and come into balance.

I'll never forget the time I asked Dave to help me do our first radio rally. We do that once a year to inspire our partners to get involved with our ministry plans. Everything is done in a radio room without an audience, so we sit in this little square box of a room with equipment all around us. I had a vision in my head of all the people out there, so I started in and introduced Dave to our radio audience.

I said, "Well, praise God, folks, we are excited to be here with you as we begin this special week of teaching. We're having this radio rally, and I believe that you will be encouraged to become a partner with us." Then I said, "Dave's here in the radio room with me, and he is going to talk to you for a minute." I said, "Now, Dave, aren't we excited?"

He took the microphone and in his peaceful and somber tone he said, "Yes." I am telling you the truth, then he added, "Yes, we are excited."

I screamed, "Cut! Throw the whole thing away," and we had to start all over. He said he was excited, but he did not sound excited. People just are different and they are the way God made them. If you want somebody to get excited with you, never tell a phlegmatic your news; save it for a sanguine.

The unexcitable phlegmatic has a good sense of humor that keeps him detached from the intensity of life. Mundane experiences are fuel for his dry wit and keen sense of reality. He delights in making people laugh. People seek him as a counselor because he is a good listener. The phlegmatic gives thoughtful and useful advice. His easygoing nature calms the storms raging in peoples' lives, and he has endurance skills that exceed all the other temperaments.

He is dependable, cheerful, good-natured, thorough, and on time. He is faithful and loyal to his friends even though he has a tendency to keep a distance from others. The phlegmatic is also "practical and efficient." He stays in the middle of the road. He's all-purpose, easygoing, and always the same every time you see him. Peace is his whole motivation in life.

Nothing bothers Dave. He can wait three months or twenty-five years for something and he just doesn't mind. Nothing disturbs him. People can talk about him, and he doesn't care. He is just your easygoing personality. I am hanging from the rafters everywhere we go, wanting to do this and that, but Dave's theme is, "Cast your care." If Dave was a preacher, he would have twenty-five tape albums on casting your care on God. He could come at it from every possible angle imaginable. He keeps excitable people like me in balance. He throws water on my fire, and I add fuel to his.

I've learned from watching my husband how to enjoy life. While I was worrying, manipulating, trying to change, struggling, fussing, and fuming all those years, my husband enjoyed life. He had peace and joy. In fact, he often does his best work under circumstances that would cause other temperaments to crack. His work always bears the hallmark of neatness and efficiency; although he's not a perfectionist, he does have exceptionally high standards of accuracy and precision.

The melancholy is more likely to be an inventor than the other personalities, but it is the hard-driving choleric who will usually produce the melancholy's invention. The melancholy has an idea, but the choleric has the determination to bring it through to a finished state. After it is invented and designed, the sanguine will be the one to sell it because he always makes a convincing sales-man; the phlegmatic, who did nothing, will buy it and enjoy it.

It doesn't take long to list the weaknesses of the phlegmatics because they are so few. They just enjoy what is going on around them. They are hard to motivate. But Dave is one of the freest individ-uals I have ever seen in my whole life. Nothing intimidates him.

The phlegmatic is prone to be lazy, often appearing to drag his feet when he feels coerced into action against his will. He is content to watch without participating and seldom initiates projects or plans he is very capable of executing.

To avoid motivation from the other personality types, the phleg-matic person gives a cold shoulder to the enthused sanguine, teases the pessimistic melancholy, and meets the choleric's excitement with levelheaded common sense to diffuse his vision of grandeur. If pushed, he can use his cool wit as a defense until everyone else is upset while he remains composed. I can talk to Dave about something and he knows just which buttons to push until I am almost exasperated while he remains as cool as he can be the whole time.

The phlegmatic weakness is selfishness. He seems to resist change more out of stubbornness than lack of interest. Most of the time, phlegmatics will let you have your way about whatever you want because their main goal in life is peace. But they have an iron-clad will, and if they ever do make their mind up that you're not going to do something, you might as well chill out because they will not be moved. Dave gets like that with me, and I cannot move him, manipulate him, or talk, beg, plead, cry, or throw fits enough to get him to change his mind.

Although selfishness is a basic weakness of all four temperaments, the phlegmatic may be cursed with the heaviest dose. This weakness leads to indecisiveness over the years that leaves him lagging behind the activity of the others. The price he has to pay to get or accomplish what he wants often outweighs his desire to have it. But through the work of the Holy Spirit, the phlegmatic can keep you steady when the storms of life are raging. They are solid rocks when you are seeking peace.

Sometimes people have other blends in their personality that for one reason or another have been repressed. The stronger part of their nature takes over, but the secondary temperament may need to be developed. This has been the case with Dave. After he came to work in the ministry full time in 1986, I noticed he was acting more like a choleric in many instances. Over the years this has increased to the point that he often seems as bossy as I am. He has a lot of important responsibility at the ministry, and I believe God developed this latent part of his personality at the time in life when he needed it. Had Dave been very strong willed when we got married, we might have killed each other. God brought out the phlegmatic side of him because that was all I could handle at the time.

After years of me bossing Dave around and him not saying much about it, he started confronting me one day. He politely and calmly told me that God had held him back all those years because I could not have taken direction from anyone else, but God had told him that the time had now come for him to begin confronting me. My flesh went wild and for a while I am sure Dave felt as if he was trying to break a wild horse, but in the end it was good for both of us. When you're in a battle, always remember that the end result may be worth enduring the battle you're in.

Actually, Dave has gotten stronger and I have gotten milder over the years. I really don't mind letting other people be in charge; I've carried enough responsibility in my lifetime to last forever.

Understanding the various personality types and how they function can bring positive change to your relationships. You can learn how to draw from each other's strengths to accomplish mutual goals.

Understanding the various personality types and how they function can bring positive change to your relationships. Instead of trying the change the unchangeable, you can learn to draw from each other's strengths to firmly establish the mutual goals you are working toward. I have tried to give you enough information about the four personalities to initiate your path to this vital interpersonal tool for understanding each other. (You may also want to listen to my teaching album "Understanding Your Mate's Personality" for more information.) You can learn to love and appreciate your differences instead of letting them agitate and separate you from each other.

Our personalities are God-given. I love to watch my grandkids interact with each other according to their personalities. One of our grandchildren is so melancholy — it is just unbelievable. He is a perfectionist who watches to see that he is getting what everybody else is getting. Another one is the bossy choleric. Another is the bubbly sanguine, always getting into trouble in school for talking and moving around. One is phlegmatic, and the fifth one at this time is a baby and we can't tell yet about her. The five of them came from two of our children, and yet they all have different personalities — they were born different.

They are just born with a certain approach, and the best part of understanding them and myself is to realize that we're not weird; we're just different. This understanding will go a long way toward improving relationships.

16

TWO ARE BETTER
THAN ONE

*Behold, how good and how pleasant it is
for brethren to dwell together in unity!
It is like the precious ointment poured on the head,
that ran down on the beard, even the beard of Aaron
[the first high priest], that came down upon the collar
and skirts of his garments [consecrating the whole body].
It is like the dew of [lofty] Mount Hermon and the
dew that comes on the hills of Zion; for there the Lord
has commanded the blessing, even life forevermore
[upon the high and the lowly].*
Psalm 133

A godly marriage results in unity between the married partners. In this place of agreement, the Lord commands blessing and life as God's promised anointing comes upon a dwelling that is filled with peace. My hope is that once you see the blessing in store for couples who come into agreement, you will be eager to find and protect that place of peace in your own marriage.

I once speculated what would happen if two strong cholerics got married. Somebody offered, "They would kill each other." Another couple in my seminar responded, "We are both choleric and we have been having a rough time. But we are glad to be hearing the teaching on personalities; now we realize that if we ever get in agreement on a goal, everyone else had better watch out because it is finished! It will happen."

The Bible says,

Two are better than one, because they have a good return for their work:

If one falls down, his friend can help him up. But pity the man who falls and has no one to help him up!

Also, if two lie down together, they will keep warm. But how can one keep warm alone?

Though one may be overpowered, two can defend themselves. A cord of three strands is not quickly broken.

Ecclesiastes 4:9-12 NIV

> *As two people become one in agreement with each other, a power from heaven is released to bless their lives.*

The three-strand cord is a picture of the power that takes place when two people agree for something in line with God's will for them. As two people become one in agreement with each other, a power from heaven is released to bless their lives. Read Matthew 18:19-20 to understand the blessings that await couples in unity with each other:

Again I tell you, if two of you on earth agree (harmonize together, make a symphony together) about whatever [anything and everything] they may ask, it will come to pass and be done for them by My Father in heaven.

For wherever two or three are gathered (drawn together as My followers) in (into) My name, there I AM in the midst of them.

It took me three years before I started to give in and try to come into agreement with Dave. The first issue I tried to see his way was over golf. While we were in "disharmony" I was the one that was miserable. Well, I eventually made him miserable, too, but my suffering became unbearable. I had no idea the fun that awaited me if I would just come into agreement with Dave.

When you demand your own way, you are the one who ends up suffering more than anybody else. God knew I needed something to do, some kind of entertainment or hobby to give me rest from the work I love. When I learned to play golf with Dave, it gave us time together that after all these years we still enjoy.

Don't be bullheaded. Determine in your heart that you will take a new look at every disagreement you have with your spouse to see what God can do for you if you come together in agreement. You are most likely missing out on the very answer you have been hoping to receive.

You can have such fun in your marriage when you begin to agree with each other. Do you know that God did not put you together to be miserable? He didn't put you together to fight, to pick on each other, to try and change each other, or just to buy a house together. The Bible says that a woman is to enjoy her husband. Think about that. I very rarely ever hear a woman say, "You know what? I really enjoy my husband." And God wants us to enjoy each other. He wants us to have fun together. You need to laugh together and have fun together.

Genesis 2:24 says, *Therefore a man shall leave his father and his mother. . . .* If you are married, but you haven't left home (both physically and mentally) you need to take care of this first step right away. *. . . and shall become united and cleave to his wife. . . .* Sometimes a wife clings to her mother, and her mother's opinions about what she ought to do, or a man runs to his father for advice when they should be trusting and leaning on each other. *. . . and they shall become one flesh.*

Now the word "cleave" means "to adhere firmly and closely or loyally and unwaveringly,"[1] to "be joined (together)," "stick."[2] In other words "cleave" means to be glued to each other. Matthew 19:4,5 says,

> *He replied, Have you never read that He Who made them from the beginning made them male and female,*

And said, For this reason a man shall leave his father and mother and shall be united firmly (joined inseparably) to his wife, and the two shall become one flesh?

Notice that these Scriptures don't say the two **are** one flesh the minute they get married. It says the two shall *become* one. Now, how are two joined as one? Most of the people reading this book probably have enough teaching in the Word of God to know that you are a spirit, you have a soul, and you live in a body. You are a spirit being; you are not a body. For example, you can present an image of yourself to everybody that is a totally different person than that one who lives on the inside of you.

The real you is in the inner man. You have a personality and then beyond that you have a spirit. When a person gets born again, the Spirit of God comes to dwell on the inside of man's spirit. So you are a spirit being; you have a soul which is made up of your mind, your will, and your emotions that is demonstrated through your personality. You have a body which everyone can see.

So how do these two people who are spirit beings with very different personalities, who don't think alike, who don't feel the same about a lot of different things, who don't even many times like the same kind of food become one? We do know that it doesn't just happen when you both say, I do. "Becoming one" is a process that takes time.

The Hebrew word for "one" in *Strong's Exhaustive Concordance* is reference number 259, *echad* (ekh-awd') and means united as one. Other descriptive words are "alike" and "together."[3] It comes from the root word (#258) that means to "unify" as to "collect (one's thoughts): — go one way or other."[4] This depicts a unity or agreement in body, soul, and spirit. To be totally unified, then you must be one in all three areas.

If both people in a marriage relationship are not born again and walking with God, then they will never be joined spiritually. You become joined as one spiritually through your union with Christ Jesus. (1 Corinthians 6:17.) If you are both one with Christ in spirit, then you are one with each other in Him. Couples who do not have Christ as the center of their marriage are having trouble and most are not making it. One out of every two people who are getting married are not staying married. Even Christian marriages can have many problems, but the hope of Jesus keeps light in their relationship to direct their paths. **Jesus has to be the prime focus in the home if you want things to be the way that they're supposed to be.**

The Bible teaches in 1 Corinthians 6:16 that two people are joined in body through the sexual relationship. So the physical process of becoming one happens quickly and even our society acknowledges husbands and wives as "one body," sharing equal ownership of property and legally obligated to each other's debts.

If you are both one with Christ in spirit, then you are one with each other in Him.

If you are both born again, then the spiritual union is in place. That doesn't mean you are both on equal wavelengths, as one may be more mature in knowledge of spiritual things than the other. One may be Spirit-filled and the other one not, or one may be letting Jesus be the Lord of their life while the other one has just made a profession of faith but hasn't started submitting to God. Being born again you are still in agreement over Jesus as Savior and know that you are both heaven bound.

The longest part of the process of becoming one is usually in the area of the soul. Couples are sometimes slow to agree in the way they think about things. How does this process of mental agreement take place? Most marital problems include strife from communication problems, sexual misunderstanding, money, goals, and how to discipline the kids. All of these things get worked out between us in the soulish realm of our union. They don't have as much to do with the spirit or the body as they do with what we think about those areas. We can know spiritually what is the right thing to do, but that doesn't mean that we will end up doing it.

And so, the primary focus of our agreement needs to be in the soul — the mind, the will, and the emotions. Your mind tells you what you think; the will tells you what you want; and your emotions tell you what you feel. When God first called me into ministry, I wanted to jump in full time, but Dave didn't want any part of it. He just wanted to go to work every day. He was a great, fun-loving guy, a good father, and a good husband who played a lot of golf, watched a lot of sports on television, and was easy to get along with.

Basically, Dave's will was to continue doing what he had previously enjoyed. He didn't have goals beyond that. He was satisfied to go to work, bring home the money, watch a little television, play a little golf, and wrestle with the kids.

But God called me to preach, and I had a worldwide vision to go out and get people saved who are dying and going to hell. I wanted to help people to get their lives back together. And Dave just told me, "I don't want to do that."

We had a problem, didn't we? But God changed Dave's will in that area. I admit that for a while, I tried to change him, by harping on it, arguing with him, and nagging him with, "You're not producing anything. If we will do this, we can help a lot of people." But he firmly said, "I don't want to do that. I just don't want to do that."

Finally, one day the Lord said to me, "Joyce, why don't you just go do what I told you to, and just let Dave do what he wants to. Just love him and go do what I'm telling you to do." Dave never told me I couldn't do it; he just didn't want to do it with me.

After three weeks, Dave came to me and said, "For three weeks, God has been dealing with me." (As soon as I stopped dealing with Dave, God started working on him.) He continued, "I believe that you are called to do what you say you are called to do. I want you to know that from now on I'm going to support you in it. When you go out and teach, I'll go with you and support you in things like that."

My point is that Dave's will was set in one direction, but God wooed Dave's heart to comply with His own. If the two people are going to be in agreement where their will is concerned, they will have to lift things up to God and say, "Father, if I'm wrong about this, then change my mind or change my will." God is the One Who will bring you into agreement, both to His will and purpose for your lives. You must be willing to be brought into agreement with that other person.

The Bible says that we are supposed to be in agreement. Dave and I have personalities that are about as far opposite as we could get. Yet God has brought us more and more together to where we are starting to think more alike and want more of the same things every day. We still have two different personalities, and now we can see that God put our differences together on purpose. It was not an accident because God knew we each have strengths and weaknesses that will complete the other when we become one.

The idea of saying, "Why aren't you like me?" is no longer a question in our hearts. We realize that we need each other to be exactly who God created us to be. We no longer pick on each other's weaknesses — instead we partake of our strengths and enjoy one another.

HOW CAN WE AGREE?

Amos 3:3 asks, "How can two walk together unless they be agreed?" Two people going in opposite directions are hard to unify. Matthew 18:19, says, . . . *if two of you on earth agree (harmonize together, make a symphony together) about whatever [anything and everything] they may ask, it will come to pass and be done for them by My Father in heaven.*

If God can find two people on earth who will agree, He says, "Anything that those two people ask, I will do it." He isn't saying that you can just agree about the one thing you believe for; He is talking about living a life of agreement where you are walking in love and unity so that everything you ask will be granted.

There are no two people who are in a more important position to get in agreement than a married couple. God has done so much for Dave and me since we have gotten out of strife and learned to humble ourselves to the point that we don't have to be right all the time. Many wars are started in our homes over some nit-picky thing that doesn't make any difference at all, such as whether to go left or right out of the subdivision when both streets go to the same store.

If you want to have power in your marriage, and power in your prayer life, then you have to be rid of the spirit of strife, get all traces of it out of your home, and commit to finding your way to agreement. You can learn how to "disagree agreeably" without causing strife. I'm not saying you have to think exactly the same thing, but if you respect one another, you can disagree with manners by saying, "Well, honey, I don't really agree with that, but we don't have to agree all the time."

We have a **right** to think for ourselves. If we want to have good relationships, we need to respect the different opinions of others. One of our greatest relational problems is that we draw out our little square box of what we think everything ought to be like and then we try to cram everybody into it.

The big question is **how** do people who are not of one mind get in agreement? The will, as I have pointed out, represents your wants, wishes, and desires. As you grow in Christ, you will become less self-centered. Without Christ, you will always be focused on yourself, but if Christ is at the center of your heart, you will see the needs of others and feel compassion to help them achieve their desires, too. If you want to have a good relationship in your home, you've got to learn to lay aside your personal wants for the good of the entire family unit.

For example, Dave once had a Z28. My husband got this idea that he had to have a sports car and he wanted a Z28. It may have been a crisis of his change of life, but he was feeling his youth again and wanted the car while he was young enough to enjoy it. Some men go out and look for a younger woman, but Dave just wanted a sports car, and he wanted it with four on the floor. Thank God they didn't have his color with a four-speed transmission. They couldn't find one anywhere, so he got an automatic transmission, but he got so good at shifting that it wasn't any different than if he'd had four on the floor.

So picture Dave taking me to these meetings where I'm going to preach and here we go, Rrrrrrrrrrr, Rrrrrrrrr. We would zip around the corner, and he would shift it into another gear — Rrrrrrrrr. I'm trying to pray and read my Bible while lunging back and forth as Dave plays with the automatic gears.

I felt like I was already sitting on the floor, and then we would pull up to a meeting, Rrrrrr, Rrrrrrr, and I would have to unfold my body to get out of his toy. I hated that car. I truly despised that car. Our family wouldn't fit in it and Dave was real picky about it. He didn't want anybody to do anything to it.

I took the thing to the grocery store one day. When I drove it back into the garage and touched the garage wall a little bit, that put a little scratch on it. I was petrified to tell him. Well, he was kind to me about it, but the point is that Dave bought something that really wasn't for the good of our whole family unit. It was something **he** wanted; it cost a lot of money. The payment on it was high. But it was not meeting our needs as a family unit. He had it about a year, and I begged him and pleaded and finally he sold it and we bought a van.

Now many years have passed, and Dave actually has a few older cars that he has collected over the years, high performance cars that he really enjoys. It is a different time in our life now. We don't need to put our children in the backseat of the car, and besides, I have my own car, which is big enough for six people if need be. He drives the cars he has collected, and I rarely ever even ride in them.

At certain times in life we may want something, but it is out of season for us to get it. This time in our life is a much better time for Dave to own that kind of car than the first time he got one. It has always been a desire of his heart, and I want him to have his desires.

Dave and I are in agreement about the cars now; when he had the Z28 we were not. It took us a year, but we found a place of agreement. That is the most powerful, safest place to be. Even though I am strong willed, I won't do things that Dave does not agree with because I know the importance of unity. The only way I go ahead with something if he does not agree is when we agree that we can disagree agreeably. In other words, it might not be what he would do, but he will allow me to do it without any animosity. It took us a long time to work through all these various things, but thank God we have, and so can you.

Agreement comes when the people involved stop being selfish. A lot of Christians still deal with selfishness. All that selfishness amounts to is, "I want what I want when I want it, and I don't really care what you want because I want what I want." Selfishness is an immature focus on our own selves.

> *If each one of us will learn to voice our wants, but choose what is best and serves everybody in the family unit, then we will find peace.*

If each one of us will learn to voice our wants, but choose what is best and serves **everybody** in the family unit, then we will find peace. The key is to care about what the other person needs and be willing to humble ourselves and do what we can to meet those needs.

Parents, I encourage you to consider the opinions and desires of your children also. Obviously, we cannot allow our children to run the home, but they do have desires, likes, and dislikes even as adults do. You as an adult might like oriental food, but your children may not like it at all. It would be an act of selfishness to insist on oriental restaurants when you go out if you do it too often. Even though they are children, I believe it is pleasing to God when we consider their desires and respect them. We should never have the attitude, "Well, I'm the boss here; you just keep quiet and do what I say."

Always search to find the place of agreement. Look for a place to eat that everyone can agree on. Dave and I practice this when shopping for furniture. We frequently don't like the same thing, so we have agreed that we won't buy something that only one of us likes; we will look until we find something we both like.

There is no reward in living selfish, self-centered lives, but the possibilities are unlimited when we live in agreement with others. God then promises to give us anything we ask for — that is in His will.

17

THE LOGIC
OF LOVE

Live in harmony with one another; do not be haughty
(snobbish, high-minded, exclusive), but readily adjust yourself
to [people, things] and give yourselves to humble tasks.
Never overestimate yourself or be wise in your own conceits.
If possible, as far as it depends on you,
live in peace with everyone.
Romans 12:16,18

Jesus said we would have trouble in the world, but we could still have peace. We simply need to trust, lean, and rely on God's plan for us. The more we understand His plan, the more knowledge we gain of the order He designed for our lives, the easier it is to enjoy the peace that passes understanding. Gary Smalley wrote a book about *The Language of Love,*[1] which I encourage couples to read who want more peace and order in their relationships. Dave and I have enjoyed the lessons that are presented in his works.

Peace came to me when I understood and accepted that Dave was always going to look at things differently from me because God purposely designed him to be different. Men tend to be more logical, drawing from their left brain cells where rules are stored, and women tend to be more likely to offer several creative options

Because of different approaches to problem solving, when a man and a woman do come together, they make better decisions than when alone.

from their right brain cells than her male counterpart. For this reason men and women generally have different approaches to problem solving. As a result, when they do come together, they can see that they make better decisions together than when alone. This process causes them to become one, as they enjoy each other's strengths.

TO LOVE IS TO SHOP

Gary Smalley tells the following story[2] of the time when after five years of marriage, he learned from his wife that she "had nearly given up hope of experiencing a loving, healthy and lasting relationship with . . ." him! "Opposed to divorce, she had resigned herself to a life that offered few of the wishes and dreams for which she longed."

He relates:

I had heard this kind of story before. For years, I had regularly counseled with husbands and wives, spending countless hours talking to them about improving their relationships. Only now . . . . the woman sitting across from me wasn't a counselee — she was my own wife, Norma!

That day, I made a decision to understand what was happening, or not happening, in my marriage. . . .

After that tearful session with my wife, I decided to commit myself wholeheartedly to understanding and relating to her. . . . I could do something adventurous with Norma — like going shopping!

I'm not sure what emotional and physiological changes ignite inside my wife upon hearing the words the mall, but when I told her my idea, it was obvious something dramatic was happening. Her eyes lit up like a Christmas tree, and she trembled with excitement — the same reaction I'd had when someone gave me two tickets to an NFL playoff game.

. . . she needed to look for a new blouse. So after we parked the car and walked into the nearest clothing store, she held up a blouse and asked, "What do you think?"

"Great," I said. "Let's get it." But in reality, I was thinking, **Great! If she hurries up and gets this blouse, we'll be back home in plenty of time to watch the college game on TV.**

Then she picked up another blouse and said, "What do you think about this one?"

"It's great, too!" I said. "Get either one. No, get both!"

But after looking at a number of blouses on the rack, we walked out of the store empty-handed. Then we went into another store, and she did the same thing. And then into another store. And another. And another! . . . And that's when it happened.

Instead of picking up a blouse at the next store we entered, she held up a dress that was our daughter's size. "What do you think about this for Kari?" she asked.

Taxed beyond any mortal's limits, my willpower cracked and I blurted out, "What do you mean, 'What do I think about a dress for Kari?' We're here shopping for blouses for you, not dresses for Kari!"

That night, I began to understand a common difference between men and women. I wasn't shopping for blouses — I was **hunting** for blouses! I wanted to conquer the blouse, bag it, and then get back home where important things waited — like my Saturday afternoon football game!

My wife, however, looked at shopping from the opposite extreme. For her, it meant more than simply buying a blouse. It was a way to spend time talking together as we enjoyed several hours away from the children — and Saturday afternoon football.

. . . I thought back to our mall experience and my commitment to become a better communicator. As I reflected on our afternoon, I realized I had overlooked something important — the innate differences between men and women.

A man's logic can get in the way of his heart, if he gives into his left-sided thinking. He thought they were there to conquer a blouse, but her right-sided thinking saw so much more potential in that time together.

This knowledge helped me to understand where Dave is coming from when he does certain things.

I can say, "That's the left side of your brain at work."

If I get emotional about something, he will nod and say,

"Mmmm. That's coming out of the right side of your brain. You had better try to kick the other side in a bit."

On a trip, the left side of the brain wants to conquer the distance, the number of miles to be driven that day. The right side of the brain pulls over to rest stops and historical markers on purpose. The right brain doesn't vaguely care about football or hockey games unless they personally know the players or their wives. It stores and expresses the feelings of love, not just the definition, and would rather read *People* than *Popular Mechanics* because it's more relational.

Men tend to favor the left side of the brain where logic operates. Women are bilateral in their thinking, which means

Men tend to favor the left side of the brain where logic operates. Women tend to use both sides of their brain at the same time.

they tend to use both sides of their brain at the same time. A woman favors the right side of the brain that carries the nurturing part of the relationship. But God intended our differences to bring peace and order to our relationship.

LOGIC, ANYONE?

When Dave and I bought our new house, Dave's logic went into full swing. I had a washrag hanging over the edge of the sink and he said, "Don't put that there."

"Why not?" I frowned, "That's the sink."

He said, "Because that rag is going to get moisture on the wood and you are going to warp the wood."

Then a few days after that, I was putting lotion on my feet and just as I was about to stand up and walk on the floor, Dave stopped me saying, "You shouldn't put that stuff on your feet and walk on the floor."

I said, "Well, how am I going to get where I'm going if I don't walk on the floor?"

He said, "That lotion is greasy and you're going to get stuff all over the carpets."

I argued, "I've been putting hand lotion on my feet all my life. Our carpets aren't greasy." But Dave comes up with these things all the time, and it helped me to realize that his logic is a gift and not intended by God to be an irritant in my life.

God intended that the differences between men and women bring peace and order to our relationship.

When I want to put a picture in a certain place on the wall he resists me saying, "We can't do that; there's no stud there."

I say, "I don't care if there's a stud there or not. I want the picture in the middle of the wall."

Unrelenting, he responds, "You can't put that in the middle of the wall, it will tear the wall up."

I try reason, "Dave, I go into other people's houses and everybody has things on their walls, and their walls aren't caving in."

"I don't care; you need to put it on the stud. We'll put it over here."

There are some things I can't agree to do, so I explain, "I don't want it there. It's not in the middle of the room."

"Let's move the couch," he offers.

"I don't want the couch on one side of the room. I want it in the middle of the room, and I want the picture in the middle of the couch."

How many times have you had these same discussions with your spouse?

I said, "You know, I want to get drapes for these windows."

He answered with, "We need a shed."

"Keep that stuff in the garage; just leave one of the cars in the driveway for awhile."

He said, "I don't want to do that."

Equally unmoved, I let him know, "I want drapes."

> *Getting into agreement is accomplished through understanding, through value, and through honor.*

Life offers endless opportunities to become divided. Unless we know how to operate together, we will have war from daylight 'til dark. We are different; we feel different; and we want different things, yet God commands us to get into agreement and to be in unity. This is accomplished only through understanding, through value, and through honor. First Peter 3:7 sets the standard for husbands:

In the same way you married men should live considerately with [your wives], with an intelligent recognition [of the marriage relation], honoring the woman as [physically] the weaker, but [realizing that you] are joint heirs of the grace (God's unmerited favor) of life, in order that your prayers may not be hindered and cut off. [Otherwise you cannot pray effectively.]

We are to be considerate of each other's differences. It's not going to do any good to tell a woman not to be emotional. It's not going to do any good to tell a man not to be logical. God created us to be this way in order to enhance, not hurt each other.

When I am hurting over something, I don't want Dave to preach to me about casting my cares. I just want him to understand, but I have to help him understand what I need. He doesn't want to see me hurting, so he tries to talk me out of feeling badly, but I just want him to love me, and hold me, and even show that he hurts with me.

Once when I was hurting over something that someone had said, he tried to tell me to "cast my cares on the Lord." I told him that is not what I wanted to hear. Finally, Dave suggested that we go play golf, and while we were driving to the course, he said, "Don't let the devil ruin your day by soaking up the hurt you feel." But then he lovingly said, "But I do understand. Really, I do understand why it is hard to stop thinking about what has hurt you."

As soon as he showed that he understood why I was hurting, I could feel the pain inside me just let go and leave. Right away, I relaxed and my spirit opened back up to him. Everything was fine because he gave me what I needed more than anything. He had said, "I understand how you feel."

That is a power-packed sentence, and if you don't get anything else out of this book, the words "I understand how you feel" will help bear much fruit in your relationship with your spouse. Sometimes we don't want a lecture; we just want a friend. And sometimes we just want somebody to hurt with us. We don't always need to preach a sermon; we often need to be a sermon to someone who is in need.

UNDERSTANDING ESTABLISHES A HOME

We are to learn how to show respect to one another. Even if we don't agree about something, I don't have to talk to Dave like there is something wrong with him just because he doesn't want what I want.

First Peter 3:1,2 speaks to wives saying,

In like manner, you married women, be submissive to your own husbands [subordinate yourselves as being secondary to and dependent on them, and adapt yourselves to them], so that even if any do not obey the Word [of God], they may be won over not by discussion but by the [godly] lives of their wives.

When they observe the pure and the modest way in which you conduct yourselves, together with your reverence [for your husband; you are to feel for him all that reverence includes: to respect, defer to, revere him — to honor, esteem, appreciate, prize, and, in the human sense, to adore him, that is, to admire, praise, be devoted to, deeply love, and enjoy your husband].

> *While men are supposed to be considerate of their wives, women are to enjoy their husbands with true admiration.*

While men are supposed to be considerate of their wives, women are to enjoy their husbands with true admiration. If you study the meaning of all those words and compare them to the way that most people live in their homes, it won't take long to understand why so many homes lack the fruit of peace and joy.

Someone needs to initiate God's plan in the home. But which of you will be first? Just as a considerate husband would inspire adoration from his wife, a devoted wife who demonstrates deep love for her husband would evoke his "intelligent recognition and honor" for her. God says that marriage is a two-sided deal, and He has given instructions for the men and the women. It takes both people for this thing to work out properly.

Ephesians 5:33 recaps both points once again:

However, let each man of you [without exception] love his wife as [being in a sense] his very own self; and let the wife see that she respects and reverences her husband [that she notices him, regards him, honors him, prefers him, venerates and esteems him; and that she defers to him, praises him, and loves and admires him exceedingly].

Something wonderful has happened to Dave and me after years of marriage. I can honestly say I would rather be with my husband than anybody. I prefer him. He treats me so well that I just love being with him. It would be awfully hard to want to prefer somebody who was always talking down to me or making fun of me or not caring anything about my needs.

Marriage is a two-way street, and Dave and I have both worked at learning to understand each other, and the more we have understood where the other is coming from, the more we seem to love each other. Understanding bears good fruit in a marriage by causing us to truly care about meeting each other's needs. I believe that people crave to be understood and to understand others.

Understanding requires communication, listening, time, and transparency.

Understanding requires communication, listening, time, and transparency. People sometimes talk but can sense that no one is listening. If you want to understand your spouse you need to take time to listen. We have to train ourselves to really listen. I'm a talker and not a good listener by nature. If I am not careful, half the time when Dave is talking to me, I am already planning my response to something he said a long time before. And I am only listening for a pause to jump in with my point as soon as he gets quiet. That is a weakness in me, and I have had to train myself to listen to what he is saying.

It is a challenge to give somebody your full attention, but it is so important to pay attention to what your spouse is saying. Learn to look at each other when you talk, and acknowledge in some way that you are hearing what is being said. You might even practice repeating back what you believe is being said.

Transparency is difficult for many of us. A woman doesn't always say what she really means at all. She often wants something else than what she is saying, but would rather drop hints than come right out with her needs. For example, a wife comes to her husband, obviously tired and frustrated, saying,

"I want to go on a vacation. I think we need a break, and I feel like I need some time alone with you and a change of pace. Our routine is too much for me and it's driving me nuts. I just need a rest and want to get out of here for a while."

She honestly doesn't know what's wrong with her, but she feels her frustration is begging to be pacified by going somewhere, eating something, or buying something to break her cycle of madness. So, she goes to her husband for help by suggesting a vacation.

He responds from the left side of his brain,

"We can't afford a vacation. We only have a few hundred dollars in the bank, and we **need** a new lawnmower."

A vacation isn't logical to him when they need a lawnmower so he reinforces his point.

"You know we can't afford to go on that vacation. Why would you even ask when you know we don't have the money?"

His logic completely missed her emotional need.

Now she feels unloved, misunderstood, and rejected. He feels that she doesn't understand why taking a vacation would pressure them financially, so now he is frustrated, too. Feeling inadequate to provide for her, he now wants some reassurance that she isn't too disappointed in him. But she withdraws, and he assumes she is mad at him.

Do you recognize the scene? Neither one of them has taken enough time to understand the other person. If only we could learn to look at our spouse and recognize when something is hurting them or bothering them, and find out how to build back up their esteem. We need to learn how to trust each other more and to not always think that the other person is out to get us.

The biggest problems in relationships stem from having too much of ourselves on our minds and not enough attention on the other person. We seem to always have "us" on our minds. Love lays aside personal self-interest to attend to the other person.

A demonstration of sincere concern can be a strong building block of love. Notice each other, encourage communication, take time to dig for the truth, examine what might be really wrong. Someone once calculated that it takes five

> *A demonstration of sincere concern can be a strong building block of love.*

times of asking, "Why do you feel that way?" before you get to the real problem at hand. Get your spouse to open up by showing real interest. You might ask leading questions, such as,

"Is something wrong?"

"Did you have a bad day at work?"

"Was the traffic real heavy?"

"Honey, aren't you feeling good?"

Or, "Is there something I can do for you; is there anything I can do to help you feel better?"

I could almost guarantee that 90 percent of the time, a loving response to a grouchy man coming through the door at night could change the whole course of your evening into something that could be beautiful. *A soft answer turns away wrath . . .* (Proverbs 15:1 NKJV), but if he comes in complaining and she volleys back with the same gruff response, they are distancing themselves and missing out on God's best for them.

I JUST NEED A FRIEND

Everyone wants companionship. We were born with the need to fill ourselves with heart-to-heart relationships that only communication can build. Take walks together; spend time just sitting beside each other. God has put an ability in every one of us to give out love.

God has put an ability in every one of us to give out love.

Ask God to show you how to communicate with each other. Remember that listening more and lecturing less makes happier homes. Maybe your husband needs to sit there for just five minutes and tell you how frustrated he is with a certain situation at work. When he is opening up to you, that is not the time to tell him to watch his confession. Just listen to see if you can understand what may be causing stress in him. Ask the Holy Spirit to reveal the truth in the situation, knowing that truth always sets a person free.

When the wife says she needs a vacation, the husband should at least sit down and listen to all the things that are overwhelming her. He could say, "OK, honey, talk to me a little bit. I can see something's not right here. I want you to tell me what's wrong." Even if he cannot take her on a vacation, he can satisfy her need to for sympathy and reassure her that everything will be OK again. Most likely that is all she wanted anyway.

But ladies, we don't live in a perfect world, and I realize that fewer husbands than wives will read this book to find out what they should be doing, so you will need to communicate your needs to your husband. God has already told us that our husbands need help. Genesis 2:18 says that God made a helper for Adam. . . . *I will make him a helper meet.* . . . The *King James Version* says, . . . *an help meet.*

That word "helper," or "helpmeet," means one who corresponds to him and one who is his completer.[3] In other words, when God gave Adam a helpmeet, the man was not complete without that woman.

So when you are overwhelmed, and you tell your husband that you need a break, tell him what you really need. Make a list and give it to him saying,

"Here is what I need from you. If you tell me that we can't go on a vacation, then I need for you to sit and listen to all the things that are making me crazy right now.

"Then I need for you to hug me and be sorry that I feel so bad. Tell me you understand exactly how I feel and that you don't blame me at all for being frustrated.

"Tell me that if you were in my situation, you would feel like getting away, too, and that you probably wouldn't even be doing as good of a job at coping as I am.

"Then hug me and let me cry on your shoulder for three to five minutes before you tell me that you love me and that everything will be all right.

"Can you do that for me, honey?"

If couples could start communicating their needs, a lot of healing would take place. Dave and I have learned to validate each other's feelings when we are down, before we try to get each other back up. Value and honor one another, and watch the power of agreement grow between you.

Value and honor one another, and watch the power of agreement grow between you.

Remember that love has its own logic that must be felt from the heart. Be loving, gentle, softspoken and not harsh; be edifying and exhortive. It would be amazing what would happen in the marriage relationship if you both could learn to say, "Honey, what can I do to be more of a benefit to you? What can I do to help you more?"

Ephesians 4:29-32 explains how we can honor and value others. Post these verses somewhere in your house where everyone will be reminded of these practical points of love.

Let no foul or polluting language, nor evil word nor unwhole-some or worthless talk [ever] come out of your mouth, but only such [speech] as is good and beneficial to the spiritual progress of others, as is fitting to the need and occasion, that it may be a blessing and give grace (God's favor) to those who hear it.

And do not grieve the Holy Spirit of God [do not offend or vex or sadden Him], by Whom you were sealed (marked, branded as God's own, secured) for the day of redemption (of final deliv-erance through Christ from evil and the consequences of sin).

Let all bitterness and indignation and wrath (passion, rage, bad temper) and resentment (anger, animosity) and quarreling (brawling, clamor, contention) and slander (evil-speaking, abusive or blasphemous language) be banished from you, with all malice (spite, ill will, or baseness of any kind).

And become useful and helpful and kind to one another, tender-hearted (compassionate, understanding, loving-hearted), forgiving one another [readily and freely], as God in Christ forgave you.

Because of the background I came out of, I had a hard, rough exterior, and it was difficult for me to learn how to be kind and gentle. The ability was in me, but I was afraid I would be taken advantage of if I softened my ways. My voice tone was so gruff, I could say the right words to Dave, but it was clear that my heart wasn't in tune with my logic. My tone let him know that I was going to do what I was supposed to do, but my heart was not in submitting to his direction.

Colossians 3:8 says,

But now put away and rid yourselves [completely] of all these things: anger, rage, bad feelings toward others, curses and slander, and foulmouthed abuse and shameful utterances from your lips!

The morning I put the hand lotion on my feet and he told me not to walk on the floor, I didn't say anything to Dave, but he saw my facial expression and heard me sigh. My facial expression said to him, "For crying out loud, what is your problem?" It all counts — words, voice tones, and facial expressions are so important in a relationship because if we don't have the right attitude, we are not showing honor and value to the one we have been called to love.

Words, voice tones, and facial expressions are so important in a relationship.

Proverbs 18:21 says,

Death and life are in the power of the tongue, and they who indulge in it shall eat the fruit of it [for death or life].

And Proverbs 15:4,

A gentle tongue [with its healing power] is a tree of life, but willful contrariness in it breaks down the spirit.

Everything that you speak to your mate either ministers life or death to them. Every single act of communication through words, voice tone, facial expressions, and body language either ministers to them life or it ministers to them death. That is quite a responsibility. Choose life.

18

HOW TO GAIN
AND MAINTAIN

---

*Make every effort to live in peace with all men and
to be holy; without holiness no one will see the Lord.
See to it that no one misses the grace of God and that
no bitter root grows up to cause trouble and defile many.*
Hebrews 12:14-15 NIV

As Christians, we need to raise the standard of excellence in our marriages. The prophet Daniel had an excellent spirit. He determined in his heart not to defile himself by doing things that he knew would be pleasing to God. We all need to draw a line in the sand, and stop moving our line.

There came a point in my relationship with Dave that I wanted to be excellent. I wanted to give him the excellence that I knew would bring life and peace and joy to our relationship. I wanted to move beyond mediocrity, and so I asked God to bring integrity to our marriage. I wanted our relationship to be in line with God's biblical standards for husbands and wives. I discovered that it doesn't matter where you are in your marriage, God loves you and has a good plan for your life. Even if your circumstances seem negative, keep your eyes on God and trust Him to bring you out and up.

Isaiah 61:7 holds a wonderful promise for those who put their hope in God. It reads,

Instead of your [former] shame you shall have a twofold recompense; instead of dishonor and reproach [your people] shall rejoice in their portion. Therefore in their land they shall possess double [what they had forfeited]; everlasting joy shall be theirs.

Don't grow impatient. The journey to excellence is a life-long process. But God is no respecter of persons, and anyone who trusts in Him will get the same benefits. God will do something awesome in your life. He will bless you, prosper you, and love you into wholeness. Psalm 103:4 (NIV) says He . . . *redeems your life from the pit and crowns you with love and compassion.*

> *We try to get our security and reassurance from our spouse instead of from God and then wonder why they aren't able to fix us.*

The instruction that God has given us in His Word can be trusted to bring fruit to our marriages and relationships. His love is a healing balm, and when we demonstrate God's love to each other, that healing power is released to work between us. Too often, we try to get too much from people. We try to get our security and reassurance from our spouse instead of from God and then wonder why they aren't able to fix us. We need to stay full of love from God and then let His love pour out from us to our spouse. This is the fuel for a great marriage.

By the time this book is released for its first printing, Dave and I will have been married over thirty-three years. I think we love each other more now than we ever have. But we realize that we can't meet all the needs that the other one has. I have to go to God to keep me whole. God will never reject us. He gives us beauty for ashes and promises double blessings for former hurts and pains.

I hope our stories demonstrate that God has the power to take you from a place of no hope to a place of triumph in your relationship with each other. I was so negative when Dave and I first married, and he was so positive and full of hope in God for our future. By watching Dave and the testimony of his faith in God, I learned to get over myself and put my hope in God, too. There has been such an astounding change in my life that now I am compelled to try everything I know to do to help others find the happiness that comes from putting their hope in the only One Who can fill the longing in their hearts. Only God can show us how to give and receive love.

Don't sit around and feel sorry for yourself all your life because of what happened to you in the past. Stop taking inventory of everything you have lost and start counting up what you have left. Give what you have to God, even if it is nothing. He can even do something with nothing. It isn't that complicated to follow the Lord.

I probably tell God two hundred times a day, "I love You. I love You, Lord. You're so awesome, God. Thank You. Thank You, God, for what You've done in my life."

When your hope is in God and you realize that He wants good things to happen to you, you aren't so dependent on what kind of mood your spouse is in. If they are down, you are up because you have just been singing a love song to the Lord, and consequently, you are able to sing one to your spouse. Keep your heart full of hope. If you don't you will definitely be disappointed.

The Bible says that Abraham once felt all human reason for hope was gone, but hoped on in faith that he would become the father of many nations. No doubt or unbelief made him waver concerning the promise of God. A woman once asked for prayer because her husband of thirty-five years had just left her. I couldn't promise that if she believed God her husband would come back to her because we cannot manipulate and control other people's wills with our prayers. But, I can promise that if she hangs on to her hope in Jesus, He will either heal that marriage or He will give her somebody who will love her even better.

Like Abraham, she can have faith in the hope that God will bless her and take care of her and even be a Husband to her. Sometimes, we have to give God a little space in which to work. We can't give Him a blueprint and then get mad at Him if He doesn't do it the way we asked, but we can trust Him to give us peace and joy. With that confidence we should be full of expectancy and excited for our future.

Every day, we should say, "God, I'm excited to see what You're going to do today. I believe that something good is going to happen to me today. Everywhere I go today, the favor of God is on me."

ARE YOUR EXPECTATIONS IN THE WRONG PLACE?

God often works through people to meet our needs, but we block Him from doing that when we put our expectations in people instead of God.

The Bible teaches us in many places to put our expectation and hope in God. He is our Source, the Source of everything we need. He often works through people to meet our needs, but we block Him from doing that when we put our expectations in people instead of God.

Sometimes we are expecting people to do things that they don't even know we are expecting them to do. We end up disappointed, but it is because of our expectation, not their failure to meet it.

There have been times when I have let my mind go wild and over a period of a few days become convinced that Dave should be asking me to go out — go out to eat or to go shopping or to a movie. I am expecting him to ask me to go somewhere, and I have myself convinced that he should do that.

When he doesn't do it, I have become angry and told him he should take me somewhere. He has responded with, "You did not tell me you wanted to go anywhere. You know I'll take you anywhere you want to go." I was expecting him to ask me, and he was expecting me to tell him.

I believe many marriages fail because of wrong expectations. Many disappointments come from these expectations that are actually misplaced. We cannot really expect someone to read our minds. We must communicate and do so clearly. We cannot expect our spouse to do what someone else's spouse does. That is putting a pressure on them that is unfair. A good friend of mine named Don Clowers has written a book on right and wrong thinking. (It is scheduled to be released by Harrison House.) I highly recommend it for improving relationships.

DO-IT-YOURSELF ADVANCEMENT

It's amazing how many times Jesus' answer to somebody's problem was, "Get up." Jesus went to the man who had been crippled for thirty-eight years and was lying by the pool of Bethesda, waiting for the angel to stir up the waters so he could get a miracle. (John 5:1-9.) Jesus asked him, "Are you really serious about getting well? Do you really want to be healed?"

The man answered, "I have nobody to put me in the pool when the angel comes. Somebody else always gets ahead of me."

Jesus looked at him and said, "Get up! Pick up your bed and walk!" One version says, "Make up your bed," which gives me the picture of cleaning up your mess while you're at it to get going in some direction that will produce something positive in your life. If he was lying there for thirty-eight years, he certainly didn't have much spunk. I think in thirty-eight years I could have wiggled and squiggled over to the edge of that pool and been on the edge so far that when the angel came I would have fallen in and said, "You either heal me or I'm drowning, but I'm not living like this any more."

If you're waiting for someone to throw you into the pool, then here I am. If you have stayed with me this far to come to this point in the book and still wonder if God can heal your marriage, then let me be the one to tell you, "Get up! Get over the past, and get on with loving the person you married!"

Stop letting what other people think determine your sense of worth and value. Whatever is holding you back, make a decision to raise the standard. Say, "I'm tired of feeling condemned. I'm tired of feeling bad about myself. I'm tired of the pain of rejection. Jesus loves me, and if nobody else in the whole world ever likes me or likes my personality, I'm doing the best I can, so I'm going to serve God and love others from this moment forth."

> *To love God and to love others are the only two things God has ever asked us to do in exchange for all the blessings He wants to give us.*

To love God and to love others are the only two things God has ever asked us to do in exchange for all the blessings He wants to give us. All the law of the Old Covenant is fulfilled in those two commandments. Watch what happens when you get out of bed in the morning and start loving others regardless if they seem to love you back. Watch what happens when you decide to get over hurt feelings, bitterness, and resentment. While you are at it, get over anything else you lost to the enemy because God can give back a double portion of whatever has been taken from you.

It could seem harsh and unfeeling, but the truth is, sometimes the only thing we can do about the past is *get over it!* I had to finally make that choice, and if you have been allowing your past to threaten your future, you should try the same thing. *Get up; pick up your bed and walk.*

We are to work with God in two ways: first, to gain victory over problems and bondages and secondly, to maintain the freedom and victory we have gained. It requires a continual willingness to follow the leading of the Holy Spirit. Galatians 5:1 (KJV) tells us, *Stand fast therefore in the liberty wherewith Christ hath made us free. . . .* Yes, we must all stand fast and maintain the ground we have gained.

There were many times when Dave had to stand fast during the years he was patiently waiting for God to change me.

Fix yourself up like you would if you were not married and he was coming after work to pick you up for a date. Maybe not quite that fancy, but I am sure you get my point. If you normally wear makeup, put some on for him. Don't always wear things you clean in; put on some nicer clothes for the evening. Even if you have gained some weight over the years, you can still look nice. Remember, do the best you can with what you have.

God is on your side. Jesus came to heal the broken hearted, to open prison doors and set the captives free. He gives us beauty for ashes, oil of joy for mourning, and the garment of praise for the spirit of heaviness, that we might be called trees of righteousness, the planting of the Lord. Why? Not because we deserve it, but just because He loves us, and others will see the glory of His kindness through our testimony.

Hold on to all the good that God has given you and make plans to advance to the best that God still has for you. Whenever you see the enemy threaten your peace, take authority over depression, discouragement, despair, fear, and hopelessness in the Name of Jesus. Command those evil spirits to loose you, to loose your thinking, to loose your emotions in Jesus' Name. Be healed and rejoice for all that God is bringing to you and your household.

Speak life to your circumstances. Speak life to your future. Speak life to your mate and to your family and to your friends. Don't wait for anyone else to throw you into the pool of life. Just jump in yourself. All you need is the truth of God's Word to keep you free.

Matthew 12:34-37 shows how we can speak with faith to bring God's best into our lives.

> . . . For out of the fullness (the overflow, the superabundance) of the heart the mouth speaks.
>
> The good man from his inner good treasures flings forth good things, and the evil man out of his inner evil storehouse flings forth evil things.
>
> But I tell you, on the day of judgment men will have to give account for every idle (inoperative, nonworking) word they speak.
>
> For by your words you will be justified and acquitted, and by your words you will be condemned and sentenced.

We are to bridle our tongue and discipline our words to be under the lordship of Jesus Christ. Our words can be full of deadly poison. The Bible says the tongue is a tiny member but it starts great big blazing forest fires. We can ruin a relationship with the words of our tongue. We can drive our children off with our tongue. We can say so many wrong things about ourselves that we can talk ourselves into a poor self-image. We can gossip and backbite, but just as anger stirs strife, a gentle tongue brings healing power.

Don't expect to maintain healthy relationships if you use your tongue to murmur, grumble, and complain. When you are positive about life, you start building up power that will bring health and increase to your situation, but when you speak negative, lifeless words, you start draining your resources and steer yourself right back to zero power.

To gain ground in your relationship, understand that if you have been speaking negative words for years, it will take more than one or two positive comments to turn things around. But, you may be surprised at the welcome response even a few good words will bring to a dry and lifeless relationship. Being nice for one or two days will not undo twenty years of nagging and hurt feelings, but speaking words of life is the only way to turn your ship in the right direction.

Second Timothy 2:16 says, *But avoid all empty (vain, useless, idle) talk, for it will lead people into more and more ungodliness.* We can't avoid useless, vain thoughts that fill our heads. The enemy's only power against us is to throw fiery darts at us to inflame our thinking against the Word of God. It is our responsibility to discern these idle, empty ideas that can steal away our inheritance and keep them from settling in our hearts. For we don't control the thoughts that enter our head, but we can keep ungodly thoughts from taking root in our heart, for it is out of our heart that we speak what we believe.

It doesn't take very long to find out how we feel about somebody just by listening to what we say about them and to them. Our words should demonstrate love, and if they don't, we should ask God to create a right heart in us so that we can build up our spouse and loved ones with our words. Jesus never cut anybody down with His mouth. He told some people the truth, but He never belittled them or made fun of them.

A GODLY INFLUENCE

Proverbs 14:1 says, *Every wise woman builds her house, but the foolish one tears it down with her own hands.* Even though men are to be the high priest and head of a household, women should never underestimate the influence they have in keeping a home and family walking in the will of God.

Titus 2:5 tells women to be *keepers at home* (KJV), and thank goodness the word "keeper" doesn't just mean the one who cleans it. The Greek origin of "keeper," as defined in *Strong's Exhaustive Concordance of the Bible,* means "a guard; be 'ware.'"[1] The woman is to be conscious of the home and protect it.

I used to quickly put our relationship back to zero power when I got upset over something. I could go two or three weeks without saying one word to Dave. That sounds like a long time and it was a long time. But God gave Dave real grace during that period of time to cope with my foolish hands that kept working to tear down our home. Dave knew that he could call on God's grace to stay in a good spirit and continue to enjoy himself in spite of my actions. God's grace to rebuild our lives and homes is still bigger than our power to tear it all down, so Dave's faith kept our marriage in the covering of God's blessing until I learned to draw from God's wisdom, too.

During those foolish times of not talking to him, I was trying to drag Dave down to where I was. It would aggravate me to see that he could stay joyful in the Lord, but what I saw in Dave began to minister to me. I eventually wanted that peace that I saw in him. I wanted to be happy like he was in spite of my circumstances. I wanted to enjoy my life, too.

God brought me out of the rebellion and the upset and the self-pity that was inside of me and began to teach me how to maintain the triumph we enjoyed and how to gain the blessings that were still in store for us by trusting God and doing what He says to do.

IS MARRIAGE A 50/50 PROPOSITION?

It has occurred to me that it could sound like I am placing most of the responsibility on the woman to be the aggressor in making things right. It is no more the woman's responsibility than the man's; however, the larger percentage of people who read this book will probably be women. Someone has to get the ball rolling, and it has to be whoever has the information and knowledge needed to make positive changes. Don't allow the devil to keep you from going forward by making you feel it is unfair for you to have to do all the work. Just be willing to begin and don't even be concerned about who is doing what.

One of the problems in marriages has come from the mentality that marriage should be a 50/50 proposition. One partner thinks, "Well, I'll meet you half way, but that is all." If there is no response that they feel is fair, they refuse to do what is right, which then makes them as wrong as the other one. It gets to be like, "What came first — the chicken or the egg?" In many marriages it is practically impossible to tell what the real problem ever was to start with. I have learned that if one person does wrong and I come to their level to retaliate, then I am behaving no better than they are, and I am just as responsible for failed relationship.

If you are mature enough to make the decision to be the aggressor in solving whatever problems you may have in your marriage, don't get discouraged if your partner does not change immediately. With every opportunity for progress, we also get opposition from Satan. He despises good relationships and fears the power that comes from them. Get ready for a fight. As Paul says in 1 Timothy 6:12 (KJV), *Fight the good fight of faith. . . .*

Consistent good choices over an extended period of time will begin to turn a situation around.

I always say that it takes us years to make our messes, and we cannot get upset if one or two good choices does not get us out of them. Consistent good choices over an extended period of time will begin to turn the situation around. If an ocean liner is told to turn around and go in the opposite direction, it cannot turn immediately; it takes time. I don't share these things to be discouraging, but rather to be realistic. I would rather share reality with you and have you around to cross the finish line than to get you emotionally excited about possibilities that only happen rarely. A bad marriage can turn around overnight, but it usually does not happen that way.

By the time Dave told me that I just about had him to the point where he could not stand me, he was dealing with a lot of emotional wounds and bruises that took time to heal. I recall once asking him how he felt about me after a year had gone by of me being on what I thought was my best behavior. He said he felt better, but we still had a long way to go. I remember being discouraged and almost becoming angry with him, but thank God I kept pressing on and "little by little, day by day, from glory to glory," we got there.

Your situation will change also, but make your mind up that you will go whatever percentage of the way you need to in order to have a marriage that will bring glory to God. Don't allow the worldly 50/50 proposition mentality to get you to give up if you don't get the response from your partner you desired.

Love begins with acceptance, just as God accepted us the way we were. Dave accepted me and loved me even though I wouldn't talk to him. Love changes us. We can remodel our house, but we cannot remodel each other.

First Peter 3:3,4 explains that men are more influenced by the unfading beauty of a woman's gentle and quiet spirit than by her outward adornment of braided hair, or the wearing of gold jewelry and fine clothes. In other words, if we want some remodeling done in our relationships, we should focus on our own behavior. The Word says that a gentle and quiet spirit is of great worth in God's sight. (See verse 4 NIV.) Verses 5 and 6 (NIV) say, *For this is the way the holy women of the past who put their hope in God used to make themselves beautiful. They were submissive to their own husbands, like Sarah, who obeyed Abraham and called him her master. You are her daughters if you do what is right and do not give way to fear.*

Men want domestic peace; they want to come home and have a peaceful, gentle, quiet atmosphere. They have been out in the world all day, and they want to come home and have things in order. If you want to see God's best increase in your life and home, then have that gentle, peaceful spirit which is not anxious or wrought up but is very precious in the sight of God.

THE ATTRACTION OF VISIBLE BEAUTY

I believe that women should display gentleness which has probably, more than any other virtue, been the hardest one for me to display. I have had to really pray about this to let God work with me and bring me to the point of being meek. I still have a ways to go, but I have already seen great changes in me and continue to trust God to teach me in this area.

Gentleness is of greater value than all the jewels we can hang on ourselves. It is good to visibly look our best, but so many women paint their outside and leave their inside in a mess. God is concerned with our inner life.

> Natural beauty is admired, but inner beauty "attracts" a lasting attention from others.

Attraction is not based on natural beauty, although it is obvious that some people are naturally "more beautiful" than other people based on fashion standards of the world. Natural beauty is admired, but inner beauty "attracts" a lasting attention from others. This attractiveness of a married woman reflects the glory of her husband, and he in turn reflects the glory of God Who in the end receives the honor for the goodness in our lives.

Stay with me while I rebuild this statement from the other direction. First Corinthians 11:7 explains that men are . . . *the image and [reflected] glory of God [his function of government reflects the majesty of divine Rule]; but woman is [the expression of] man's glory (majesty, preeminence).*

When I say that a husband needs for his wife to look her best in order for him to feel good about himself, I am not talking only about natural beauty, but this inner attraction that we can carry with us. A happily married woman who has a charming, fearless approach to life makes her husband look good in the eyes of those who know them. When people see that she is at peace, beautifully adapted to her husband and family, they will think, **Her husband must be really good to her for her to be so happy.**

When they look at her husband to see why his home is full of peace and why his wife walks with confidence and grace, they will think, **His God must be good to him for his home and family to be so blessed.** Both our outward appearance (what others see) and our inner condition (what God sees) should bring honor to God through the testimony of peace that He has given to us.

Because our outer attractiveness is our first testimony to others, I believe that every woman should maintain her physical appearance as best as she can. Outer beauty is based on what we do with what we have. I believe that every person can be attractive. I always look approximately the same way. I don't run around the house in high heels and dresses, but I don't go around looking dumpy. I understand that when I look good, my husband and my Lord look good, for everyone can see the blessing that God's order has put in my life.

If a woman is wanting to gain a deeper relationship with her husband and gain God's best for their marriage, I think one of the biggest mistakes she can make is to ignore her physical attractiveness. I am a great advocate of makeup and perfume. When a woman has been cleaning house all day, and her hair is stringing down in her face, leaving her with a haggard appearance, it's no wonder her husband's eyes are more attracted to television. Take time before he comes home to fix yourself up and demonstrate to him that your relationship with him is a priority in your life.

I can already hear the arguments against this idea. Women say, "Well, I don't have time to do all that, and I have all these kids to take care of." But they can do it if they want to and if they don't, they will be the same as women who later complain that their husbands never demonstrate any personal effort to win their love and affection. They will long for the attention that they refused to give their husbands. Attractiveness needs to be a priority in your life in order to make him feel attractive, too.

Likewise, of course, men should take care of themselves. Dave takes good care of himself for me. I appreciate that he wants to look good when he is with me. We affect each other; when I look good, he feels good about himself because I belong to him. I feel good about myself when he looks good, too. Once again, I am talking about "attractiveness" not natural beauty.

Can you imagine the romance that would begin if all the women who read this book started dressing up for the homecoming of their husbands each night? Startled husbands around the world would ask, "What are you all dressed up for?" Loving wives would say, "You, I'm just dressed up for you. I love you and I want to look my best for you." Oh, I tell you the devil doesn't like this idea.

There are some awesome things we can learn from the virtuous woman in Proverbs 31. She was spiritually smart and naturally skillful. She made herself coverlets, cushions, and rugs of tapestry. Her clothing was of pure, fine linen and of colorful purple, such as was used to make clothing for the priests and hallowed cloths for the temple. Nothing is said of "natural beauty," but her character and industrious spirit caused many people to be attracted to her life.

In other words, this lady was a sharp dresser and she had some nice stuff. There's nothing wrong with having nice things. This fine woman takes good care of herself and her family. She is well-known for her spiritual strength and the way she handles herself. Her husband is famous and well-known because of his fine wife. People would say, "Oh, he is married to that fine woman dressed in purple who buys her family's food at the import store."

Ladies, we need to do all we can to enhance our husband's reputation. Just as we need our husbands to be a good father to his children, he needs our admiration and reassurance that we are looking after the needs of the family, too. Believe it or not, in most cases he is concerned about the success of you and his children. He instinctively knows that your welfare is a reflection of his manhood and ability to provide for you.

LOVE LIFTS US TO WHERE GOD WANTS US

Your admiration of him builds his confidence to be that provider. Submission is a picture of getting underneath in order to lift up the other person. Ephesians 5:33 gives a detailed list of how we truly submit in ways that will lift him up to fame and the position that God wants him to hold. I realize that I have already pointed you to this verse earlier in this book, but I hope to bring it to the attention of wives from every possible angle until the power of it is clearly understood. I remember one time when the Holy Ghost inspired me to get a dictionary and look up every single one of the following words to understand what they all meant.

*However, let each man of you [without exception] love his wife as [being in a sense] his very own self; and let the wife see that she **respects** and **reverences** her husband [that she **notices** him, **regards** him, **honors** him, **prefers** him, **venerates**, and **esteems** him; and that she **defers** to him, **praises** him and **loves** and **admires** him exceedingly].*

In practice this means that when you are both out with other people that you haven't seen for a while, don't spend the whole night talking to everyone else without paying any attention to your spouse, even if you simply go over and squeeze his hand every once in a while. It means that when he comes home and sits in front of the television, you should go and sit with him, if even for a few minutes, and embrace him to let him know that you notice him and prefer him over the duties of family life.

The number one roadblock to a triumphant marriage that is gaining ground as years progress is a lack of real commitment. Be committed to your partner. Discover each other's needs, and find out how to meet those needs.

I believe that there are things in people's hearts that need to be expressed and if we want to gain ground, we must learn to listen without taking personal offense. I still ask Dave to tell me if there is anything that I am doing that he doesn't want me to do. I still have to practice accepting his honesty without offense.

One time he told me, "I really don't like it when I apologize to you and then you give me a speech about what I should have done and how it made you feel. When I initiate an apology to you, all I want you to say is, 'Thank you; I appreciate it; you're forgiven.'"

When he shared that with me, I felt the pain of that in my soul because not one of us wants to be told that we're doing anything wrong. But bottom line, I was hurting him. When he had already realized he should be sorry, he apologized. And instead of forgiving him, I lectured him all over on how horrible he was to hurt me in the first place. We have to get beyond those fleshly feelings. We need a heart commitment to the task of pleasing our mate.

Commitment means you will say what you are going to do, then you will do what you said. A promise was made to your spouse in your marriage vows.

You care about your marriage or you wouldn't have read this far. I pray and agree that you will let God direct change in the way you treat each other. Even good marriages can be enhanced with respect and honor towards each other's feelings. Commitment means you will say what you are going to do, then you will do what you said. A promise was made to your spouse when you said the marriage vows. It is easy to repeat those words without paying any attention to what was said. At our wedding, I promised to love, honor, and obey Dave, and I didn't even understand the meaning of those words.

What did you promise at your wedding? I believe that you said something like, "I promise to love you forever, when things are good and when things are bad." I don't believe anyone has ever said on that day, "I will love you until things don't seem to be working out, then I'm heading out of here." No, I believe that you probably said, "Till death do us part." Marriage is total commitment.

19
THE PRICE
OF PEACE

But the wisdom that comes from heaven is first of all pure;
then peace-loving, considerate, submissive, full of
mercy and good fruit, impartial and sincere.
Peacemakers who sow in peace raise a harvest of righteousness.
James 3:17,18 NIV

I used to be very unstable emotionally. I would wake up one morning and be all excited because of something I was going to do that day. The next morning I would wake up in the depths of depression because I had nothing to look forward to. My emotions would go up and down from day to day, hour to hour, or even minute to minute depending on my changing mood.

My husband might come home one day, and I would run to him, throw my arms around him, and kiss and hug him. The next day he might walk in, and I would be ready to throw something at him. Most of the time my reaction had nothing to do with anything he had done or failed to do. It was all determined by my own emotional state.

Even if you have never been as abused or as mentally and emotionally unstable as I was, all of us have need of continual restoration in order to maintain proper balance and stability in our lives. Whatever your past experiences or present circumstances are, submit your mind, will, and emotions to the Lord. I have written about it to a great extent in my book titled, *Managing Your Emotions*. But I want to remind you that peace is the fruit of a righteous relationship with God. When we have peace with God, we will have peace with each other.

> *The price we must pay to have peace is so small, and yet its benefits are eternally immense.*

The price we must pay to have peace is so small, and yet its benefits are eternally immense. We simply receive peace from Jesus, through the power of the Holy Spirit, and agree to forgive people for their offenses against us. John 20:21-23 (NIV) confirms,

Again Jesus said, "Peace be with you! As the Father has sent me, I am sending you."

And with that he breathed on them and said, "Receive the Holy Spirit.

"If you forgive anyone his sins, they are forgiven; if you do not forgive them, they are not forgiven."

Jesus gives us the power to have peace by breathing His own Life, the Holy Spirit, into us. But if we don't forgive others, the grief of the sin against us will remain with us forever. Our price is small, but the price Jesus paid for us to have the gift of the Holy Spirit is incomprehensible.

JESUS LAID DOWN HIS LIFE FOR US

When Judas betrayed Jesus, He had insight to know what Judas was doing but He just stood there and let him continue with his greeting, his embrace, and his kiss. Then in Matthew 26:50, *Jesus said to him, Friend. . . .* (You ought to circle the word friend in your Bible.) Knowing that Judas was betraying Him, He still called him, *Friend, for what are you here? Then they came up and laid hands on Jesus and arrested Him.*

Peter, ready to defend Jesus drew his sword, struck the servant of the high priest, and cut off his ear. Whack! Old lion-like Peter was full of fleshly zeal. He whipped out that sword and chopped off his ear. You know what Peter was thinking? **Bless God, we don't have to put up with this!** Whack! **You're messing with God's anointed!**

But Jesus said, *"No more of this!" And he touched the man's ear and healed him* (Luke 22:51 NIV). Then Jesus told Peter to put his sword back into its place for all who draw the sword will die by the sword. (Matthew 26:52.) I have more understanding on this today than I've ever had before. Peter's use of the sword represented an abrasive way of life. More than just being a sword that he pulled out of his sheath, it represented a manner of behavior.

Peter was always talking when he didn't need to be talking, doing things when he didn't need to be doing them. Peter needed to learn how to wait on God, and he needed to learn humility and meekness. God wanted to use Peter in a mighty way, but if Peter wanted to preach the Good News of the Gospel, he couldn't do it by taking his sword out and chopping off ears when he felt angry.

Our abrasive words can cut off hearing, just as Peter's sword cut off the servant's ear. We just can't come against people whenever we feel like justice is needed. We must be submissive to God, and if He says, "Say nothing," we are to stand there and just let them think they are right even though we know they're not. We have to say, "Yes, Lord," and accept that He doesn't even owe us an explanation.

Jesus asks us to trust Him because He loves us. There was no greater way for Him to prove His love than the fact He laid down His life to pay the price for the sin that separated us from the blessings of God. Jesus was willing to be our scapegoat; He was the One Who bore the blame for all of us. None of us would have our names written in the Lamb's Book of Life if Jesus hadn't been submissive or if He had opened His mouth when He shouldn't have.

How many times do we prevent somebody's salvation because we can't control what we say? How many times do we prevent somebody's spiritual growth or how many times do we prevent the blessings of God from coming on our own life because we don't have that control of the words that come out of our mouth?

When Jesus took our sins, He carried them off into a land of forgetfulness so we could enjoy the freedom of a relationship with God and release the fruit of His Spirit that dwells in us. People who don't know God misunderstand meekness as weakness. But when God said the meek will inherit the earth, he was talking about the patient, long-suffering believers. It takes great strength to patiently endure injury without resentment.

Meekness is not weakness — it is strength under control.

I so badly wanted to learn the meaning of meekness that I read its definition in my *Vine's Dictionary* so often that the page finally fell out of the book. For a long time I carried the folded-up page in my wallet, and I reread it whenever I thought to do so. One definition says that meekness is not weakness — it is strength under control. First of all it says that meekness "is an inwrought grace of the soul."[1] Now "inwrought" means it has to be worked in us.[2] In other words, it doesn't just suddenly happen; it has to be worked in you. "It is that temper of spirit in which we accept His dealings with us as good."[3]

God revealed to me that I do not have the authority to retaliate to anyone unless He authorizes me to do so. Instead, we are to trust **God** to take care of the situation. **God** will retaliate for us. He promises, "**I** will pay them back. **I** will balance out the scales of justice." So often we miss miracles in our lives that we could get because we get involved with solving an issue when we should wait and trust God.

Jesus was meek. In the Garden of Gethsemane, He had the strength and the power to call twelve legions of angels, but He didn't confront anyone because the Father didn't give Him permission to do so. Sometimes, God asks us to simply be a scapegoat for someone else, instead of confronting them with justice.

WHO'S BEEN TAKING YOUR BLAME LATELY?

A few years ago, Dave was behaving in a way that I knew was wrong, and I could **not** get him to admit that he was wrong. To make it worse, he was blaming his actions on me. Now isn't it hard when somebody else is doing something wrong who won't admit it, and they even lay the guilt of it on you? I was upset about it for several days, during which time I entertained some heavy groaning about the situation.

"God," I complained, "This is not right; it's just not fair." That's when God led me to the teaching in Leviticus 16 about the scapegoat. He showed me how Aaron put his hands on the goat and confessed all the sins and iniquities of Israel before sacrificing it on God's altar. The innocent "scapegoat" was a picture of what Jesus did for us as the Lamb of God.

I was complaining about Dave during the season of time that I was also studying this illustration, when God spoke to me in answer to my complaints. He said, "Joyce, for years Dave was your scapegoat." When Dave and I first married, my problems were impenetrable, but Dave was called and anointed by God to marry me. God knew the call on my life was going to take someone who was strong in the Lord and who was able to stand with me and be my scapegoat to show me the *agape* love of God. I did not know what love was — I had only seen selfish, self-seeking greed — until Dave loved me with the unconditional, accepting love of God.

I had always talked myself through conflicts, trying to manipulate others the way others had tried to control me. I would get mad and stay mad for long periods of time. I had a bad temper and I would sink into deep self-pity. Dave would try to have fun and I would get mad, but he never came against me. He was a lover of peace, and he just put up with my moods and never confronted me. Many times I blamed him, and he trusted God to reveal truth to me.

Sometimes I didn't respect him for it and thought, **Why don't you just tell me to shut up?** But God was using him to demonstrate His own patience and agape love. Then after several years of letting me rant and rave, as I mentioned previously, all of a sudden, Dave started confronting me. I violently disliked his new challenge. I had gotten by with my way for a long, long time, and now God had put somebody in my path to confront me. Even though the spiritual part of me wanted it, my flesh was having a fit.

All of a sudden, Dave started taking over various responsibilities that I had willingly controlled. I ran my present ministry all by myself for a long, long time before Dave quit his job and came on board. He took over the finances, and I didn't know how much money we had half the time, and I never saw my paychecks because he took them straight to the bank. He made decisions about where I would speak and where I wouldn't speak and what engagements I would take and which ones I wouldn't take and so on and so forth.

I felt I had been emptied of all control, and he started to confront me by saying, "I'm not putting up with that anymore." I would think, **Why not? You have as long as we've been married!** I did get to choose where I wanted to go to eat, but all of a sudden, he started saying, "No, I don't want to go there. I want to go here." I would just get in another fit over not getting to go where I wanted to eat.

I was a terrible mess, far from understanding what meekness or humility was, but greatly needing those qualities in my life in order to follow through with the next level of ministry that God was calling us to step into. One day Dave told me, "Joyce, I don't have any choice. God is telling me that I have to confront you."

He even bought a book by David W. Augsburger called *Caring Enough to Confront*[4] and read it. I was nervous when he **bought** it, but it was even worse knowing that he was **reading** it! Just as I feared, he began to use his newly learned confrontational skills on me.

We had been having a good conversation one night, when he began, "Joyce, I believe that the Lord has shown me that because of the wounded position you were in when I married you, if I had confronted you sooner, you would have left me."

It's true, I probably would have, not because I didn't love him, not because I would have wanted to leave him, but because of the way I was mistreated as a child; I wouldn't have known any other way to react except to run. I had so much rebellion in my flesh that I had to be left alone for God to work with me for a long period of time.

God definitely sent my husband to me. I'm confident that God has sent people to help you mature in Him, too. Or perhaps God may be ready to use you to help someone grow in the knowledge of His fullness or lead them into His kingdom. If so, you may have to be that scapegoat until God says, "It's time to confront."

That's what Dave did for me. He loved me; he just kept persisting and consistently loving me and showing me the love of God. Now if I get downright rude with Dave, he tells me, "Knock it off." But I did so many things that I would never have tolerated from others, yet he just overlooked my faults until God told him to deal with me.

He was just like Jesus waiting like a lamb led to the slaughter. He was being mistreated and picked on, and I was just getting by with it and nothing was happening, nothing was changing, but God had a plan. God sees what we are and what we will become.

If God asks you to be a scapegoat in a situation, it is because He is trying to give that person some space of time to change. He knows who that person will become, and He needs you to carry the load for that person for a period of time. Just as it was important for Dave to avoid confrontation with me for a while, it was also important to move when God said, "Now, it's time to confront her."

Dave told me one night, "Can I tell you something, Joyce? In the natural, I don't want to challenge you on these things." He said, "Why would I want to fight with you and argue with you every time I turn around? I don't really care where we go to eat. It doesn't make that much difference to me, and I would just as soon let you have your way." He explained, "I'm doing this because God is telling me that I've got to do this now if we're going to progress and go on to the fullness of what God has for us."

When a person gets far enough along in the Lord, they should be able to submit to whatever authority God puts in their lives. If I would have resisted Dave's leadership at that point, I wouldn't be in ministry today. We wouldn't be flying all over the nation, or teaching on television and radio stations around the world. If you will do things God's way, God will honor you. You will come to be that lionhearted, but only if you do things God's way.

SUBMIT TO THE ANOINTING

In the ministry, a person quickly learns that you cannot operate without God's anointing. And you quickly learn what God will anoint and what He will not. God anoints humility and obedience. To demonstrate our willingness to be obedient, there must be authority in our lives.

When God established authority in our home, He had a big plan in mind. As wives demonstrate the humility needed to submit to their husbands, husbands must also humble themselves and submit to God. God tells them to love their wives, so women wind up with a double portion of love, both her husband and her Lord are looking after her. God's plan for everyone to be subject to someone is explained in Romans 13:1,2.

> *Let every person be loyally subject to the governing (civil) authorities. For there is no authority except from God [by His permission, His sanction], and those that exist do so by God's appointment.*

> *Therefore he who resists and sets himself up against the authorities resists what God has appointed and arranged [in divine order]. And those who resist will bring down judgment upon themselves [receiving the penalty due them].*

We are supposed to have a godly fear of authority. The devil can wreak havoc in homes where the man isn't submitting to God by loving his wife and the woman isn't submitting to her husband. Respect needs to flow in our homes. The devil works on women trying to make them feel like doormats. But, the Hebrew word for helper in Genesis 2:18 is best illustrated by picturing the "opposite bookend." A woman needs to be as strong as her husband, complementing his efforts to hold up the family. But there must be humility in her life to lean towards her husband, as God commands her to, and not away from him, or everything that God wants to hold together in the family will fall.

We must be able to respect authority to be able to handle the power that comes with any anointing God gives to us. I have a gift to teach and preach, but I still don't have the right to be the head of my home. The Word clearly teaches that authority is in our lives as a divine order and a covering, not as a ranking of superiority or inferiority. In the context of telling men they are the head of the family, God also tells them to remember they came from woman and would not have life without her. God keeps everything in balance.

I believe any woman who is trying to operate in any kind of ministry who won't come under her husband's authority will miss the anointing that God has for her, unless she comes into obedience to the order He established for the family. It doesn't matter if her husband has anything to do with her ministry or not. She still

We must be able to respect authority to be able to handle the power that comes with any anointing God gives to us.

must be willing to humble herself to be in line with God's principles if she wants power to be released through the work of her hands.

God dealt with me over the years about things that needed to change in me. He covered my shortcomings by His grace for a certain period of time, and He let me get by with things. There is so much wrong with each one of us when we first come to Him that if He revealed it all at one time, we would just say, "Take me home, Lord, and forget it."

But God uncovers things in us that need to change one issue at a time. His grace gives us the power to do the right thing, after He shows us where we need to grow. God uncovered things in my personality that He wanted changed one step at a time. At that point in my life, I needed to trust God's order and authority if I wanted to move on to the next level of His plan.

We go from glory to glory to glory. It is tremendous to think that all those bad things in our lives can be turned into glories – that God can take each one of our bad habits and bad attitudes and He can turn them into another story of His goodness and power.

God is long-suffering, and He sent just the right person to help me learn the lessons I needed. I believe that every couple is put together to help each other reestablish fellowship with God. That is our divine purpose, to help each other get home again, spiritu-ally, mentally, and physically. You don't know what your husband is capable of. You don't know the talents and the gifts that are in him, but if you will love him and help him bring out his full potential, you will both enjoy God's divine plans for you.

PREFER ONE ANOTHER

God began to deal with me that if I wanted His anointing to increase on my life, then I also had to stop being harsh. It was my nature to be tough. I couldn't even tell one of the kids to take the trash out without sounding like an army sergeant. I could make my point loud and clear, "All right, let's get it out! Go! Go! Go! Move! Get that trash! Get it out there! Go! Go! Go!"

It was even hard to for me to say, "Honey, would you please get me a glass of water?" I preferred, "Give me a glass of water, will you? Be quick about it!" Maybe that's a little bit of an exaggeration, but when God began to show me the price of peace, I saw many areas that demonstrated my need for humility.

When God starts to uncover pride in our lives, He lets us feel it in an exaggerated manner so we get the weight of what we are like compared to His holiness. God showed me that I needed to be sweet and gentle and humble and meek and kind and lowly. He taught me to say "please" and "thank you." I learned that it didn't hurt so much after all.

Another area that God taught me a lesson in humility was through our finances. I do believe that both the husband and wife should be involved in the financial standings of a household. For a while I was totally ignorant of our finances and I started feeling resentful and left out. Now I know how the bills are being paid, even though they are Dave's responsibility. Sharing this knowledge keeps us in agreement about major purchases and financial goals.

If we want to buy something of major value, we talk about it and stay in agreement. If we absolutely cannot get into agreement, then we realize that it may not be the time to buy it. There is a time to get and a time to lose. We can trust God for the anointing of agreement to indicate the time to buy.

I have seen God's anointing at work when it is time to shop. I know that sounds funny, but when it's the right time it doesn't take me but about one hour to buy five outfits. I mean every one of them will fit me perfectly. God's anointing will be on it — it is God's timing, the money is there, and everything is right. There have been times when I have gone up and down the mall in vain, wearing myself out and listening to Dave say, "Can we go home? I can't stand this anymore."

I could have been looking all day and half the night and have nothing but a pair of shoes I didn't even like, and one dress that didn't fit me right. It is better to shop when God is ready to place His blessing on it.

If you are trying to buy a house and you are not in agreement over it, it may not be God's timing. The most important thing in a godly home is that you have no strife. You've got to get the strife out of your lives. And a lot of strife comes over money because one wants to do one thing and somebody else wants to do something else. I believe that if you are both seeking God, you can come into agreement.

But what if we have the money to buy something and he wants to buy a boat and I want to buy a couch, or what if he wants to buy golf clubs and I want to buy a new coat? Who wins? I believe the one who wins is the one who gives in first, and not the one who gets his or her own way. The Bible says it is more blessed to give than to receive.

Dave and I were arguing about something; I wanted one thing and he wanted something else, and I finally argued him down and I got what I wanted. For a minute I felt pretty smug. He went to get a cup of coffee, and I unexpectedly felt the presence of the Holy Ghost come all over me. He said, "You know, you didn't win; you lost." He said, "The one who wins in a situation like this, Joyce, is not the one who gets what they want, but the one who gives in first."

If you can be obedient to the heart of God like that, if out of pure honor to God you prefer the desire of your spouse, you will have peace that passes understanding flowing through your life. You won't have to say, "Lord, I don't think this is fair, but to honor You, I'm going to let it go." God will see to it in the long run that you get what's coming to you. God will bless you when you have an attitude of meekness and humility.

ENJOY PEACE

Let's look in Matthew 11, starting in verse 28: *Come to Me, all you who labor and are heavy-laden and overburdened, and I will cause you to rest. [I will ease and relieve and refresh your souls.]* When we are trying to take charge of our own life, and trying to make things work out the way we want them to, and we're resisting about 50 to 75 percent of everything that comes our way because we don't like it, or want it, or it doesn't feel good, or because we don't understand it, we are not enjoying the rest that comes through humility.

If you are not enjoying the peace of God, you are not resting in God, and you are probably heavy-laden and overburdened. Jesus says, *Take My yoke upon you and learn of Me, for I am gentle (meek) and humble (lowly) in heart, and you will find rest (relief and ease and refreshment and recreation and blessed quiet) for your souls. For My yoke is wholesome (useful, good — not harsh, hard, sharp, or press-ing)...* (Matthew 11:29,30). Harsh, hard, sharp, and pressing is the way of the flesh. Harsh, hard, sharp, and pressing is the way of the world. Humble, gentle, meek, and lowly is the way of the kingdom. That's a kingdom law.

When I think about those four words — gentle, meek, humble, and lowly — I initially think of "pain." The flesh prickles with resistance to humility, gentleness, meekness, and lowliness. For example, do you love correction? The Bible says if you are humble, you will love correction.

Even the things that don't feel good right now, God is going to make them all work out all right in the end.

I have learned something that has brought me much, much peace and rest, and that is, God is sovereign. We are in God's hands and God loves us and He cares for us. If I keep my big brown eyes on Him, He's going to make it all work out all right. Even the things that don't feel good right now, He's going to make them all work out all right in the end. All I need to do is learn to be gentle, meek, humble, and lowly. In Colossians 3:12, the Bible says,

Clothe yourselves therefore, as God's own chosen ones (His own picked representatives), [who are] purified and holy and well-beloved [by God Himself, by putting on behavior marked by] tenderhearted pity and mercy, kind feeling, a lowly opinion of yourselves, gentle ways, [and] patience [which is tireless and long-suffering, and has the power to endure whatever comes, with good temper].

As God's chosen ones, we have the power to endure whatever comes, with good temper. Romans 8:28 says, *We are assured and know that [God being a partner in their labor] all things work together and are [fitting into a plan] for good to and for those who love God and are called according to [His] design and purpose.*

Ephesians 1:11 says, *In Him we also were made [God's] heritage (portion) and we obtained an inheritance; for we had been foreordained (chosen and appointed beforehand) in accordance with His purpose, Who works out everything in agreement with the counsel and design of His [own] will.*

You might think that it doesn't include what you are going through, but the Word says He works out **everything.** Just because something doesn't feel good, doesn't mean it's not good. And just because it looks awful right now, doesn't mean that it's going to look awful down the road when we will see God fit even the most awful thing into a plan for our good.

Trust is trusting God when it doesn't make any sense at all, and you don't see any way that it could possibly fit in. But yet you're saying, "God, I'm in Your hands. I have put myself in Your hands by faith. And I believe, because You're God, that You're going to work it out to my good. I believe that! I believe You're going to work it out!"

We received a letter from a young woman who paid us a good compliment. Here is a summary of her comments:

I thank God for your ministry because it has filled in the gaps . . . I could preach a series on prosperity and healing, but thank God, I can also preach a series on suffering. It's just as much a part of the Word as all the rest of it. If we leave that part out, we're going to leave people in confusion because you're going to have the fiery trials; you're going to have the tribulation; you're going to have the affliction; you're going to have the suffering — because the Bible says you are.

The Bible says it's part of God's plan to grow us up. It's part of God's plan to get us to the point where we frankly don't care what's going on, we're the same all the time because we're not operating because of what's going on out there; we're operating because of what's going on in here [our heart].

I thank God for the teaching that I had about faith and healing and prosperity, but it wasn't working without the part about dying to self! I was wearing myself out all the time! I was confused because I didn't understand why I couldn't get everything I wanted, the way I wanted it, when I wanted it.

I couldn't understand what was wrong with me, what was wrong with my faith. I thank God for the teachings I've got on faith, prosperity, healing, knowing the Word, knowing how to pray, and how to chase the devil off my property. But I thank God that you filled in the gaps. We've got to have the whole counsel of the Word of God.

Years ago, the church was in extremes the other direction. All Christians wanted to do was suffer, suffer, suffer, suffer — but we suffer so we can get resurrected, not so you can just go around suffering in the same area all your life! When God deals with you in an area of life, you will come out on the other side of it free! But, I might as well tell you that He will always be dealing with you about something.

God chastises those whom He loves. He loves you more than you will ever know. Yes, God wants us to prosper. Yes, He wants to see us with healthy bodies. Yes, He wants our marriages to work. Yes, He wants us to have favor because we are the ones who are to bring Him the glory in this earth, but we have to be willing to do it God's way. Jesus said, "Follow in My footsteps." The Bible says man's mind plans his way, but God directs his steps. Put everything that concerns you in God's hands; He will give you what is right.

Philippians 4:6-7 says,

. . . *in every circumstance and in everything, by prayer and petition (definite requests), with thanksgiving, continue to make your wants known to God.*

And God's peace [shall be yours, that tranquil state of a soul assured of its salvation through Christ, and so fearing nothing from God and being content with its earthly lot of whatever sort that is, that peace] which transcends all understanding shall garrison and mount guard over your hearts and minds in Christ Jesus.

Here's an example of how to take everything, all of our wants, to God. Suppose that Dave decides he wants us to go somewhere and I don't want to go.

I tell him, "I really don't want to go there, Dave. I just don't want to go! Could we not go?"

He is firm, "Well, yes, we're going to go."

I concede, "OK, we're going to go."

So then I go to God, I say, **God, I really don't want to go. I'd like it if You'd change Dave's heart. I just really don't want to go. However, God, I'll put myself in Your hands, and I'll believe that if You want me to go, I'll go, and if You don't want us to go, then You will change his heart.** How many fights and wars would be avoided if we took our wants to God and trusted Him to work things out on our behalf? It never ceases to amaze me what God will do for us if we will simply ask Him.

> It is amazing what God will do for us if we will simply ask Him.

God won't leave you hanging. First Peter 5:10 promises, *And after you have suffered a little while, the God of all grace [Who imparts all blessing and favor], Who has called you to His [own] eternal glory in Christ Jesus, will Himself complete and make you what you ought to be, establish and ground you securely, and strengthen, and settle you.*

We can stand anything for a little while, but don't give up until His work is complete. Continue to love your spouse until you see that you have become one. Continue to obey God's Word until you see His promises complete in you. God will do a work in our lives that we will not be able to believe or understand.

20

HELP ME —
I THINK I'M IN LOVE!

*Bid the older women similarly to be reverent and devout
in their deportment as becomes those engaged in sacred
service, not slanderers or slaves to drink. They are to give
good counsel and be teachers of what is right and noble,
So that they will wisely train the young women to
be sane and sober of mind (temperate, disciplined)
and to love their husbands and their children.*
Titus 2:3,4

The day I said to Dave, "I give up — teach me to play golf,"
may have been the day I learned to truly love him. We have
enjoyed golf together for a good number of years now. It is a time
that we can get away together and enjoy the solitude of the course,
the fresh air, and the exercise.

Sitting in the fishing boat all day may not be your idea of a perfect
date with your husband, but you may be surprised at the pleasure
you'll take in seeing him within his favorite element. It could be so
good for your relationship that he agrees to walk through the craft
show with you the next weekend. Whatever it is your husband is
able to find refuge in, take the challenge to "adapt yourself to him"
and say, "You know, I'd like to go with you sometime."

With a shocked expression, your husband will probably say, "What? You would?" I can't wait to get your letter telling me that you took the assignment and went with him to his favorite get away. Maybe it will simply be watching a football game with him, cuddled up at his side while you hold the popcorn bowl for him. Maybe you will spend a day puttering in his workshop with him, holding a piece of wood steady while he cuts it in two.

I'm sure that one part of your testimony will be the same as the other women who offer to spend the day with their husbands doing "whatever" they most enjoy. You will write and say, "You know, Joyce, I think I might go with him again someday soon."

When you spend this day with him, use the time to just notice him while he leads you through his adventure. Leave behind all your agendas, grudges, and payback plans. Take an interest in him, and see what surprises God has for you through your relationship with your husband.

We go in search of an experience with God, we look for our "ministry" and wonder if God can use us in some way, when all the time God has already given us the assignment to love our husbands as unto the Lord. We need to start giving our time, our attention, our sacrifice, and our service to our spouse.

Once you are good at loving each other, God will give you bigger assignments. When the two of you are in agreement, God will cause you to do ten times what you would have been able to do alone.

You and your spouse have to have fun together; you need to laugh together.

Dave goes out and plays golf a lot of times when I don't want to go — I don't feel about the game what he does. If I tell him I really don't want to go that day, it's fine. But we have great memories of the times we have played together. You've got to have fun together; you need to laugh together.

Dave and I still wrestle sometimes. Even though we're older, we still chase each other around. It's a little dangerous for me because once we start wrestling, he gets in his conquer mode and he's going to win or else. I tell him sometimes it's dangerous to horse around with him because I am bound to wind up with bruises before the game is over.

Several years ago, probably twenty-five years ago, we were chasing each other through the house one night, playing, "I got you last." I would run and hit him, then take off running and shout, "I got you last." Then he would chase me and say, "I got **you** last." Then I would chase him again, and he would chase me.

Well, I ran outside, through the front door, and around our cul-de-sac. I was running as fast as I could go, then I turned to run back to the house. The overhead garage door was partially opened, but it was dark outside and I didn't realize that the dark brown door was not opened all the way. It was suspended a few feet from the ceiling and I ran right into it, hitting the top of my head. The impact knocked me off my feet and cut my head open.

Dave had to take me to the hospital to get stitches. The first thing the nurses and doctors look for is abuse. So there I was with a gash in my head and they were probing for the story, "Honey, can you tell us what happened? Did he beat you up?"

I said, "Actually we were playing, 'I got you last.'"

The nurse said, "You were doing what?"

I said, "We were playing 'I got you last.' I was chasing him, he was chasing me, you know, 'tag — you're it, I got you last.' Then I ran . . ."

She said, "Honey, I've worked here a long time, and I have seen every kind of situation. But we have never had a case of 'I got you last.'"

Seriously, couples need to take every opportunity available in a day to laugh. Seize the moment, and make each other laugh about something. I was always so serious, sober, and a deep thinker, always thinking about something, always trying to solve some problem. I have learned in the last few years to be more childlike and more lighthearted.

The things that Dave used to do that would make me mad for two or three days just make us laugh now. Likewise, I did plenty of things that would irritate him, and now we just laugh when we look back on those days. Take every opportunity that you can to laugh.

Your husband needs a helpmate, not a nag, a boss, a critic, a teacher, a potter who wants to keep reworking him on the wheel all the time. He doesn't need you to be a personal advisor, unless he asks for it. But he does need a friend and a place to come home where he is championed, in spite of what he had to put up with through his day. He may not want to relive the stresses he went through at work by telling you about it, but he certainly will enjoy the escape to your warm embrace when he comes home. Help him to realize there is more to life than what he experienced at work.

Have fun! Plan playtime together. Look for the humor in a situation. Call it out at unexpected moments. Don't be so serious all the time. Laugh at yourself!

One precious lady came to me at a conference and could hardly say what she wanted to say to me, but finally she admitted, "I really didn't want to come. I was glad when I called the first time and you were out of tickets, but then somebody gave us tickets, so I came.

"We have been married twenty-four years and have seven children and I came here with no hope — I was ready to get a divorce and give up." Tears started running down her face as she said, "I'm not even sure why, but somehow this weekend some hope has slipped into my heart."

Dropping her voice a little, she said, "My husband and I have not made love for two years," then she leaned over and whispered in my ear, "but tonight I really want to make love to my husband." God's Word changes people's hearts. There's hope and help in God. People without the Lord are without hope, but in Christ Jesus there is a bright future.

LIKE A PAIR OF BOOKENDS

Dave and I are one and becoming more alike all the time. When I'm with Dave, it's like being by myself. I'm so comfortable with him; I can just do anything I want to when we are together. I don't have to talk if I don't want to or I can talk if I want to. Sometimes Dave and I take trips, and we will ride two or three hours without saying one word. But yet, there's a silent communication going on between us.

I really don't care to do many things without my husband. I just don't enjoy being apart from him much. Dave goes shopping with me; if I go to the grocery store, he goes with me. I still have to watch him to keep him from throwing food at me when we go, but even these trips to the store are filled with wonderful memories of the two us shopping, with kids hanging out of the carts. I see Dave chasing us while I tried to restore the purpose and intent of the serious expedition we were really there to achieve.

A lot of times if I don't want to play golf or don't feel like it, he will want me just to come and ride on the cart. He says, "You can read or study or do what you want to." Dave keeps me balanced; he keeps me looking at the world from new angles that I wouldn't otherwise enjoy.

Now there are times when he goes by himself, and there are times when I go by myself. I'm not trying to sound unbalanced, but I am trying to share a principle with you. When the Bible says to leave your father and mother and to cleave to each other, it doesn't mean to get married and then for the man to play on three softball teams a week and bowl two nights and play golf at least once after his sixty-hour workweek.

There are plenty of marriages that have irreparable damage done to them because the man was gone all the time doing what he wanted to do while his wife was home alone trying to raise the kids. Let me just say again — don't avoid each other.

If your husband wants to play ball, go park yourself in your lawn chair and sit right there and watch him. You don't have to thoroughly enjoy it, but you need to be there and be there **with** him.

Invite your husband to go to the store with you. When he says he doesn't want to spend his time at the store, tell him you need his company. These gestures of companionship will change your love life.

The Bible says a man should leave his father and his mother and he should **cleave** unto his wife. And remember "cleave," as we saw before, means to be glued to, to stick with, and to follow. To "cleave" to a person is to go where he goes, to be attached, devoted, and hang upon each other as an expression of love. "Cleave" means to be made fast, to be permanently attached as with adhesive, soldered together or welded so as to adhere firmly and closely or loyally and unwaveringly.

A lot of times, I just hang on Dave. "What God has joined together, let not man put asunder." I believe that the purpose for marriage is strength because the Bible says that one can put a thousand to flight, but two, ten thousand. (Deuteronomy 32:30.)

The Bible says, *Can two walk together, unless they are agreed?* (Amos 3:3 NKJV).

> I believe that God's purpose of marriage is enjoyment. God wants you to enjoy each other the way He wants you to enjoy Him.

I believe that God's purpose of marriage is enjoyment. God wants you to enjoy each other the way He wants you to enjoy Him.

Satan works so hard to destroy marriages by bringing strife into the relationship. He must know something that we don't know. The devil is threatened by the power of a loving marriage relationship where two people are in unity and in harmony with each other. He knows love never fails, so his only hope is to destroy the love between two people.

What do we really think that means when it says, "one can put a thousand to flight, but two, ten thousand"? How many enemies do you think you've got out there trying to destroy you? You have strength when you are in agreement. Agreement is the key to answered prayers. Strength comes from agreement. The Bible says a house divided cannot stand. When we live in strife, we destroy our strength.

The Bible says if men mistreat their wives, God is not going to answer their prayers. So many people are not getting their prayers answered, and I believe disagreement in their home is one of the main reasons why.

THE BALANCE OF LOVE

We have so much balance now. Dave used to tell me that I was always running out ahead of God. And I said, "Yeah, and you're ten miles behind Him." But I am no longer running ahead of God, and Dave is no longer behind. God gave Dave a vision once of a wild team of white horses pulling a chariot with a driver who was trying to hold them back. The horses were in a frenzy and the guy in the chariot had the brake on so it was digging a rut in the road.

The Lord told Dave, "That's you and Joyce. She's the wild horses and you're the guy in the chariot trying to hold her back. You're trying to slow things down. And she's trying to run ahead."

And so God has brought us together and changed Dave's heart. We cannot change our husband's heart but God can. In Ezra 7:27 (NIV) we see how God changed the heart of the king to come in line with God's plan. *Praise be to the* LORD, *the God of our fathers, who has put it into the king's heart to bring honor to the house of the* LORD *in Jerusalem in this way.* The Lord told Dave, "I need you to work together so you can flow together."

I have come to trust Dave. I know he loves me and he is not out to get me. He still can get cranky once in a while or make a decision that I don't think is fair to me about money or something, but he will usually always rectify it if I don't get angry and try to make a big deal out of it. I know I can trust God to either rectify the situation or give me the grace to let it drop.

After you are married to somebody for a long time, you learn how to work with them. If Dave feels strongly about something, and I see that our debate is starting to get heated, I just back off. Then if it's something that is really important to me, I might try again a week later.

A lot of times he will feel differently about it, but if he still feels the same way then, I just realize I've got to let it go. If I ever come to Dave and say to him, "This is what God said to me," he will always let me do what I want. But I never abuse that. I mean I never tell him that unless I really, really feel like God did tell me something.

I appreciate the freedom that Dave lets me have with God. I suppose it is because Dave knows he can trust God, too. Dave never tries to tell me what to do in the pulpit. He lets me run the meetings and never gets involved in that aspect of what I'm trying to do. He never tries to tell me how to hear from God. Now if I was doing something wrong, he would tell me, but there has only been a couple of times he has corrected me about anything. One time he said, "I don't think you should say that, that way."

We have a wonderful relationship now. But we know each other so well and we respect each other. I respect Dave's authority and he respects the gift that God has put in me. He doesn't intrude on what God has put in me and recognizes the authority God has anointed me to have on the platform.

When asked about how it feels to see me in the focal point of the ministry, he says that God has put me in that position, and he is at peace with the work of God in our lives. Of course if he wasn't in agreement, this ministry would not flow in the anointing that is on it.

BUT WHAT ABOUT THE KIDS?

In the beginning of the book, we looked at the fact that God wants order and balance and love to flow between a husband and wife so that there will be godly offspring released into the earth. I am convinced that much of the rebellion that we see in teenagers today is caused because of strife between the parents.

The best parenting advice we can give to couples is to love each other and be openly affectionate in front of your children. If you fight all the time, it will affect your children. In the earlier years when Dave and I would get in a fight, they would get upset and go to their rooms and cry. There is no greater pain for a child to experience than the threat of their parents not loving each other. But it doesn't work to pretend to love each other just for the sake of the children.

The person we are married to is the most important person in our life, besides the Lord Jesus Christ. Your spouse is more important to you than your children. Your children will grow up and get married and leave for their own life, and they leave the nest quickly. We had four children with us, and in a matter of twelve months' time, two of them married, and another one became engaged.

If you pour all your life into your children, someday you may regret that you did. Your children should not come before your spouse. Take good care of your children, but don't place them above God or your marriage. Be generous with your children while they are with you. Teach them the principles of giving by letting them see your offerings and assistance to people in the body of Christ, but be sure to let those principles operate toward them, too. God convicted me years ago to give to my children.

I know a man right now who refuses to be a Christian because his father gave all their money to the church and let his own children go barefoot, even in the winter. They bore the discomfort and embarrassment of going to school with no shoes on, and it created a bitterness in his heart that he has never gotten over.

If you tithe and give offerings according to the leading of the Lord, I believe you will always have enough to meet your family's needs and more besides. But the Bible does teach in Proverbs to use wise thoughtfulness. Sometimes we can get a personal satisfaction out of giving to others and get so caught up in it that we forget our own family. In Isaiah 58 the Bible says not to forget the needs of your own flesh and blood.

When I first started learning the principles of giving, I was giving offerings, taking clothes out of my closet and things off my walls and giving them to people. I wanted to be involved in giving! One day, the Lord quickened my heart saying, "Your own kids are running around with holes in their shoes, and you're busy giving everything you have to somebody else." Sometimes we get so religious with a godly principle that we miss the heart of how it is supposed to work for the people we live with.

We give to strangers and bless people through the church, and it makes us feel good. If we do it to be well liked by the people who see us give, then we are being religious instead of godly. We need to give to our own spouses and children just because we love them, not for any other approval.

I always encourage men to be involved with the discipline of the children. The dad should establish the consequence of disobedience. No woman will ever discipline a child like a man could, and no child will ever fear a mother properly — and I'm talking about a right kind of fear — like they will for the father.

> When the children see their parents' agreement, their security is established and they learn to submit.

Mothers may have to help get the dads involved, since they are with the children more than he is. My son tried to talk me into stuff and argued and made deals with me to convince me. If that didn't work, he would cry and play on my emotions. But not so with Dave. If Dave told him something, that was it because a man is anointed with authority in the home. He is supposed to walk in it with love, and the wife is supposed to submit to it with her support of it. When the children see their agreement, their security is established and they learn to submit, too.

Unconditional love needs to be balanced with encouragement for a child to do his best. The home should not be a place of pressure where your children feel the need to perform just to make you feel good. Encourage your children to do their best in school, but don't ever compare them with another sibling or child you know.

It is pitiful what some people go through by the time they are grown. The most important thing we can teach our children is how to have healthy, loving relationships. They need to learn to get along with their siblings and treat people with the same respect they see their mom and dad treating each other.

If the relationships in your home need repair, God is in the healing business. There is a move of the Holy Spirit right now to bring healing to past hurts and direction for a fruitful future.

Build esteem in your children by loving each other first. To do this, you need to have time alone, away from them. Spend time together as a couple; go on dates. Maybe that sounds silly to you because you are married, but you need to be dating!

I can remember when Dave and I were first married, and we didn't have much money. We might have $40 left over for a month, and that was if we didn't have a flat tire, or some other surprise expense. Every once in a while, somebody would give Dave tickets to a show or a ball game or something so we could go out together. All day long I would get ready to go out with Dave. The process of the bubble bath, the perfume, the makeup, combing the hair, all built great anticipation for our time together.

A GOOD MARRIAGE HAPPENS ON PURPOSE

Good marriages are not an accident. If you want to have a great relationship with anyone, you have to deliberately work at it. It doesn't matter if you are building a friendship with a neighbor, a relative, your child, your spouse, or God, you have to keep communication flowing to and from the one you love. This involvement causes love to keep growing between you. It is . . . *by understanding it* (a life, a home, a family) *is established [on a sound and good foundation]* (Proverbs 24:3).

> *Good marriages are not an accident. If you want to have a great relationship with anyone, you have to deliberately work at it.*

Find out what your spouse would enjoy doing on a night out. Get a baby-sitter if you still have small children at home and spend the night out. The kids will do fine. They would rule you if you let them! But they are going to grow up and go their way and live happily ever after, while you two are going to be with each other for life! Do something now about making sure you have something you want to live for later on!

Go to dinner and perhaps occasionally stay in a nice hotel, even if it is close to home. Don't let your life get boring! There are so many people who just are bored with their lives. Do something about boredom! Be creative! Pray and ask God for ideas. Everybody craves change, even when they are afraid of it.

Protect these outings between the two of you. Be sure they happen frequently enough to keep your outlook stirred with new scenery. Go out every one or two weeks and discover what it is like just to be alone in each other's company. Hold hands, rub shoulders, hug and show respect to each other. Demonstrate to the world what God's love looks like between two people.

THE WORD OF OUR TESTIMONY

Revelation 12:11 (NIV), speaking of believers in defense against the accuser, says, *They overcame him by the blood of the Lamb and by the word of their testimony; they did not love their lives so much as to shrink from death.*

To love someone is to die to self, but dying to self is the only way to gain the life God has planned for us. Dave and I share a testimony of God's power to overcome the devil's war against us. We have endless memories that we can talk about even when we are too old to enjoy traveling to new places. We understand that our days are short, packed with activity and events, but our retreat home to each other remains a highlight for each new day.

The Word of God changes people; it certainly changed me. Radical changes, for all areas of life, are in store for those who will put their hope in God. I honestly don't know how people are living without Jesus; I can hardly comprehend getting through one day without the Lord lighting our path to the greatest of all eternal things — love.

In closing, I think the letter to you from Peter, as paraphrased in *The Living Bible*, best summarizes this testimony of hope that we have in God:

God paid a ransom to save you from the impossible road to heaven which your fathers tried to take, and the ransom he paid was not mere gold or silver, as you very well know. But he paid for you with the precious lifeblood of Christ, the sinless, spotless Lamb of God. God chose him for this purpose long before the world began, but only recently was he brought into public view, in these last days, as a blessing to you.

Because of this, your trust can be in God who raised Christ from the dead and gave him great glory. Now your faith and hope can rest in him alone. Now you can have real love for everyone because your souls have been cleansed from selfishness and hatred when you trusted Christ to save you; so see to it that you really do love each other warmly, with all your hearts.

For you have a new life. It was not passed on to you from your parents, for the life they gave you will fade away. This new one will last forever, for it comes from Christ, God's ever-living Message to men.

Yes, our natural lives will fade as grass does when it becomes all brown and dry. All our greatness is like a flower that droops and falls, but the Word of the Lord will last forever. And his message is the Good News that was preached to you.

1 Peter 1:18-25

Our lives should be full of reward — full of testimony of God's power in our lives. Peter went on to testify in his first letter to the church, chapter 2:15 (TLB), that, *It is God's will that your good lives should silence those who foolishly condemn the Gospel without knowing what it can do for them, having never experienced its power.*

The testimony of your and your spouse's love for each other can be used by God to win others to Himself.

God is wonderful. He is awesome, and it is the greatest thing to know God, to be saved and to enjoy the benefits of living within His divine order and grace. He didn't just save us from dying and going to hell; He saved us from having to live in hell while we're here on the earth.

The testimony of your love for each other can be used by God to win others to Himself. The mystery of how God causes you and your spouse to become one flesh in perfect agreement through marriage is great, but within your testimony of how God makes this happen lies a revelation of God's love for you and the world.

God didn't just save us from dying and going to hell; He saved us from having to live in hell while we're here on the earth.

God is the Author of life's greatest love stories. Let Him finish writing the one you have begun.

PRAYER FOR A PERSONAL RELATIONSHIP WITH THE LORD

God wants you to receive His free gift of salvation. Jesus wants to save you and fill you with the Holy Spirit more than anything. If you have never invited Jesus, the Prince of Peace, to be your Lord and Savior, I invite you to do so now. Pray the following prayer, and if you are really sincere about it, you will experience a new life in Christ.

Father,

You loved the world so much, You gave Your only begotten Son to die for our sins so that whoever believes in Him will not perish, but have eternal life.

Your Word says we are saved by grace through faith as a gift from You. There is nothing we can do to earn salvation.

I believe and confess with my mouth that Jesus Christ is Your Son, the Savior of the world. I believe He died on the cross for me and bore all of my sins, paying the price for them. I believe in my heart that You raised Jesus from the dead.

I ask You to forgive my sins. I confess Jesus as my Lord. According to Your Word, I am saved and will spend eternity with You! Thank You, Father. I am so grateful! In Jesus' Name, amen.

See John 3:16; Ephesians 2:8,9; Romans 10:9,10; 1 Corinthians 15:3,4; 1 John 1:9; 4:14-16; 5:1,12,13.

ANOTHER BLESSING
AVAILABLE TO YOU

There is one more very important thing you need to know.

The Bible calls another blessing available to you the baptism of the Holy Spirit. Matthew 3:4-6,11 tells us that John said when Jesus came, Jesus would baptize people with the Holy Ghost and fire. John had been baptizing people in water, and they had been repenting of their sins, but this baptism was in the Holy Spirit.

In Acts 1:5-8, Jesus talked about this Spirit baptism. He said they would receive power (ability, efficiency, and might) when the Holy Spirit came upon them, and this power would cause them to be witnesses to Jesus.

When you received Jesus, you received the Holy Spirit into your human spirit. But the baptism of the Spirit is a filling completely. He fills you, and you are placed into Him. It is like asking the Spirit to fill you through and through with the power and ability to live the Christian life and serve God according to His will.

If you need power, ability, strength, and miracles in your life, you need to be baptized in the Holy Spirit.

HOW TO RECEIVE THE BAPTISM IN THE HOLY SPIRIT

Ask God to fill you and to baptize you in the Holy Spirit. Simply pray, *Father, in Jesus' Name, I ask you to baptize me in the power of the Holy Spirit with the evidence of speaking in tongues.*

Be relaxed and at ease in God's presence. He loves you and wants you to have His best. Wait on Him quietly and believe you are receiving. Believe before you **feel** any change. You may **feel** a change taking place, but you may not. Do not be led by your feelings; be led by God's promises.

To speak in tongues, open your mouth, and as the Spirit gives you utterance, speak forth what you hear coming up out of your inner man. **This will not come out of your head.** Remember, your mind does not understand this.

That is why it is so hard for many people. We are accustomed to our minds running our lives. This whole book is about spiritual life and learning to live spiritually, not naturally.

You will hear or sense syllables, phrases, groanings, or utterances that are unusual sounding or foreign sounding to you. Take a step of faith and utter them; speak them forth. Acts 2:4 (KJV) says, *they . . . began to speak with other tongues, as the Spirit gave them utterance.*

You may now use this language (which will grow as you grow and as you exercise the gift) anytime you pray or just to edify yourself. Do not speak in tongues around people who do not understand. Tongues brought forth in a church setting should be interpreted or explained.

Enjoy your new life in the Spirit!

ENDNOTES

Chapter 4

[1] "marriage." *Merriam-Webster OnLine:/WWWebster Dictionary.* 2000. http://www.m-w.com/dictionary.htm (7 August 2000).

Chapter 10

[1] James E. Strong, "Greek Dictionary of the New Testament" in *Strong's Exhaustive Concordance of the Bible* (Nashville: Abingdon, 1890), p. 10, entry #283, s.v. "undefiled," Hebrews 13:4. (Abbreviations have been spelled out in this and in all other endnotes from Strong.)

Chapter 14

[1] Strong, "Greek Dictionary," p. 58, entry #4139, s.v. "neighbour," Romans 15:2.

[2] "neighbor." *Merriam-Webster OnLine.* (7 August 2000).

Chapter 15

[1] One available test: C. Peter Wagner, *Finding Your Spiritual Gifts: Wagner-Modified Houts Questionnaire* (Ventura: Gospel Light Publications, 1978, 1985, 1995 by C. Peter Wagner).

Chapter 16

[1] "cleave." Based on definition in *Merriam-Webster OnLine.* (7 August 2000).

[2] Strong, "Hebrew and Chaldee Dictionary" in *Strong's Exhaustive Concordance of the Bible* (Nashville: Abingdon, 1890), p. 29, entry #1692, s.v. "cleave," Genesis 2:24. Based on this definition.

[3] Strong, p. 10, entry #259, s.v. "one," Genesis 2:24.

[4] Strong, p. 10, entry #258, s.v. "one," Genesis 2:24.

Chapter 17

[1] Gary A. Smalley with John T. Trent, *The Language of Love* (Colorado Springs: Focus on the Family Publishing, 1991).

[2] "Shoooopping" in "Why Can't My Spouse Understand What I Say?" "husbands & wives." http://www.family.org/married/comm/a0009640.html.

[3] Strong, "Hebrew and Chaldee Dictionary" p. 87, entry #5828, "help meet," Genesis 2:18. Based on definition.

Chapter 18

[1] Strong, "Greek Dictionary," p. 51, entry #3626, s.v. "keepers," Titus 2:5. From p. 51, entry #3624, "keeper," Greek origin of the word.

Chapter 19

[1] W.E. Vine, *Vine's Complete Expository Dictionary of Old and New Testament Words* (Nashville: Thomas Nelson Inc., 1984), "An Expository Dictionary of New Testament Words," p. 401, s.v. "MEEK, MEEKNESS," B. Nouns.

[2] "in-wrought." *Merriam-Webster OnLine* (6 August 2000). Based on the definition, "2: worked in especially as decoration."

[3] Vine, "New Testament Words," s.v. "MEEK, MEEKNESS," B. Nouns.

[4] David W. Augsburger, *Caring Enough to Confront* (Ventura: Gospel Light Publications, 1980).

RECOMMENDED READING

LaHaye, Tim. *Spirit-Controlled Temperament*. Wheaton: Tyndale House Publishers, 1993.

Littauer, Florence. *Your Personality Tree*. Nashville: Word Publishing, 1991.

Smalley, Gary A. with John T. Trent. *The Language of Love*. Colorado Springs: Focus on the Family Publishing, 1991.

ABOUT THE AUTHOR

JOYCE MEYER has been teaching the Word of God since 1976 and in full-time ministry since 1980. She is the bestselling author of more than seventy inspirational books, including *Approval Addiction*, *In Pursuit of Peace*, *How to Hear from God*, and *Battlefield of the Mind*. She has also released thousands of audio teachings as well as a complete video library. Joyce's *Enjoying Everyday Life*® radio and television programs are broadcast around the world, and she travels extensively conducting conferences. Joyce and her husband, Dave, are the parents of four grown children and make their home in St. Louis, Missouri.

To contact the author write:
Joyce Meyer Ministries
P. O. Box 655
Fenton, Missouri 63026
or call: (636) 349-0303

Internet Address: www.joycemeyer.org

Please include your testimony of help received from this book when you write. Your prayer requests are welcome.

To contact the ministry
in Canada, please write:
Joyce Meyer Ministries, Inc.
Lambeth Box 1300
London, ON N6P 1T5
Canada
or call: (636) 349-0303

In Australia, please write:
Joyce Meyer Ministries, Inc.
Locked Bag 77
Mansfield Delivery Centre
Queensland 4122
Australia
or call: (07) 3349 1200

In England, please write:
Joyce Meyer Ministries, Inc.
P. O. Box 1549
Windsor
SL4 1GT
United Kingdom
or call: 01753-831102

The Joy of Believing Prayer

Never Lose Heart

Being the Person God Made You to Be

A Leader in the Making

"Good Morning, This Is God!"

Jesus—Name Above All Names

Making Marriage Work
(Previously published as
Help Me—I'm Married!)

Reduce Me to Love

Be Healed in Jesus' Name

How to Succeed at Being Yourself

Weary Warriors, Fainting Saints

Life in the Word Devotional

Be Anxious for Nothing *

Straight Talk Omnibus

Don't Dread

Managing Your Emotions

Healing the Brokenhearted

Me and My Big Mouth! *

Prepare to Prosper

Do It Afraid!

Expect a Move of God in Your Life . . . Suddenly!

*Enjoying Where You Are on the Way to
Where You Are Going*

The Most Important Decision You Will Ever Make

When, God, When?

Why, God, Why?

The Word, the Name, the Blood

Tell Them I Love Them

Peace

The Root of Rejection

If Not for the Grace of God *

JOYCE MEYER SPANISH TITLES

*Las Siete Cosas Que Te Roban el Gozo
(Seven Things That Steal Your Joy)*

*Empezando Tu Día Bien
(Starting Your Day Right)*

BOOKS BY DAVE MEYER

Life Lines